IN PURSUIT OF
THE GOOD

IN PURSUIT OF
THE GOOD

INTELLECT AND ACTION
IN ARISTOTLE'S *ETHICS*

Eric Salem

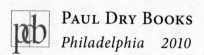

PAUL DRY BOOKS
Philadelphia   2010

First Paul Dry Books Edition, 2010

Paul Dry Books, Inc.
Philadelphia, Pennsylvania
www.pauldrybooks.com

Cover: Statue of Aristotle in Stagira,
Greece. © iStockphoto.com / Snezana Negovanovic

Text type: Minion
Display type: Diotima
Designed and composed by P. M. Gordon Associates

Printed in the United States of America

Library of Congress Cataloging-in-Publication Data
Salem, Eric.
   In pursuit of the good : intellect and action in Aristotle's ethics / Eric Salem.
— 1st Paul Dry Books ed.
      p. cm.
   ISBN 978-1-58988-050-4 (alk. paper)
  1. Aristotle. Nicomachean ethics. 2. Ethics. 3. Happiness. 4. Good and evil.
I. Title.
   B430.S25 2009
   171'.3—dc22
                                                      2009002648

To my mother and father

CONTENTS

PREFACE

> Every art and every inquiry and likewise action as well as choice seems to aim at some good.
>
> Aristotle, *Nicomachean Ethics* (opening line)

WHY DO WE DO everything we do? What end or good are we pursuing when we make our choices and live our lives? What is the ultimate aim of human life? This is the question Aristotle sets out to answer in the *Nicomachean Ethics*.

Naming the human good turns out to be fairly easy. What people want more than anything else is to live well and prosper, to flourish, to be happy: *Happiness* is the one thing we want simply and solely for its own sake. But finding a name for the good is just the first step in a very long journey. The domain Aristotle traverses in the *Ethics* is vast and various. Deliberation and choice; virtue and vice; pleasure and pain; honor and friendship; the heights of intellectual activity and radiant moral action, the degrading ugliness of moral weakness, morbidity, and brutishness—all fall within the scope of his inquiry. No wonder Aristotle calls his search for the good, his pursuit of happiness, "the philosophy concerning human things." Every human thing, every human possibility, has its proper place within his inquiry. Nothing human is alien to Aristotle.

What is happiness? What role does luck play in the life of a happy man? Is the good life a life of ease and pleasure-seeking? Is the pursuit of honor compatible with living well? Must the happy man have certain excellences or virtues, and if so, which ones? Is the life of moral excellence a happy one? What about a life devoted to inquiry and reflection? What is the happy man's relation to other human beings? Do happy human beings need friends? These are among the questions that Aristotle addresses in the *Ethics*. They are also questions that I take up in my own inquiry. My intention throughout is to make sense of the varying and sometimes contradictory answers that Aristotle gives to these questions.

In order to do this, I must uncover and trace the underlying argument of the *Ethics*, its "logic." I begin with the end of Aristotle's inquiry. A central difficulty concerning the relation of thought to action emerges in Book X. I articulate that difficulty and place it within a larger framework (Introduction). I then do what I think Aristotle means us to do—re-read the book with that difficulty in mind. I begin with a long look at Aristotle's initial sketch of happiness in Book I (Chapter One); consider the moral virtues and moral life through Aristotle's snapshots of the great-souled man and complete justice in Books IV through V (Chapter Two); and work through Aristotle's account of the intellectual virtues in Book VI (Chapter Three). I then return to the end of Aristotle's inquiry and view the difficulties elaborated earlier in light of his extended treatment of friendship in Books VIII and IX (Chapter Four). In the *Ethics*, as in life, friendship proves to be a key that unlocks many doors.

I make a number of assumptions in the course of my inquiry. Let me briefly consider two of them here. To begin with, I suppose that Aristotle's initial question is meaningful: There is something called human happiness, and it makes sense to investigate it. In addition, I suppose that we can understand the *Ethics* on its own terms and learn something about human happiness from Aristotle.

Many objections can be leveled against these assumptions. Someone might insist that we all have our own individual views of happiness, views developed on the basis of our individual experiences; there is no *one* thing we can call human happiness—and even if there were, human reason is too weak to comprehend it. Also, Aristotle lived long ago and far away. His world is too distant from ours for us to be able to grasp his thoughts about happiness or anything else. Moreover, while his thoughts about happiness may have been meaningful to his contemporaries or near contemporaries, they cannot possibly be meaningful to us: Our circumstances are different, and different circumstances dictate different understandings and different forms of happiness.

I find none of these objections convincing; they certainly don't prove that making the *effort* to understand Aristotle is not a worthwhile undertaking. For one thing, all the objections I've listed rest on presuppositions that are themselves questionable. Take the first one. Different people have different views of happiness. Does it follow from this that there is not some one thing called happiness? One view might be right and the others wrong. Or perhaps—and this is closer to my approach and, I think, Aristotle's—happiness is something complex, and each claim about it brings into view one aspect of it, one part of its total truth. The first verb used in the *Ethics*, "aim," is also used of arrows, which are literally "sent at" or "released toward" their objects. Perhaps that is our case. We have been sent or released by nature. We are like arrows speeding toward the same target from different angles. Is it any surprise that the target looks different to each of us? Or take the second objection. How could we know in advance that reason is too weak to make progress with Aristotle's question concerning happiness? *Our* reason may be too weak, perhaps from lack of practice as much as anything else. But wouldn't it make sense to watch a master-reasoner—say, Aristotle in the *Ethics*— wrestle with the question before drawing any conclusions?

I take a slightly different approach to the objections based on the distance between Aristotle's thought-world and our own. Aristotle's initial question about happiness is not one that we ask ourselves very often. We tend to keep our heads down. We pursue particular goods, aim at particular ends, and let our actions be shaped by our characters, our settled opinions, and the usual constraints that life imposes on us. But now and then we find ourselves diverted from the usual course of our lives. We start to wonder what we should do with ourselves and what really matters. We suddenly want to know whether it's good to be good, what friends are for, whether the esteem of others is worth caring about. We may even start to wonder whether the asking of such questions is a feature of the good life—whether, that is, the unexamined life is really worth living. These are precisely the sorts of questions that Aristotle addresses in the *Ethics*: At such moments our kinship with Aristotle becomes apparent. We find ourselves in, or at least on the border of, Aristotle country. We have been *grazed* by Aristotle's question, and if we then turn to the *Ethics*, we will find that the more we read, the more we will see ourselves and our concerns reflected in Aristotle's own inquiries. Of course there are things that are hard to understand in the *Ethics* and in Aristotle's other works. But these reflect not a distance in time between us and Aristotle but a difference in depth of understanding. In short, the best solution to worries about the possibility of reading Aristotle fruitfully is to plunge right in.

Before I plunge in there are a number of people I must thank: first and foremost, Leo Paul de Alvarez, for showing me how to read the *Ethics*, for guiding my inquiries, and for prodding me to produce the first version of this text some twenty years ago; Tom West, for pressing me to be clear and keep my focus on human things; Glenn Arbery, J Keyser, Ron Millen, Ron Mawby, and Mark Shirey, for the right conversations about the right things at the right times; Joe Sachs, for the twelve years of Aristotle study groups that helped me to re-think the version he was kind enough to read; Pamela Kraus and Laurence Berns, for helpful comments on sections of the manuscript; Eva Brann, for scads of comments, and for three hours of *Ethics*-conversation, coffee, and cookies while we worked through the manuscript at her kitchen table; Paul Dry, for his keen eye, editorial advice, and patience; Peter Kalkavage, for serving as editor, for dozens of helpful suggestions, and for much-needed support in the home stretch.

And finally, thanks to Karen, for endless conversations about the subject matter of the *Ethics*, for keeping the home fires burning, and for putting up with my attempts to juggle teaching, studying, and writing.

IN PURSUIT OF
THE GOOD

INTRODUCTION

M IDWAY THROUGH THE TENTH and final book of the *Nicomachean Ethics* Aristotle re-opens the question he first raised in Book I: What is happiness? There he defined happiness, or the human good, as an "activity of the soul in accordance with virtue" (1098a16–17). But this definition can hardly be said to provide a satisfactory answer to his question. Aristotle himself likens it to a mere "outline" or "sketch" (*perigraphē*) of happiness, and for good reason (1098a20–24). His initial definition leaves us wondering *what* activity constitutes happiness, and *what* virtue happiness is an activity in accordance with. Now, ten books later, having discussed "the virtues and friendships and pleasures," Aristotle proposes to fill in the sketch (1176a30–32).[1]

Happiness, he argues, does not lie in the enjoyment of bodily pleasures, in the "childish amusement" (*paidia*) so prized by most men, including "those in power" (1176b9–1177a11). Nor does it lie in the exercise of the moral or ethical virtues. Although Aristotle is careful to say that the happy man will practice such virtues as occasion dictates, the life of action, the life of beautiful deeds undertaken for their own sake, is not, it seems, the happy life (1178b3–7). Happiness rather lies in contemplation (*theōria*), in knowing, in "seeing" (*theōrein*) for its own sake; happiness is the activity of the intellect in accordance with wisdom (*sophia*) (1177a12–18; 1179a29–32).

Aristotle's rejection of "amusement" should come as no surprise to the reader of the *Ethics*. As early as Book I, Aristotle staunchly refused to identify happiness with bodily pleasure; his "sketchy" definition of happiness itself implies that virtue rather than pleasure lies at the core of happiness (1095b19–22). And although Aristotle comes close at times to identifying the activity that is happiness with certain pleasures, and claims repeatedly

1

that the capacity to take pleasure in virtuous activity is a mark of virtue, he never ceases to distinguish the pleasures of the happy man from those summed up in the ordinary meaning of *paidia* (1099a7–21; 1175a12–22).

What is surprising, even shocking, is Aristotle's rejection— and rejection is not too strong a word—of the claims of the active life in favor of the contemplative. After all, Aristotle spends by far the greater part of the *Ethics* discussing the virtues that fulfill themselves in action (*praxis*)—courage, moderation, generosity, justice, and the like. Book II and most of Book III are an account of moral or ethical virtue "in general." The remainder of Book III and Books IV and V treat the particular moral virtues (and their corresponding vices). Most of Book VII is devoted to a discussion of continence and incontinence, dispositions of the soul that share the same sphere and the same objects as moderation and its opposite. Even in Book VI, Aristotle's account of the intellectual virtues, the focus is primarily on action. Not wisdom (*sophia*) or knowledge (*epistēmē*), but prudence (*phronēsis*), the intellectual virtue aligned with the moral virtues, is the chief topic of Aristotle's discussion of the part of the soul that "possesses *logos*." The question forced upon us by Aristotle's claim in Book X is clear: If happiness truly lies in *theōria* rather than *praxis*, if human life reaches its peak and end in the activity of wisdom rather than in action in accordance with moral virtue, why spend so much of the *Ethics* discussing the practical life, and so little discussing the theoretical?[2]

This question acquires even more force when we consider the "tone" of the *Ethics* as a whole, and then take into account its concluding chapter. From the first, Aristotle seems to assume that the good or happiness lies in action rather than thought. Action (*praxis*) and activity (*energeia*) function as virtual synonyms in the opening argument of the *Ethics* (1094a3–6). Aristotle addresses his book to those who "fashion their appetites and act (*prattousi*) according to reason" and characterizes it as a "sort of political" inquiry (1094b10–11; 1095a10–11). He calls the end he seeks "the highest of all goods achievable through action (*praktōn agathōn)*" (1095a14–17). In Book II Aristotle remarks—and the remark is characteristic of the *Ethics*—that "the present business is not for the sake of *theōria*, as the others are," as if acting rather than knowing were the ultimate end of his inquiry (1103b26–30). The very absence of the word *logos* from his definition of happiness in Book I, and the postponement of any account of *logos* until after his lengthy discussion of the moral virtues suggest that thought in any form, and *a fortiori* theoretical thought, plays at best a subordinate role in the happy life.

The final chapter of Book X of the *Ethics* points to the same conclusion. For Aristotle begins it by returning to the position that thought, including theoretical thought, exists for the sake of action: "Or just as is said, the end in actions is not to contemplate *(theōrēsai)* each of the things and to know them, but rather to do *(prattein)* them" (1179a35–1179b1). The remainder of the chapter seems to bear out this shift. Nowhere in the final chapter does Aristotle mention *theōria*. The question discussed there is how best to lead the young to virtue. Given what Aristotle has just finished saying about contemplation, we might expect him to suggest ways through which the young might be induced to care for wisdom. But this is precisely what Aristotle does not do: He never mentions wisdom, and instead makes the inculcation of *moral* virtue his theme. In short, *theōria* makes a brief appearance in the final book of the *Ethics*, only to be bundled off stage in its closing moments.

What are we to make of this curious state of affairs? If true happiness lies in *theōria*, and if Aristotle knows this before he reaches Book X, what possible reason could he have for spending such a large part of the *Ethics* treating the "practical" virtues, that is, the moral virtues and prudence? And why conclude the *Ethics* with what amounts to a call to action once the superiority of *theōria* has been established? Several possibilities come to mind. It might be the case, for instance, that knowledge of contemplation and of the contemplative life is available only to those who have first thought deeply about the moral virtues, prudence, and the life based upon them. Aristotle's lengthy account of the intricate workings of the moral virtues and prudence may serve as a kind of paradigm for understanding the still more intricate, or at any rate less accessible, workings of wisdom. Can *theōria* perhaps be *understood* only by way of *praxis*?

Again, Aristotle's discussion of the active life may be intended to show us the limits of that life and to prepare us for his claim that the theoretical life is superior to it. Here two possibilities present themselves. Aristotle's lengthy account may be a sort of *reductio ad absurdum*, the ultimate purpose of which is to display the defects inherent in the practical life, and thence the necessity of preferring the contemplative life to it. Or Aristotle may simply mean to show us the incompleteness of *praxis* without *theōria*—and perhaps at the same time the incompleteness of *theōria* without *praxis*. Is the happy life a judicious mixture of action and contemplation, and is *theōria* in the fullest sense available only to those who also (and already) *possess*, and not merely understand, the moral virtues and prudence?

Or, to sketch out yet another alternative, perhaps *theōria* and *praxis* are not completely different activities—which may or may not be appropriately united within a single life—but instead aspects of the *same* activity. Does Aristotle separate out *theōria* in Book X only in order to make visible a not easily seen aspect of the *one* activity that is happiness—is he exaggerating for the sake of clarity? Are *theōria* and *praxis* perhaps separable only "in speech"?

Answering these questions will require a careful examination of the *Ethics*. If we are to understand what Aristotle has to say about the relation between *theōria* and *praxis*, we cannot simply point to what he says about that relation in Book X. On the contrary, we must first understand the "elements" of that relation; that is, we need to take a close look at the moral virtues and prudence, on the one hand, and theoretical wisdom and its components, on the other. And as we do, we must ask ourselves why he presents these elements in the order he does and as he does. What Aristotle says in Book X about *theōria* and *praxis* must be understood in light of the unfolding argument of the *Ethics* as a whole.

The need for a careful reading of the *Ethics* becomes even clearer if we attend to the way Aristotle proceeds in that book. The question that explicitly guides and informs Aristotle's inquiry throughout is *not* whether contemplation is superior to action. This may turn out to be the most significant form of the question "What is the good or happiness?" But it seems equally significant that Aristotle does not raise this question explicitly at the outset of the *Ethics*—in fact, does not set contemplation over and against action until its final book. If we wish to understand Aristotle as he understands himself, we must beware of approaching his inquiry with a question that emerges only late in the course of that inquiry; otherwise we run the risk of losing sight of the grounds of that question, the horizon within which it first becomes intelligible. Only a close reading of the *Ethics* can show us why Aristotle is ultimately forced to call into question the very assumption upon which his inquiry seems to rest, the assumption that happiness lies in action rather than thought.

There are other reasons for proceeding with care in the study of Aristotle's work. We live in a world shaped in large measure by Aristotle's thought—or rather by interpretations and transformations of his thought. For instance, many of the key terms and distinctions employed by Aristotle in the *Ethics* (and elsewhere) have become part of the very warp and woof of our thinking. When we use words like science, intuition, induction, and demonstration; when we speak of prudence or morality or ethics; above all, when we distinguish between theory and practice, or between science and "life," we are thinking in Aristotelian terms. This fact alone would justify an inquiry into Aristotle's understanding of the relation between *theōria* and *praxis*: What better way to reflect on our own understanding of the distinction between theory and practice or, in general, on the place of knowledge and its pursuit within human life, than to return to the author chiefly responsible for establishing that distinction?

And yet the very fact that Aristotle's distinction has become commonplace for us, the fact that we take science and the so-called "life of the mind" for granted—as we do even if we disdain them—means that we are liable to take as self-evident a distinction that for Aristotle is at once hard won and somewhat questionable. Moreover and more important, virtually every one of Aristotle's key terms and distinctions has been the subject of repeated interpretation. And more often than not, the interpreters have been enemies of Aristotle (or at any rate of Aristotelianism) who deliberately set out to "stand Aristotle on his head," either by jettisoning important elements of his thought, for example, the notion of final cause, or by subtly transforming his vocabulary.

This holds true of *theōria* and *praxis* as well as other key terms in the *Ethics*. What Aristotle means by science or theoretical knowledge underwent a radical transformation at the hands of two of his most determined opponents, Bacon and Descartes. Along with this new understanding of *theōria* came a new notion of *praxis*: the new science was linked, indeed fused, with the task of mastering nature in the name of improving the human condition. Put in Aristotle's own terms, Bacon and Descartes radically undermined the distinction between *epistēmē*, *praxis*, and *technē*. In terms more familiar to us, science became the handmaiden of technology and was permitted to keep intact her sense of dignity only so long as she acknowledged the claims of her mistress.[3]

The lesson to be learned here is clear enough: Even the most innocuous translation of Aristotle's words may conceal interpretations of his thought that distort his meaning. We need to pay close attention to Aristotle's language, to the very words in which he couches his insights, lest we ascribe to those words meanings not intended by Aristotle. In short, if we wish to recover the thought of the author chiefly responsible for the distinction between theory and practice, we must avoid making over that distinction in the image of our latter-day understanding of it.

The difficulties—and rewards—inherent in any attempt to grapple directly with Aristotle's thought become still clearer when we compare his enterprise with that of two of his most influential interpreters, Thomas Aquinas and Descartes. It is hardly an exaggeration to say that Aquinas, certainly one of the deepest and most "friendly" of Aristotle's readers, tends to take the Philosopher's thought and language for granted, on faith, so to speak: Aquinas's categories, in the broad as well as the narrow sense, are largely Aristotle's. To be sure, Aquinas disagrees with Aristotle at times, above all when what Aristotle says conflicts with Christian doctrine. But even in such cases, Aquinas does not so much use conflict as an occasion for thinking a serious question through "from the ground up" as he does seek a position wherein the thought of Aristotle and the teachings of the Bible can be reconciled. It is no accident that even Aquinas's disagreements with Aristotle are couched in Aristotle's terms. In a decisive sense, Aquinas is an Aristotelian, albeit a Christian Aristotelian; that is, he makes *Aristotle's thought* the object and guide of his own.

The same thing cannot be said of Descartes. Although his arguments and conclusions in the *Meditations* and elsewhere often seem to have about them the odor of scholasticism or Aristotelianism, to deny that Descartes seriously intends to leave behind the education he repudiates in the *Discourse on Method* would be to deny the power of the drama of doubt we see played out in the *Discourse* and *Meditations*. Moreover, one can argue that Descartes is forced to wear the mask of an Aristotelian in order to overcome Aristotle and Aristotelianism.[4] But it is precisely here that the kinship between Descartes and Aquinas becomes apparent: However pure, however free of the taint of Aristotle's views Descartes' position may appear to be, it is nevertheless true that Descartes arrives at that position *by negating* the thought of Aristotle. He is just as surely an anti-Aristotelian as Aquinas is an Aristotelian. In other words, the thought of Descartes, as well as that of Aquinas, is in a decisive sense determined by Aristotle. Each thinker defines himself in terms of an *already given* philosophic tradition.

With Aristotle this is not the case. To be sure, he always takes into account the opinions of "the wise," in the *Ethics* and elsewhere. As John Burnet amply demonstrates in his commentary on the *Ethics*, Aristotle is often engaged in conversation with his contemporaries and predecessors even when he does not make this apparent by mentioning names.[5] But this is just what distinguishes Aristotle from authors like Descartes and Aquinas. Though he sometimes agrees and sometimes disagrees with the opinions of his fellow philosophers, these opinions never form the primary subject matter or the principal focus of his inquiries. They rather serve as occasions for reflecting directly on the things themselves. Put otherwise, when Aristotle engages in conversation with his fellow lovers of wisdom, he does not so much look *to* their views (whether in the mode of negation or affirmation) as he looks *with* them, in common with them, at the world. Or to say the same thing in yet another way: Although Aristotle concerns himself with the views of the philosophers, his primary concern always lies in understanding, sifting through, and then ascending from what might be called the pre-scientific or pre-philosophic understanding of things. The commonsense understanding of the world, the understanding of things that human beings *as* human beings always already have, always forms the principal point of departure of his inquiries.[6]

Here we have one explanation for the fluidity and apparent incoherence of Aristotle's discourses, especially those that focus on human affairs: Our everyday understanding of the world is riddled with ambiguity; words mean different things in different contexts, and even within the same context our most deeply held convictions are often at odds with one another. Because this is so, and because Aristotle stays so close to "what seems to be the case," his attempts to sort out and articulate what we say and think about the world necessarily share in this ambiguity. Thus it is often difficult to know exactly when Aristotle is speaking in his own voice and when he is giving voice to one aspect or another of "everydayness;" when he is using words precisely, that is, with their most proper (*oikeios*) or authoritative (*kurios*) meaning, and when he is imitating and exploring the apparently arbitrary, but nevertheless revealing, way in which human beings ordinarily speak.[7] What's more, even when Aristotle speaks precisely and in his own voice, his claims and conclusions betray their origins in the hurly-burly of everyday speech and experience. His conclusions are necessarily hypothetical and tentative, and even his most basic distinctions, not to mention the edifices erected upon them, need to be examined again and again—something Aristotle lets us see if only we are willing to look. In short, the task Aristotle imposes upon his readers is not that different from the task he imposes upon himself: We, too, are forced, again and again, to return to, reflect upon, and think through our ordinary experience of the world, a task made more rather than less difficult by the "history of philosophy." Like Plato, his friend and fellow lover of wisdom, Aristotle the inquirer writes his books for inquiring—and patient—minds.

But the almost limitless patience that Aristotle's writings demand of their readers has its rewards. In the case of the *Ethics* in particular, if we are willing to follow Aristotle's own path, to make the attempt to understand Aristotle as he understands himself, we may come to see how *theōria* and the difference between *theōria* and *praxis* show themselves within the natural understanding of human things. We may come to see how they look, not from the vantage point of an already established philosophic tradition, which takes for granted the existence, and in some sense the superiority, of "theory," but from a point of view that lets *theōria* and the life that contains it appear as the strange and perhaps questionable things they are.

No doubt the best way of doing this would be to undertake a line-by-line examination of the *Ethics*, something along the lines of Aquinas's own painstaking commentary. For a variety of reasons, such an examination is out of the question here. But something approximating it is not. We can begin with a close reading of the first book of the *Ethics*. This will allow us to see how our questions concerning *theōria*, *praxis*, and their relation can be framed in Aristotle's own terms, how those questions arise "naturally" in the course of his inquiry. Beginning where Aristotle begins will also allow us to pick and choose passages in the remainder of the *Ethics* in a fitting way. Finally, a careful examination of Book I will help to give us a sense of the character of Aristotle's inquiry, that is, his understanding of his own enterprise as well as his peculiar way of writing. Thus looking closely at Book I should serve to confirm and amplify some of my claims about his way of proceeding.

1

||||||||||||||||||||||||||||||||||||||||||||||||||

HAPPINESS

THE FIRST BOOK OF the *Nicomachean Ethics* looks like a mess. At first glance, it seems more like a heap of loosely related arguments and fragments of arguments than a well-ordered whole. To be sure, Aristotle raises a question in the first chapter of Book I, answers it, though "sketchily," in chapter seven, and then goes on to defend his answer in chapter eight. Moreover, chapters four and five contain the beginnings of an inquiry into this question—the beginnings of a search for the "highest human good." To this extent, Book I is more than a patchwork. But the remainder of Book I is given over to discussions and digressions that seem only faintly related to the question at hand. The argument of chapter four is interrupted—as it is preceded—by a series of terse reflections on the nature of inquiry. And the line of reasoning "developed" in the brief chapter five breaks off abruptly and is followed by a lengthy, not to say obscure, critique of the Platonic understanding of "the good itself," a critique that Aristotle admits "would be more at home in another philosophy" (1096b31).

Again, in the latter part of Book I, rather than continuing the defense of his definition of happiness or perhaps clarifying some of its obscurer points, Aristotle spends his time considering apparently peripheral questions like "Can a man be called happy before he is dead?" Even chapter seven, where Aristotle at last names and defines the human good, lacks clarity and resolution. The line of reasoning that leads to his definition of the good is highly compressed, to say the least, and it is followed by yet another of those reflections on inquiry that at once interrupt and undermine the development of his argument. In short, if we approach the first book of the *Ethics*—as well we might a work by the author of the *Prior* and *Posterior Analytics*—expecting to find displayed there the virtues of clarity and distinctness, we seem doomed to disappointment. We find a book riddled with obscurity and plagued by confusion, a book lacking both clarity in its arguments and a due sense of order in their presentation.

Is it any wonder, then, that serious scholars long regarded the *Ethics* as a rather badly edited compilation of Aristotle's lecture notes on ethical matters?[1] Given what we now know or believe we know about the manner in which Aristotle's works were assembled, and given what *we see* when we first read Book I, the efforts of Aquinas and other early commentators on Aristotle to find consistency and order in the *Ethics* (and elsewhere in the Aristotelian corpus) seem fruitless, naive, even somewhat ridiculous. Charity, if nothing else, bids us regard it as the work of some other hand than Aristotle's.

And yet, a second glance at Book I, a reading of it that proceeds on the assumption that Aristotle not only wrote the *Ethics* but also knew what he was doing when he wrote it, reveals a method in the apparent madness of Book I. The more carefully we read Aristotle's highly compressed arguments, the more sense they make. The more carefully we attend to his reflections on inquiry, the more clearly we begin to see why he *must* include them, and why his inquiry in Book I *must* have the shape that it has, *must* seem confusing at first sight. Above all, we begin to see that Book I is, after all, a well-ordered argument, a *logos*, that centers on Aristotle's definition of happiness in chapter seven.

All roads in Book I lead to that definition—this is what reflection shows us. The "false" starts in chapters four and five pave the way for the claim that the good is happiness as Aristotle defines it. His discussion of apparently unrelated questions in the latter part of Book I does, in fact, serve to clarify, ground, and fill out his "sketch" of the good in chapter seven. Even Aristotle's critique of

Platonism in chapter six turns out to have a purpose within Book I, defined, once again, by his argument in chapter seven. It is no accident that Aristotle puts his definition of happiness at the very center of Book I: its place within the text reflects its place within the *logos* of Book I.

The centrality of Aristotle's definition suggests a point of departure for our own inquiry into the *Ethics*. I cannot hope to illuminate every dark corner in Book I, to show that every sentence or even every argument in Book I belongs of necessity within Aristotle's *logos*. What I can do is attempt to make sense of Aristotle's definition and in so doing show, at least in outline, that Book I is indeed an ordered whole. At any rate, it should become clear as we proceed that much of what seems obscure and out of place in Book I is indispensable to an understanding of his definition of happiness.

I. COMPLETE VIRTUE
AND A COMPLETE LIFE

It is not quite true to say, as I did earlier, that Aristotle defines happiness or the human good as an "activity of the soul in accordance with virtue," for he qualifies this formulation in two ways immediately after making it. He adds, "and if the virtues are several, in accordance with the best and most complete [virtue]" and ends with, "and further, in a complete life" (1098a17–18). Thus the full definition of happiness that Aristotle gives us in chapter seven would run roughly as follows: Happiness or the human good is an activity of the soul in accordance with the best and most complete virtue, in a complete life.

The words "activity of the soul in accordance with virtue," even apart from Aristotle's qualifications, pose a serious problem for the reader of the *Ethics*. Most human beings would deny that happiness has anything to do with virtue. Most would probably agree with what Aristotle undertakes to show in the first half of chapter seven, namely, that happiness is *the* human good or that happiness is the most appropriate name for the human good. As

Aristotle points out at the close of that argument, this is "no doubt (*isōs*) . . . something agreed upon" (1097b22–23). But most people would "no doubt" be inclined to say that, all things being equal, human happiness lies in pleasure rather than virtue, in joy rather than excellence. Accordingly, if we are to make sense of Aristotle's definition of happiness, we must at some point understand why it includes virtue and excludes pleasure.

Yet in a certain sense, Aristotle's two qualifications present an even greater and more pressing problem than his initial formulation. Not only does he defend this formulation in chapter eight, and indeed seek to "harmonize" it with the view that happiness is pleasure; he also arrives at the formulation "activity of the soul in accordance with virtue" by way of a closely reasoned argument in chapter seven. The same thing cannot be said of his two qualifications. He gives no reason at all for the first qualification, and none to speak of for the second; the gloss he provides for the words "in a complete life," namely, "for one swallow does not a spring make, nor one day" can scarcely be regarded as a sufficient reason for their inclusion in his definition (1098a18–19). How should we understand these qualifications? What do they mean, and why does Aristotle add them to his original formulation?

ONE POSSIBLE REASON FOR Aristotle's first qualification becomes apparent when we consider his definition of happiness in light of Books II through VI of the *Ethics*. In those books Aristotle discusses a total of thirteen virtues, and it is natural to assume, as we work through his discussion, that these are the virtues of the happy man, that he means to say that the happy man will be courageous in war, moderate in his pursuit of pleasures, generous with his wealth, and so on. But the words "if the virtues are several, then in accordance with the best and most complete [virtue]" suggest that this is not Aristotle's meaning at all. On the contrary, Aristotle thinks happiness is an activity in accordance with only one of the many virtues. His first qualification thus serves as a kind of warning to the reader. It tells us to read the *Ethics* not as a straightforward presentation of the several virtues of the happy man but as a search for the *one* virtue whose exercise constitutes happiness.

This reading of the passage bears on the way we understand the relation of *theōria* to *praxis*. I began this inquiry with the puzzled observation that in Book X Aristotle suddenly argues for the superiority of contemplation to action, and thus, in effect, for the superiority of wisdom to all the other virtues. But we can now see that his apparently abrupt setting off one virtue against the others at the end of his inquiry was in the works from the beginning; it was embedded inconspicuously in his very definition of happiness.[2] To be sure, we have not yet examined Aristotle's reasons for thinking that *sophia* is "the best and most complete" of the virtues. Nor have we seen why Aristotle believes that happiness must be an activity in accordance with only one virtue: why *shouldn't* happiness consist in the activity of all the virtues, each in their proper season? But clearly Aristotle thinks that happiness lies in the exercise of only one of the many virtues.

Or is it clear? Another reading of Aristotle's first qualification keeps open the possibility that *all* the virtues he considers might play a significant part in the happy man's life. Aristotle's words *could* mean that the virtues are many and that happiness is an activity in accordance with only one of them. But they could also mean that *if* the virtues are many—and this is an issue worth pursuing—then happiness will be an activity in accordance with only one of them. If not, if the several virtues are in some sense one, then happiness will be, or may be, an activity in accordance with all the "virtues." In other words, if we take the "if" clause seriously, if, that is, we take it as a *question*, we are obliged to ask ourselves whether the many virtues Aristotle discusses are perhaps many only in appearance: perhaps the same virtue shows itself now as courage, now as moderation, now as justice and now again as . . . wisdom.

This second interpretation of Aristotle's words has somewhat less support in the text than the first. Had Aristotle wished us to read his "if" clause as contrary to fact, he could have made this perfectly clear. On the other hand, he could also have made it perfectly clear that only one of the many virtues lies at the core of happiness simply by modifying or leaving out the "if" clause; that he leaves it in place suggests that we are to take it seriously.[3] Moreover—and this will become clear as we make our way through the *Ethics*—Aristotle *is* in fact on the lookout for a kind of unified field theory of the virtues, that is, a single virtue that both presupposes and in some sense comprehends the remaining virtues. Consider, for instance, his discussion of prudence at the end of Book VI.

Though these two interpretations of Aristotle's first qualification seem to be at odds with one another, they have much in common. Both invite us to read his account of the virtues *actively* and with an eye to their wholeness or completeness. The first encourages us to search for the one virtue that is best and most complete, the second to investigate the possibility that all the "virtues" might be parts or aspects or modes of a larger whole. Moreover, each interpretation requires us to sacrifice some part of our "everyday" understanding of virtue and happiness. Suppose we find persuasive Aristotle's claim that happiness is an activity in accordance with virtue, that happiness lies in "being virtuous." Then the first interpretation requires us to say that, for instance, being courageous and being moderate are not both aspects of being happy, while the second asks us to believe that courage and moderation are not distinct virtues. Aristotle's first qualification of his definition of happiness—if we take it seriously—not only obliges us to read the *Ethics* with a view to the question of wholeness or completeness; it pushes us to think para-doxically, that is, to think past or beyond (*para*) our everyday opinions (*doxai*) concerning virtue and happiness.[4]

What about Aristotle's second qualification? Like the first, the qualification "and further, in a complete life" admits of more than one meaning. To be sure, Aristotle's gloss on these words implies that duration or continuity belongs to happiness. Just as a single sunny day or the song and flight of a single swallow do not necessarily mark the arrival of spring, so, too, one radiant deed, a single burst of virtuous activity, does not sufficiently signal the presence of happiness. The true mark of happiness is the steady exercise of virtue throughout a life. This much is clear, but the meaning of the words "and further, in a complete life" is nevertheless obscure.

The qualification may specify an additional condition for happiness, beyond that of virtue. Aristotle may mean that happiness both requires the presence of complete virtue in the soul and, in addition, a complete life within which to exercise that virtue—a life in no way guaranteed by the presence of virtue. Or the qualification might have a simpler meaning. Aristotle's view may be that virtue and its exercise are *of necessity* enduring, but he may wish us to avoid making the error of the man who mistakes one beautiful day for spring. Aristotle may simply wish to remind us that happiness, like spring, takes time.

Chapter seven does not help us to decide which of these views is Aristotle's; nor does it discuss the implications of each view. Fortunately, however, the later chapters of Book I—chapters that appeared earlier to have no place within Aristotle's inquiry into the human good—serve as an extended gloss on the words "in a complete life." Let us turn to them now.

In chapter nine Aristotle investigates the sources of human happiness. Alluding to Meno's initial question to Socrates concerning virtue, he asks whether happiness, that is, activity *in accordance with virtue*, is "something learnable or acquired by habituation or also somehow acquired through practice in some other way or comes to be according to some divine lot or even on account of chance" (1099b9–11).[5] In chapters ten and eleven, Aristotle addresses the "Solonic" question—a question also at work in Greek tragedy—whether a man can be counted happy before he is dead.[6] But the issue that underlies and gives rise to both of these inquiries is the one that Aristotle first broaches in the closing lines of chapter eight: What part do external goods or, more generally, fortune (*tychē*) or good fortune (*eutychia*) play in the life of the happy man?

Aristotle approaches this question with delicacy and even diffidence. At the end of chapter eight, he admits that external goods do make a difference. After all, who would be so bold as to call happy a man who lacks children and friends, or worse still, a man whose children are bad and whose friends are scoundrels (1099b3–6)? In chapter nine, however, Aristotle initially backs away from this view: "To entrust the biggest and most beautiful thing to fortune," he says, "would be too discordant" (1099b24–25). Yet he concludes the chapter with a statement that returns us to his initial position and to the language of his definition of happiness: "For, just as we said, both complete virtue *and* a complete life are necessary. For many changes and all sorts of fortunes turn up in life, and it is possible for one who has led an exceedingly upright life to fall into great misfortune in old age, as the tale is told of Priam in the Trojan stories; and no one calls happy the man who has met with such fortunes and died miserably" (1100a4–9).

In chapters ten and eleven, Aristotle again wends his way between the view that external goods make no difference and the view that they make all the difference in the world. The focus here, however, is on the primacy of virtue and its exercise. For instance, Aristotle observes that "what is beautiful" in the virtuous man "shines out," that is, is actively, radiantly present in the world, even in the midst of great misfortune, namely, "whenever someone bears with good temper many and great misfortunes, not on account of insensitivity to suffering, but because he is noble and great-souled" (1100b30–33). Moreover, he insists in chapter ten that "steadfastness" belongs to nothing in human affairs so much as "activity in accordance with virtue," as if to say that the life of the happy man arises directly from his enduring and virtuous activity rather than being an external condition on which that activity depends (1100b12–13). And yet, even as he argues for the primacy of activity in accordance with virtue, Aristotle remains aware of the problem posed by great misfortune and great suffering. He returns again to the plight of Priam in chapter ten, and even goes so far as to admit, in chapter eleven, that the sufferings of children and friends, even after a man's death, have some limited effect on his happiness (1101a6–8; 1101b1–10).[7]

Where exactly does Aristotle stand on the question of external goods or chance, and how, accordingly, are we to understand the words, "and further, in a complete life"? If what counts in regard to happiness is the condition of a man's soul, if the make-up of the soul is what makes for happiness or its opposite, then the presence or absence of external goods would be of little moment, and Aristotle's second qualification would simply mean that happiness properly names virtuous activity as it shows itself over the course of a man's whole life. The "complete life" of the happy man would simply be the unfolding, the externalization, of the soul's inner excellence. Happiness would be like a play that can be performed any time, anywhere, on any stage. On the other hand, if external goods do make a decisive difference, if human happiness stands or falls by fortune, then Aristotle's second qualification would mean that a "complete life," in the sense of a life replete with external goods as well as one "full of days," is an added condition for happiness: stage, staging, props, and even audience would all be of vital importance.[8] Aristotle presents persuasive arguments for both views. Perhaps, then, the most one can say about the second qualification is that, like the first, it raises a serious question, again concerned with completeness, which we are meant to keep in mind as we read the *Ethics*. Just as Aristotle's first qualification invites us to ask where completeness is to be found among the virtues—in one virtue or in "many"—so his second qualification encourages us to ask ourselves where completeness is to be found in the happy man's life. Is the man who possesses complete virtue sufficient unto himself—is he complete and happy simply because of the condition of his soul? Or do his happiness and completeness depend as well on the presence of external goods, and hence in some measure on chance?[9]

Though Aristotle does not answer these questions in the second half of Book I, I want to emphasize that he does not leave us entirely in the dark about the place of fortune in a happy life. Even as Aristotle argues for the importance of external goods, when, for instance, he observes in chapter eight that "without equipment it is impossible or not easy *to do beautiful things*," he makes it clear that such goods are subordinate to virtue and the beautiful deeds it generates.[10] He rejects out of hand the common view—implicit in the ordinary meaning of the word *eudaimonia*—that happiness *is* good fortune or comes about solely through the "agency" of chance: good fortune may be a necessary but it is in no way a sufficient condition for happiness.[11] In short, never for a moment does Aristotle back away from the claim that virtue or activity in accordance with virtue forms the core of happiness. The only question for him is whether and to what extent external goods are requisite for that activity.

II. PLEASURE AND VIRTUE

To say that Aristotle subordinates fortune to virtue in chapters nine through eleven is to say that Aristotle's inquiries in this section of Book I—like his division of virtues in the final chapter of Book I, his discussion of the moral virtues in Books II through V, and his examination of the intellectual virtues in Book VI—rest on the assumption that happiness lies chiefly in activity in accordance with virtue. Can we make sense of this claim, especially since most people, as I observed earlier, identify happiness with pleasure rather than virtuous activity? For surely this is the most paradoxical of the claims Aristotle makes in Book I. It may be difficult to believe that good luck is not the chief source of happiness. To suggest that courage, generosity, and good manners in conversation may all be aspects or parts of the same human excellence severely tests our convictions about virtue. But the claim that virtue rather than pleasure is central to the meaning of happiness, that virtuous activity rather than enjoyment is the good that all men "really" aim at and long for, runs counter to our deepest beliefs about human happiness.

Before we begin to consider Aristotle's reasons for making this claim, two observations are in order. First, Aristotle does not define happiness as he does in ignorance of the fact that most of us identify happiness with pleasure. Pleasure is the first of the "clear and apparent things" that he lists in chapter four as possible candidates for the title of happiness or the human good (1095a22–26). And "the life of enjoyment" is the first of "the three most prominent" ways of life that he mentions in chapter five (1095b14–19). In other words, Aristotle knows full well that most human beings explicitly seek a life of pleasure and ease; he knows that "the many" as well as "many of those in power" are "in sympathy with Sardanapollos" (1095b21–22).[12]

Awareness of an alternative, however, is not a sufficient ground for rejecting it. We are more likely to trust an author who shows himself aware of alternatives to his own views than one who does not, but simply to accept his judgment in so important a matter as our happiness would be foolish. Given that most men identify happiness with pleasure and that Aristotle knows this to be the case, shouldn't we expect him either to show that his view of happiness and the ordinary view are compatible with one another or to give sound reasons for his rejection of the ordinary view?

At this point our second observation becomes crucial. For Aristotle *does* in fact try to show that his view of happiness and the view that happiness is pleasure are in accord with one another. Though the word "pleasure" does not appear in his definition of happiness, Aristotle claims in chapter eight that the life of "noble and good men," that is, men who are truly happy, is "pleasant in itself" (1099a7). For such men, pleasure is not a mere "appendage," something to be pursued apart from their engagement in activities in accordance with virtue. On the contrary, the good man's pleasure is *natural*. Homegrown and organic, it arises directly out of his activity, so much so that the delight a man takes in virtuous activity can be regarded as a measure of his virtue (1099a15–21). Although Aristotle is unwilling to say that pleasure, even the noble and good pleasures of noble and good men, *is* the good—the absence of the word pleasure from his definition makes this clear—he does admit that pleasure and happiness somehow belong together. The good is *pleasant*, if not pleasure. Pleasure belongs to the happy man in much the same way that seeing belongs to the healthy eye: given the appropriate conditions—light in the case of the eye, perhaps external goods in the case of the happy man—it enters naturally into his life, without, however, defining it.[13]

In chapter eight, Aristotle is striving to accommodate his view of happiness to the view that happiness is pleasure. This much is clear. The express purpose of chapter eight is to show that what he has arrived at by means of reason in chapter seven "sings together" with "the things said" about happiness (1098b9–12). Whether Aristotle succeeds or believes he has succeeded in bringing his view and the ordinary view of happiness into complete accord is another matter. Presumably most people who identify happiness with pleasure do not mean the pleasure that accompanies virtuous activity. They mean sensual or bodily pleasure, and Aristotle knows it. Only this can explain the apparent contradiction between chapter five, where Aristotle denounces the pursuit of pleasure in the strongest terms, and chapter eight, where he calls happiness, not only "best" and "most beautiful," but "most pleasant" as well (1099a24–25).

We are back where we started. How does Aristotle address the problem that most of us identify happiness with *bodily* pleasures? Chapter five gives us no help in this regard. There Aristotle simply says that "most men show themselves to be completely slavish in choosing a life of cattle," that is, he gives no *reason* for rejecting their view of things (1095b19–20). For reasons, we must turn now to chapter seven and Aristotle's working out of his definition of happiness.

After concluding in the first part of chapter seven that "the good" or "the best" is happiness, Aristotle now tries to say "more clearly what it is (*ti estin*)" (1097b22–24). This might be done, he says, if "the work (*ergon*) of man could be laid hold of" (1097b24–25).[14] How so? Consider any craft or any bodily organ. The end or the good of each surely lies in the work that each does, in the activity proper to each of them. The point of house-building is to build good houses; the point of musicianship is to make good music. Eyes are for seeing well, hands are for handling well, and so on. So, too, Aristotle supposes, in the case of man: assuming that man has a work that is proper to him, that he is not "by nature workless (*argon* = *a-ergon*)," it seems reasonable to look for the human good in that work, for "the good and the well seem to be present in the work" (1097b26-27).[15]

What is the work proper to man as man, not man as butcher or baker or candlestick-maker? Aristotle attacks this question, as he does so many questions in the *Ethics*, by proceeding from the general to the particular, by gradually bringing the issue at hand into sharper focus.[16] In this case, instead of ascending from the variety of particular works human beings engage in to the work that is common to every human being, he descends from the work common to every living thing to the work peculiar to that living thing which is man. Thus the work of man cannot consist simply of "being alive" (*to zēn*), for this work "appears to be common even to plants": mere life, in the sense of absorption and transformation of the external world, belongs to plants as well as animals, but we are seeking the work "peculiar" (*idion*) to man (1097b33-34). We must "mark off" from the range of possibilities "the life of nourishment and growth" (1098a1). Nor can the work of man consist of the work that "follows" this one, namely, "a sort of life of sensation ([*zōē*] *aesthētikē*)," for this life or work, too, is "common both to horse and cow and every animal (*zōon*)": animals other than man also take in and absorb the world through seeing, hearing, touching, and so on, and so once again these works cannot constitute the *sumbebēkos idion*, the "private property," of man (1098a1-3). What "remains," Aristotle concludes, is "a sort of active (*praktikē*) life of that which possesses reason (*logos*)" (1098a3-4).[17]

Aristotle's derivation goes on—at this point he has only uncovered the characteristically human activity, not located the good "in" it—but we have seen enough to understand why he might reject, and how he might argue against, the view that happiness lies in bodily pleasures. Insofar as such pleasures are rooted in the activity of sensation—Aristotle will later argue that they are rooted in touch, the sense common even to the lowest forms of animal life—they cannot be regarded as properly human and hence cannot qualify as candidates for the human good.[18] Insofar as such pleasures are rooted even more deeply in the functions of nourishment and reproduction—in De Anima Aristotle includes reproduction among the activities of the "vegetative soul"—they qualify still less.[19] Apparently Aristotle is speaking in chapter five with more precision than we thought. When he says that human beings who devote themselves to the pursuit of bodily pleasures— our "party animals"—choose "the life of cattle," he means just that: such people turn away from the realm of the properly human and devote themselves instead to "works" that are common to animals, and even plants.[20] And when he calls such people slavish, he means that as well: they "show themselves to be slavish" insofar as they abandon the work that belongs to them as human beings and choose to give themselves, their human being, over to a way of life (bios) common even to the lowest forms of life (zōē). They vegetate.[21]

However cogent these reasons for rejecting the identification of happiness with bodily pleasure may be, they still leave unanswered a number of questions. For instance, the definition of happiness is supposed to answer the question Aristotle raises in the first chapter of the Ethics, "What is the good we wish for solely on account of itself?" But large numbers of human beings apparently wish for and pursue a good that is in no way compatible with the human good. What does Aristotle make of this very strange fact? Does he mean to exclude such people from the "we" whose good he is seeking to bring to light? Would he say they exclude themselves from consideration by choosing to pursue a good that is not properly human? After all, their lives seem to be based on the negation of the premise upon which the Ethics as a whole rests, namely, the claim that there is a human good, a properly human work. Or would Aristotle say that those who choose a life of bodily pleasure are somehow aiming at the good as he defines it— or would aim at it if only they understood it or their own desires more fully? Is their view of happiness compatible with Aristotle's at some level that we have not yet grasped?

Another cluster of questions raised by Aristotle's treatment of pleasure in Book I concerns not the relation of "sensualists" to the good but the relation of "good and noble men" to bodily or sensual pleasure. How do those who are happy in Aristotle's sense of the word regard such pleasures? Do they confine themselves to pleasures that accompany the exercise of virtue? Hold themselves away from bodily pleasures on the grounds that to do otherwise would involve participation in a life that is less than human? Or is there a place in the happy man's life for the enjoyment of bodily pleasures? After all, human being is no more separable from the being of animals than animal being is separable from the being of plants: Man is partly *zōon* and partly *phyton* as well. Doesn't the problem lie not in his participation in these subhuman realms but in his participation in them to the exclusion of the properly human?

III. VIRTUE AND REASON

We cannot answer these questions—all concerned, in one way or another, with the relation of pleasure to the highest human good— within the context of Book I. I raise them now, as I earlier raised questions concerning external goods and complete virtue, so that they might serve as guides and signposts for our inquiry into the rest of the *Ethics*. Still, we have learned enough about pleasure to understand, at least provisionally, why it is missing from Aristotle's definition of the highest human good: bodily pleasures are not, strictly speaking, human goods, while the "natural" pleasures of the happy man lie at the fringe rather than the core of his happiness. What we have yet to see is an account of the *presence* of virtue in Aristotle's definition. Is his inclusion of virtue any less paradoxical than his exclusion of pleasure—does virtue play any part in the "natural" understanding of happiness?

Aristotle's answer is a qualified "yes." While he is willing to admit that many men, perhaps most men most of the time, identify happiness with pleasure, Aristotle also thinks that at least some identify it with virtue; at any rate, their notion of the good at some level includes the notion of virtue. To see how virtue enters into the natural understanding of happiness or the human good, we must turn once again to chapter five.

The second life that Aristotle considers in chapter five is "the political way of life." As in the case of "the life of enjoyment," Aristotle is critical of those who engage in political life, but his criticism of such men—he calls them "the cultivated and active" (*hoi charientes kai praktikoi*)—differs markedly from his criticism of the "Sardanapollists" (1095b22).[22] He does not denounce them; instead, with great delicacy and even gentleness, he shows them, and us, that their understanding of the good points beyond itself. "The cultivated and active," he observes, understand the good to be honor, "for this is nearly the end of political life" (1095b22–23). "Nearly" or "close to" (*schedon*) is the key word here, for Aristotle gives two reasons why honor is not the end that is sought or, at any rate, the end that should be sought by such men.

In the first place, honor is "more superficial than the thing sought" because it lies "in those who honor more than in the one honored" (1095b24–25). Honor comes from the outside; it is a matter of fortune, an external good, and a fragile one at that. It depends upon those who choose to, or choose not to, bestow it.[23] To treat honor as the good would be to put oneself, one's happiness, at the mercy of others (and let us remember what Aristotle has just said about most men), but "we divine that the good is something that is one's own (*oikeion ti*) and hard to take away" (1095b25–26). To be sure, an honor-seeking man of action might respond to this objection by claiming that the good opinion of the fickle and pleasure-seeking multitude is no concern of his; *he* cares only about the respect of men as cultivated as he is. But this is where Aristotle's second reason comes into play. Adopting or anticipating this point of view, Aristotle observes that honor-lovers seek honor, not for its own sake, but "in order that they may be sure *they are good.*" The tell-tale signs of this are that "they seek to be honored by men of sound judgment (*tōn phronimōn*) and by those who know them *and for virtue*" (1095b26–29). Love of honor points beyond itself; it points to the wish to *be good*, to *have vir-*

tue. "It is clear, then," Aristotle concludes, that "according to these men, at least (*ge*), virtue is better [than either pleasure or honor]" (1095b29–30).

The view that happiness somehow involves virtue *does*, then, have a place in the natural understanding of things. That view is inchoate in the understanding of men who engage in political life—or at least some of them.[24] Aristotle is not so naive as to believe that everyone engaged in political life is even "ultimately" concerned with virtue. After all, he has just told us that "many of those in power are in sympathy with Sardanapollos" (1095b21–22). Some men, those whom Aristotle regards as the genuine representatives of and genuine participants in the political way of life, somehow connect virtue with happiness—this is what matters.

We should not lose sight of the significance of this fact and of Aristotle's mention of it. That the subject of virtue should first arise in the *Ethics* in the course of Aristotle's working out of the self-understanding of the political man may suggest several things. It may imply that in Aristotle's view virtue first becomes an issue for human beings in the context of political life. The importance of cultivating and recognizing virtue or excellence in oneself and others may first become apparent when the common good becomes an object of common deliberation.[25] It may also imply that in Aristotle's view the true understanding of happiness, the view that happiness somehow involves virtue, first comes to sight within the same context. The recognition that human flourishing is not just a gift of the gods or a matter of supine self-indulgence, the recognition that it involves human effort and human striving and human excellence, may first become apparent to men as they shape a common life with one another. But if in Aristotle's view political life is the "natural" source and locus of our appreciation of virtue and our identification of it with the good, he might be "naturally" inclined to allow his inquiry to be shaped by the political understanding of virtue and happiness, that is, to allow his inquiry to ascend from the understanding of "the cultivated and active" rather than, say, the understanding of those who sympathize with Sardanapollos. We are not yet in a position to follow up the full significance of these suggestions, for example, to see how they get worked out in Aristotle's presentation of the various virtues. Still, I think they help to explain two curious features of Aristotle's working out of his definition of happiness in chapter seven.

In the course of establishing his definition, Aristotle finds the work that belongs to man as man to be a work of "that which possesses reason (*logos*)."[26] Since the human good is to be found in the work of man, it is no exaggeration to say that his whole derivation turns on this "discovery" that reason is what distinguishes man from the rest of the animals, not to mention plants. Accordingly, we might expect the word reason to appear in Aristotle's definition. In fact, since the words "work" (*ergon*), "life" (*zōē*), "activity" (*energeia*), and "soul" (*psychē*) all function as virtual synonyms in this passage, we might expect Aristotle to say that happiness lies "in" the life of reason or "in" the activity of thinking or "in" the reasoning soul, and to conclude that the human good consists in thinking or reasoning well (*eu*).

He does not. In the course of working out his definition, Aristotle does use the phrases "activity in accordance with reason" and "activity of the soul with reason." In fact, the first major premise in the very long sentence that issues in his definition runs thus: "If the work of man is an activity of the soul in accordance with reason or not without reason . . ." (1098a7–8). But both phrases containing the word reason have dropped out by the time Aristotle reaches his conclusion. In the final form of his definition reason is conspicuously absent. What are we to make of this? For that matter, what are we to make of the weak or diluted phrases "according to reason," "with reason," and, worst of all, "not without reason," all of which suggest that *logos* has been shifted from its original position as the very core of man's work, to a secondary position as the mere modifier of that work or activity?

Aristotle gives no explanation in chapter seven for these shifts and omissions. But suppose we were right to suggest that his inquiry takes its bearings by the political understanding of the

human good. Suppose Aristotle's inquiry was addressed primarily to men who embody that understanding, not simply in order
to persuade them that he is on their side, but because he *is* on their
side, that is, because he regards their understanding as the best
and truest point of departure for his inquiry. Such men would
surely be willing to admit that reason played some part in their
lives and had something to do with the good. But if, as Aristotle
suggests, honor and action form the principal foci of their lives—
we must remember he calls them *praktikoi*, men of action—they
would presumably be unwilling to admit that reasoning well
forms the core of the good life. In other words, to men for whom
the good life consists in seeking honor through noble actions, reason would at most seem to be a needed instrument rather than a
defining feature of their happiness. To say or even to imply, as the
qualifying phrases that Aristotle omits might, that happiness is to
be found primarily in thinking, that it is an activity (*en-ergeia*) to
be found anywhere but in deeds (*en ergois*), would run counter to
human life as they understand it: it would needlessly offend the
sense and sensibilities of his closest allies. Hence, I suggest, Aristotle's omission of reason from the final form of his definition.

The second curious feature of chapter seven that our interpretation of chapter five helps to explain involves another omission. In this case, however, the omission does not concern the
argument of chapter seven as such, but the relation between that
argument and the discussions that follow it, especially Aristotle's
discussion of the particular moral or ethical virtues in Books III
through V. Aristotle fails to articulate, or even mention, a principle that might connect the virtues discussed in those later books
of the *Ethics* and the term "virtue" as it is used in chapter seven.
In order to see the problem, we need to look closely at the way in
which virtue enters Aristotle's argument in chapter seven.

As we saw earlier, Aristotle supposes that "the good" or "the
well" is to be found in the work or activity proper to man. That
is, just as the good for a musician or sculptor lies in his sculpt-
ing or playing music well, so the good for man lies in his working well at the activity that is proper to him. But just as there must

be something in the man who plays the lyre well, that is, the serious (*spoudaios*) lyre player, which distinguishes him from the man who merely plays the lyre, so there must be something in the man who works well at being a man, that is, the serious or good man, which distinguishes him from the man who is merely a man (1098a7–15). This something Aristotle calls virtue, "for each thing is accomplished well (*eu*) according to its proper virtue" (1098a15).[27] Here "virtue" means nothing more than the internal condition, the disposition of soul, which makes for the difference between working and working well. The phrases "activity in accordance with virtue" and "being at work well" are thus virtually synonymous.[28] They differ only in that the first characterizes the human good in terms of its inner cause (virtue), while the second lays stress on the effect of that cause (good activity).[29]

As I said a moment ago, there is nothing inherently problematic about this rather bare meaning of virtue. The problem lies in understanding how to connect it with the rich and varied discussion of the virtues later in the *Ethics*. How is Aristotle able to move from virtue understood as the condition or disposition of the soul that allows a man to work well at the activity proper to him (whatever that might turn out to be) to the "virtues" that are more or less known to us—courage, moderation, generosity, justice, and so on? What allows him to suppose—as he already does in chapter eight of Book I—that *these* dispositions of soul, and not others, are the ones that satisfy his definition of happiness in chapter seven (1099a10–12; 17–24)?

Again, I suggest, the answer lies in chapter five and in Aristotle's willingness to take his bearings by the political understanding of virtue and happiness. For the dispositions of soul that Aristotle discusses in Books III through V seem to be precisely the ones that "the cultivated and active" would be inclined to recognize as virtues. Most issue in some form of action. And at least four of them—courage, magnanimity, the unnamed virtue which follows magnanimity, and justice—have something to do with honor, the primary concern of political men. In other words, just as Aristotle unfolds the political man's desire for honor in chapter five and finds virtue at its core, so, too, he unfolds the political man's understanding of virtue in Books III through V and finds the moral or ethical virtues at its core. Those books presuppose familiarity with the language of virtue and vice, and that language is in the first instance the language of "the cultivated and active."

This is not to say that such men would agree with everything Aristotle says about the moral or ethical virtues. Aristotle's account of the moral virtues *arises from* the political understanding of things; it does not follow that the moral virtues *are* the political virtues or that his account is merely a *description* of the virtues of the good citizen. Still, the "middle term" that allows Aristotle to bridge the gap that exists between virtue in chapter seven and the virtues discussed in Books III through V is the implicit assumption that "the cultivated and active" are generally right in what they think about the virtues. At any rate, the things they call virtues as well as the topics that concern them—honor and action—provide an adequate starting point or source (*archē*) for his inquiry.

What does Aristotle ultimately think about this assumption? We have already seen that he appears to omit reason from his definition in order to accommodate his inquiry to the understanding of "the cultivated and active." What we have just seen suggests that he adjusts his inquiry into the virtues to much the same purpose: Aristotle's account of the virtues begins with the moral virtues and perhaps especially with the virtues of courage, moderation, and generosity, because men of action (*hoi praktikoi*) recognize and appreciate precisely these virtues.[30] But given that reason *should* have a place in Aristotle's definition of happiness, can we suppose that he is satisfied with a definition that fails to include it? And given that, according to the terms of chapter seven, happiness *should* consist of some form of reasoning activity and not, as is the case with many of the moral virtues, activity in the sense of action, can we suppose that Aristotle is satisfied with the assumption that happiness is primarily to be found in virtuous *praxis*?

Let us return to our opening question about the *Ethics*. At the outset of this inquiry, I observed that throughout much of the *Ethics* Aristotle focuses on action and its attendant virtues while leaving reason, especially theoretical reasoning, in the background. I then asked why this should be the case, since, after all, he affirms the superiority of *theōria* to *praxis* in Book X. We are now in a position to understand more clearly the force behind this question, that is, to see how it arises directly out of Aristotle's discussion even in Book I. Aristotle's definition of happiness is the ruling principle and source, the *archē*, of Book I, if not of the *Ethics* as a whole. The working out of that definition hinges on the "discovery" that reason is the peculiar possession of man. And yet reason has no place in the definition's final form. But if Aristotle had left reason in place, had he said that happiness lies in the life or activity of reason, the *possibility* that *theōria* constitutes happiness would have become visible at the very center of the first book of the *Ethics*. After all, happiness or the human good is what we choose simply and solely for its own sake, and *theōria* seems to mean, at a minimum, thinking, that is, the activity of reason, exercised simply for its own sake. By leaving reason out of the final form of his definition, Aristotle pushes this possibility to one side, displaces or even conceals it, so that the reader of his definition will be inclined to assume that happiness lies in a life of virtuous action.

Aristotle's treatment of the virtues points in the same direction. By focusing initially on the ethical virtues, by moving immediately from virtue in chapter seven to the virtues of generosity and justice in chapter eight, Aristotle encourages the reader to assume that activity (*energeia*) and action (*praxis*) are synonyms. The possibility that the properly human activity (*energeia*) could lie anywhere but in deeds (*en ergois*), for example, in *theōria*, is left out of the picture. In short, Aristotle's accommodation of his inquiry to the perspective of "the cultivated and active" displaces from the first part of the *Ethics* what from the perspective of Book X would seem to be the highest human possibility. In its early stages, Aristotle's inquiry into the human good omits the very thing that, in its final stage, turns out to be its goal.

Chapter five beautifully captures this displacement of the possibility that *theōria* might constitute happiness. Aristotle spends the first few lines of the chapter on the life of pleasure. This seems fitting. The view that happiness is pleasure is somehow first for us; it is the natural view of happiness in some sense of the term "natural." The second and therefore central way of life that he considers, and the one he spends by far the most time on, is the political way of life: it occupies center stage in chapter five just as it occupies center stage in the greater part of the *Ethics*. To the third possibility, the theoretical life, Aristotle devotes a total of one sentence: he brings it up only to tell us it will be considered "in what follows" (1096a4–5). The place of the theoretical life in chapter five mimics its place within the *Ethics* as a whole—postponed or displaced, it gets mentioned only in the end, and then, as it were, in passing.[31]

To be sure, Aristotle's taking notice of the theoretical life, if only in passing, need not be lost on the reader. The reader of the *Ethics* who thinks he already understands the good life is liable to pass over Aristotle's mention of the theoretical life and focus instead on the life of "the cultivated and active." But to the reader who reads as if his whole way of life might depend on the outcome of his reading, Aristotle's mention of the theoretical life might serve as a clue. He might wonder where the theoretical life fits into the grand scheme of things and even whether the theoretical life is mentioned last in chapter five precisely because it is the highest way of life.[32] The, in some sense, *conspicuous* absence of reason from Aristotle's definition and his sudden shift from virtue in chapter seven to the ethical virtues in chapter eight might set this reader wondering along the same lines. In short, while the focus in Book I is clearly on the moral virtues and *praxis*, Aristotle seems to say just enough to leave us wondering whether he thinks—and whether we are to think—that the perspective of "the cultivated and active" is entirely adequate. As in the case of the two qualifications of his definition of happiness and his treatment of pleasure, Aristotle's presentation of virtue and reason in Book I raises a cluster of questions to keep in mind as we proceed.

Since "reason" seems to dictate that reason have some part in the happy life, we must ask what part it plays in the ethical life, how it enters into Aristotle's discussion of the moral virtues, and whether the life of action can be regarded as the properly human one. Since Aristotle does mention the theoretical life, and since some features of chapter seven point to the possibility that happiness might lie in *theōria*, we must weigh this possibility as well and examine closely those passages in which Aristotle discusses the virtue that governs *theōria*, that is, wisdom. Moreover, since Aristotle's focus on *praxis* and his gestures in the direction of *theōria* suggest that each of these activities has some claim to be the activity that constitutes happiness, we must think about the relationship between them. For instance, we must ask whether each of necessity forms the center of a way of life—in which case a choice would have to be made between them—or whether *theōria* and *praxis* might together form a harmonious whole. In short, we must try to understand how Aristotle's sketch of happiness is to be filled in—for whatever else can be said about his definition, it has become clear that it is indeed only a sketch, an outline of possibilities which lacks, as yet, a fully determinate content.

IV. ACTIVITY

There is one feature of Aristotle's sketch that we have not yet considered directly. In the course of trying to understand why Aristotle's definition excludes pleasure and includes virtue, we looked briefly at his reasons for supposing that the good lies in man's work, and work (*ergon*) seems to be a virtual synonym for activity (*en-ergeia*). But for the most part we have taken Aristotle's claim that happiness is some form of activity for granted. Yet activity is the most fundamental feature of Aristotle's sketch; he returns to it again and again in the course of defending his definition in chapter eight.[33] Aristotle's focus on activity—in chapter seven, in chapter eight, and indeed, everywhere in the *Ethics*—obliges us to attempt to explain its presence within his definition.[34]

As in the case of virtue, Aristotle finds reasons within the everyday understanding of happiness to include activity in his definition. I noted earlier his conclusion in chapter five that "according to these men at least [that is, the cultivated and active] virtue is better" than honor. But Aristotle goes on:

> And perhaps even more [than honor] someone might understand this [namely, virtue] to be the end (*telos*) of political life. But even this appears rather incomplete (*a-telestera*). For it seems possible for one who has virtue either to remain asleep or to remain inactive (*a-praktein*) throughout life, and in addition to these things to suffer evil and suffer misfortune with respect to the greatest things. But no one, except someone defending a position, would call one living thus happy (1095b30–1096a1).

The words "and in addition to these things to suffer evil and suffer misfortune with respect to the greatest things" obviously point ahead to the problem of external goods and their relation to happiness, while the rest of Aristotle's sentence clearly suggests a connection between activity and happiness. The more closely one looks at chapter five, the more evident it becomes that this brief chapter implicitly contains virtually all the fundamental issues in Book I—and frames them all in terms of completeness. In particular, if we assume that Aristotle is at this point still articulating the political understanding of happiness, the passage implies that in the eyes of at least some men, namely, "the active" (*hoi praktikoi*), a definition of happiness that left men inactive (*a-praktein*), a definition that did not include some notion of activity, could not be ultimately satisfying.

Moreover, Aristotle indicates elsewhere that there is virtually universal support for the view that happiness is some form of activity. His inquiry proper begins in chapter four—chapters one through three forming what he calls his "proem" (1095a11–13). It is here in chapter four that Aristotle first introduces the notion that happiness is the good. And the first thing he says about the good is this: "In name, then, it is agreed upon by nearly all men; for both the many and the cultivated say [the good] is happiness, and they understand living well (*to eu zēn*) and faring well (*to eu prattein*) to be identical with being happy" (1095a17–20). Aristotle cannot immediately go on from here to establish a definition of the good agreeable to all because "the many" and "the cultivated" differ in their understanding of the content of happiness. Indeed, at first glance Aristotle seems to be saying they share only a common name for the good, "happiness," along with some synonyms for that name, "living well" and "faring well." And yet, in representing the shared understanding of "the many" and "the cultivated," Aristotle uses articular infinitives (*to zēn*, *to prattein*), that is, *verbal* nouns, each modified by the adverb "well" (*eu*). He thus suggests that the very words all of us use to describe the good we long for imply that it is some form of activity (*energeia*), and indeed some form of being at work well (*energein eu*). He invites us to wonder whether all men, if only they reflected on their own experience and the very way in which they describe the good, would agree that the good or happiness is to be found in some form of activity. Of course, since the many identify happiness with pleasure, one interesting consequence might be that pleasure, too, would turn out to be a form of activity; if so, perhaps *activity* is the element we were looking for earlier that is common to every human being's understanding of the good.[35] More about this later. What matters now is to see that Aristotle's claim about activity has roots in our everyday understanding of happiness, perhaps deeper roots than any other feature of his definition.

Now while the reasons just adduced at least in some measure justify Aristotle's inclusion of the *notion* of activity in his definition, they do not, I believe, sufficiently illuminate his choice of the word *energeia* to signify that activity. It is true that *energeia* is well suited to the task; *energeia* is a substantival form of the adjective *energos* (or *energēs*)—itself built from *en* (in, at) and *ergon* (work, deed)—which means something like "busy," "active," or "productive." But it is also true that if all that were needed was a word to denote the opposite of sleep or inaction, or the activity implied by the verbal nouns *to zēn* and *to prattein*, Aristotle could have used some other word, for example, *kinēsis* (motion), *praxis* (action) or even *zōē* (life). Instead he uses *energeia*, which along with its virtual synonym, *entelecheia*, is the most fundamental word in his vocabulary. Why *energeia*? What makes this the most suitable name for the type of activity that forms the core of human happiness?

The primacy of *energeia* and *entelecheia* becomes apparent when we notice that key notions in Aristotle's key works are characterized in terms of them: motion in the *Physics*, soul in *De Anima*, being in the *Metaphysics*, and, in our case, the good in the *Ethics*. But *energeia* and *entelecheia* come into their own in the *Metaphysics*, and we must turn to this work to understand the significance of Aristotle's decision to define the human good as a type of *energeia*. Now this may seem rather strange. After all, Aristotle's inquiry in the *Ethics* is firmly rooted in our experience of the world and informed by questions that bear directly on our lives and the way we are to live them. By contrast, the *Metaphysics* is the most theoretical of Aristotle's theoretical works; the level upon which Aristotle operates in it would seem to be at the furthest remove from ordinary human experience. What possible connection could there be, then, between "first philosophy" or "theology"—Aristotle's own names for the enterprise in which he is engaged in the *Metaphysics*—and the "philosophy of human things," which we find in the *Ethics* (1181b15; *Meta.* 1026a19–32)?

A little reflection on the books Aristotle actually wrote points the way toward an answer, for while it is true that the *Ethics* is firmly rooted in our experience of the world, the same can also be said of Aristotle's other writings. Taken as a whole, those writings constitute a sustained reflection on our everyday experience and on the articulations of that experience in human speech or opinion. The *Metaphysics* is no exception to this rule.[36] In fact, the task of first philosophy is in large measure to bring to light what lies at the very root of our ordinary experience. To look to the *Metaphysics* for help in understanding the meaning of *ener-*

geia is not to look away from experience. Nor is it to suggest that Aristotle's own understanding of happiness ultimately rests on "extra-experiential" considerations, that is, on "metaphysical" considerations in this sense of the term. On the contrary, I hope it becomes clear as we examine what Aristotle says in the *Metaphysics* that the meaning of *energeia* that emerges in the course of its argument embodies, as few other words could, what "we divine" to be true about happiness, and that Aristotle chooses to define happiness in terms of it largely for this reason (1095b24–26).[37]

THE SUBJECT MATTER OF the *Metaphysics* differs from the subject matter of all the other sciences or knowledges (*epistēmai*). All the others, Aristotle says at the outset of Book IV, cut off some part of being (*to on*) and investigate its attributes (*Meta.* 1003a23–26).[38] First philosophy, on the other hand, "looks at being as being (*theōrei to on hē on*) and what belongs to this as such" (*Meta.* 1003a21–22). It seeks "the first principles and highest causes" of beings, not insofar as they are human or living or even natural beings, but simply insofar as they *are* (*Meta.* 1003a25–26). Accordingly, we might expect Aristotle to answer the question "What is being?" in the course of the *Metaphysics*. That is, just as in Book II of *De Anima* he sets out to find a definition of soul that includes everything that has life, so, too, in the *Metaphysics* we might expect him to seek out the common defining characteristic of everything that *is*.[39] But Aristotle does not do this, and he does not because, as it turns out, he cannot.

The difficulty is that being is always already divided into certain ruling kinds (*genē*), into "categories" so distinct from one another that no common definition of the being of the things that are can be given.[40] When we call a man and a piece of paper white, we mean or intend by "white" the same thing in each case. But when we say "the man is white" and "the man is five feet tall," the verb "is" refers to decisively different kinds of beings: "to be such and such" and "to be so great" are different modes of being, neither of which can be reduced to the other.[41] This is not to say that the verb "to be" is used equivocally, that there is simply no connection between the various meanings of "is" (1003a33–34). "Being" is not like the word "pen," which can equally well refer to an instrument for writing and a place to keep pigs (or criminals). Rather it resembles the adjective "healthy," which refers to quite different things—what produces health, what preserves health, what possesses health—but only to things that are related to one another by being related to the one condition we call "health." In other words, being is one, but one only *pros hen*, "in relation to one": All the various, irreducible meanings of the word "being" are united by being related to one primary meaning of "being," and all the various, irreducible beings are united by being related to one primary kind of being (*Meta.* 1003a34–b6).[42]

This being Aristotle calls *ousia*, often translated, or mistranslated, as "substance" (1003b17–19). Because beings as such admit of no common definition, and because the primary being is *ousia*, Aristotle's search for the being of *ta onta* becomes, by Book VII, a search for the being of *ousia*: he is, after all, forced to cut off and look into a part of being. "And so the question asked long ago and now and forever, and always causing perplexity, namely 'What is being (*to on*)?' this [question] is 'What is *hē ousia*?' . . . and so for us, too, our looking for 'What is it?' must be most of all and first and, so to speak, only concerned with being in this sense" (*Meta.* 1028b2–7).

By *ousiai*, Aristotle means, roughly and in the first instance, things as opposed to the features of things: houses, horses, and human beings, in contrast to their shapes, sizes, colors, and locations. There are several ways of seeing the primacy of *ousiai*. Qualities, quantities, positions, and so on are predicated of things, but things themselves never act as predicates, are never "said of" anything (*Meta.* 1028b36–37). Invert the word order in a simple sentence: Turn "The horse is sixteen hands high" into "Sixteen hands high is the horse." It makes no difference—"horse" will remain its grammatical subject, "sixteen hands high" its predicate. This primacy of *ousiai* in speech mirrors their primacy in being. There are no free-floating colors or sounds or shapes or locations. A given quality (or quantity) cannot exist apart from some thing—qualities are always qualities *of* some thing—but a given thing can exist apart from a given quality: A man can blush with shame or turn pale with fear while still remaining a man (*Meta.* 1028a10–32). *Ousiai*, in other words, are separate (*chōristai*); they have a kind of independence or self-sufficiency lacking in their features.

Moreover, this separability or separateness of things extends beyond their relation to their features. Things—and Aristotle's very way of proceeding in Books VII and VIII makes it clear that he regards "natural bodies" and especially living things as the primary instances of *ousiai*—possess a kind of distinctness or separateness from the world to which they belong.[43] To see this we need only attend closely for a moment to our most basic experiences. The world we inhabit, the world given to us in experience, is not a mass of confused perceptions; it comes before us *already* articulated, *already* organized, *already* ordered into an array of distinct things with distinct features, all competing more or less eagerly for our attention. Noisy children, purring cats, leafless trees stand out from their surroundings; they ex-ist, here, there, and everywhere. Thus Aristotle can say that to be an *ousia* is to be a "this something (*tode ti*)," that is, the sort of being that one points out and *can* point out only because it already stands out.[44] But to say that an *ousia* stands out and apart from its surroundings is to say that it *endures* as none of its features can. Of course things that live also die. But, as we saw just a moment ago, things can change their qualities and quantities and still preserve their identities. A dog grows, changes its shape, moves from place to place, even changes its color while still remaining what it is, namely, a dog. Indeed, dogs (and all *ousiai*) seem to endure in the world precisely *by* moving and changing, by *working* at what they are. They maintain or preserve themselves *as* dogs by eating what dogs eat; they perpetuate themselves, and thus endure in some sense, by producing others like themselves, that is, other dogs; and when they are not preserving or reproducing what they are, they are "at work" doing just those things that allow an observer to say that "this here thing (*tode ti*)" is a dog and not a cat or a man or a rat.

At this point *energeia* and *entelecheia* enter the picture. Suppose we were to ask ourselves what it is that characterizes a thing as a thing, an *ousia* as an *ousia*. Or rather, suppose that we were asked to find *words* that somehow capture what it means to be an *ousia*. The word *entelecheia*—like *energeia*, a noun of Aristotle's own making—carries the connotation of endurance, in part from the presence in it of *echein*, which can mean "to be" in the sense of remaining in a particular condition, and in part from its resemblance to the noun *endelecheia*, which means continuity or persistence.[45] Thus, insofar as *ousiai* are distinguished from their attributes by their endurance or persistence, *entelecheia* is admirably suited to capture their fundamental character. But each *ousia* endures as a "this something (*tode ti*)" and as "thises," as beings that stand out and apart (*chōris*) from their properties and surroundings, *ousiai* possess (*echein*) a kind of completeness or perfection (*enteles*) that other beings lack; they are fully formed, determinate, *there*, ready to appear and thus draw our attention. Again, *entelecheia* is clearly a fitting name for the being of *ousiai*.

Moreover, a thing endures as "this thing right here" precisely by being at work at what it is. Although the stuff or material (*hylē*) that makes up a thing "matters"—without it, the thing would lack the power (*dynamis*) to be what it is—this material does not constitute its being what it is. A dead cat *is* its material, but is nevertheless a cat only in name. Nor is the being of a thing sufficiently constituted by the ordered arrangement of its stuff, its "look" or "form" in this sense. A thing is what it is only when, or above all when, it is at work doing just what it is "intended" to do. A sleeping cat *is* a cat, but it only sleeps *in order that*, when awake, it might *do* what cats do: pounce, play with its tail, stretch in a certain way—all those recognizably "catty" things that allow even an infant to point it out and say "kitty." *Energeia* names the manner in which the "whatness" of a thing is most fully revealed—it is the be-*ing* of the being—and from the point of view of the thing's capacity, whether understood as material or the well-ordered arrangement of those materials into powers (*dunameis*), *energeia* shows itself as an end (*telos*), that *for the sake of which* those powers are first there.

Here the virtual identity of *energeia* and *entelecheia* becomes apparent. An *ousia is*—endures as something complete and separate (*entelecheia*)—precisely by being at work (*energeia*) at what it is. But since its work or being at work *is* its end, an *ousia* stays (*exein*) at (*en*) its end (*telos*) precisely when it is "at work." To be at work is to be at an end, and to endure at an end, to be complete, arises out of being at work. Thus Aristotle can say in Book IX, in his defense of the priority of *energeia* over *dunamis*, "the work is an end and the being-at-work is the work, and since being-at-work (*energeia*) is named from the work it also extends to being-at-an-end (*entelecheia*)" (*Meta.* 1050a20–23).

THIS IS A ROUGH and incomplete account of Aristotle's inquiry in the *Metaphysics*, rough because it leaves out so much of what Aristotle says in Books I through IX, and incomplete because it neglects entirely what he has to say in Books X through XIV. Still, we have learned enough about *energeia* and its relation to *entelecheia* to see how its meaning is "at work" in Book I of the *Ethics*. For example, we can now see why Aristotle's pursuit of the human good resolves itself into a search for the distinctively human work, or why it is natural for him to suppose that the good lies "in" the work of man. Since "the work is an end and the work is being at work," since the very notion of end is inextricably bound up with the notion of activity, to raise the question "What is the good or the end of human life?" *is* to raise the question "What is the activity or work proper to man?" Again, we can see why the self-sufficiency of the happy man with respect to external goods—including honor—becomes an issue in Book I, why, that is, the question of the relation of *the* good to good fortune arises naturally in an inquiry into the human good. Our notion of being at an end, being complete, is inseparable from the notion of separateness or distinctness from the surrounding world. What we see to be true of all genuine things, that they have their good or end "in" themselves, we also "divine" to be the case with "human things."

Integrity matters: the good, faring or being at work well, must somehow be "our own" and "hard to take away" (1095b24–26). Once again, since being at work at an end entails *enduring* at that end, we can see why *duration* is regarded as an essential feature of happiness, that is, why for Aristotle—and for all of us—happiness is not a matter of "a day" or "a little time" but "a complete life."

Above all, our reflection on *energeia* allows us to see more clearly than before the *seriousness* of Aristotle's question concerning the meaning of happiness. We sometimes regard happiness as a feeling, highly treasured, no doubt, but still a feeling not different in kind from the other feelings or moods or passions (*pathē*) that overcome us from time to time. We say, for instance, "I was sad [or angry], but now I am happy." Clearly nothing could be further from the object of Aristotle's pursuit. If happiness is to have any claim to be the appropriate name for the human good, it cannot be a changeable, incidental feature of the human soul, a momentary *pathos* or shifting mood. Rather, to ask the question "What is happiness?" is to ask the question "What does it mean to *be* human?" It is to ask what the distinctively human *energeia* is, the work in which "the what it is to be (*to ti ēn einai*)" for human beings comes fully to light. It is to ask what it would mean for me, a human being, to be fully present in the world—to be, for once, *all there.*

There is, however, one feature of Aristotle's definition of happiness that his treatment of *energeia* in the *Metaphysics* does not directly illuminate: the modifying phrase "in accordance with virtue." Aristotle's account does help us to see why virtue alone cannot constitute happiness. If virtue is, as Aristotle will later explicitly argue it is, a disposition or ordering (*hexis*) of the soul, it cannot be the end of human life, for the end of an *ousia* lies, not in its disposition toward activity, but in that activity itself: the end *is* the being at work.[46] In other words, Aristotle, following common opinion, is speaking quite precisely when he likens the mere possession of virtue to being asleep: to say that happiness *is* virtue would be like saying a cat is most of all a cat when it is asleep (1095a31–32; 1098b31–1099a2). What Aristotle's treatment of *energeia* in the *Metaphysics* does *not* explain is why the phrase "according to virtue" has a place at all in his definition of happiness. That is, if to be at work *is* to be at an end, if *energeia* and *entelecheia* are true synonyms, one would think that *energeia* itself would sufficiently define the human good and that, accordingly, the phrase "according to virtue" is superfluous. One would think, in other words, that Aristotle would say that the end of man *is* the work of man rather than saying, as he does, that it is present *in* that work.

Why does Aristotle define happiness as being at work *well*, that is, as being at work *in accordance with* virtue? The answer seems to lie in something that distinguishes human beings, for better or worse, from all other *ousiai*. A rock cannot fail to be completely a rock. To be at work as a rock is already to be at work well as rock; it makes no more sense, in this case, to add the additional qualification "well" (*eu*) than it does to distinguish between good and bad rocks. All rocks are, if you will, good rocks by nature. The case of living things other than man is somewhat more complicated. Animals must grow up, and an animal, while young, is not yet at its end. Moreover, although nature, in the sense of the form or "whatness" of a given animal, is always at work in it, bringing itself to light as *this* animal, it does not always succeed in bringing itself forth fully. The internal or external materials an animal needs in order to be complete may on occasion be lacking. But given the right stuff, an animal will in time become full-grown (*enteles*); "for the most part" its *energeia* will become *entelecheia*.

Clearly the same thing cannot be said of human beings. Those with severe mental handicaps aside, human beings cannot fail to possess and exercise their capacity for speech or reason. We talk, we think, we count, we compare, we notice things all the time. *Logos* infuses everything we do. But for human beings it is one thing to possess and exercise what distinguishes them from the rest of the animals, and another to exercise it well. There is a gap within human being between being merely human and being fully human, a gap reflected in Aristotle's distinction between the work of man and the good "in" that work. If this gap is to be filled, if human beings are to achieve their proper human shape, something additional is needed, a disposition beyond that disposition of powers, that is, the soul, which all men by nature possess. This additional something is reflected, in turn, in the adverbial phrase "according to virtue." In short, were all human beings by nature in a position to reach their end, all men would be happy by nature, and there would be no *need* for inquiries into the nature of happiness, that is, for inquiries such as the *Ethics*. But because they are not, because a gap between *energeia* and *entelecheia* does exist, the question of happiness or the human good must be raised, and because virtue is needed to fill that gap, Aristotle's inquiry into happiness—his pursuit of the good—must become an inquiry into the virtues. To be more precise, it must become a search for "complete (*teleia*) virtue," that is, that disposition of the soul which lets us become full-grown (*en-teles*) or complete (*teleios*) in the fullest sense of these terms.

V. CONCLUSION

We have come full circle, back to the subject of complete virtue. Our first two questions about Aristotle's definition of happiness had to do with the qualifying phrase "and if the virtues are several, in accordance with the best and most complete [virtue]." We have not yet answered one of them: whether "the best and most complete virtue" Aristotle seeks is only one of the many virtues he discusses or a complete whole somehow formed of them all. But at least we can answer the other: it is now clear why Aristotle introduces the qualification in the first place, why, that is, the adjectives "best" (*aristēn*) and "most complete" (*teleiotatēn*) come to modify the word virtue. Just as "courage" appropriately names what makes possible the doing of courageous things and "justice" appropriately names what makes possible the doing of just things, so, too, "best and most complete" virtue is the fitting name for that condition of soul which makes possible the distinctive activity which is "the best thing" (*to ariston*) for man, "that which is most of all his end" (*to teleiotaton*). Aristotle qualifies his definition as he does, and thus makes completeness in virtue a major theme of his inquiry, because completeness, being at one's end, *entelecheia*, is its paramount goal.

Indeed, the more one thinks about it, the clearer it becomes that completeness or wholeness is at issue in all the various questions we have come upon in the course of reflecting on Aristotle's definition of happiness—and that it is precisely this issue that unifies the apparently disparate parts of his inquiry in Book I. Obviously this is so in the case of the question we raised concerning external goods. There we asked whether complete virtue alone suffices for happiness—whether the man who possesses complete virtue is complete or sufficient unto himself, or whether, in addition, a "complete life" in the sense of a life replete with external goods is needed to complete the acquisition of happiness. But the issue of completeness is no less present in the questions we raised about the relation of pleasure to happiness. For instance, in thinking about pleasure we were led to wonder whether the life of virtuous activity, which Aristotle seems to say has pleasures that form a sort of natural whole with that activity, also has a place within it for bodily pleasures. Here the question is whether the work, and thus the happiness, of man is entirely separable from the "works" he shares with other living things, including plants, or whether happiness somehow involves the whole soul, man as *zōon* and *phyton* as well as man as man.

Finally, the questions we were provoked to ask by the conspicuous absence of reason from Aristotle's definition of happiness clearly have to do with completeness. We asked whether the life of action has a place for reason within it that satisfies the requirements implicit in Aristotle's derivation of his definition, that is, whether the distinctively human part of the soul can be satisfied, can reach completion, within a life focused on deeds. But this led us back to the question in which the issue of completeness perhaps reaches its fullest form, namely, our initial question concerning the relation of *theōria* to *praxis*. Is each of these activities to be regarded as a self-sufficient whole, independent of the other and perhaps incapable of being brought together with it within a single life? Or is the happy life a whole within which both *theōria* and *praxis* play essential parts?

Since completeness is at issue in all four of these questions or question-clusters, and since it seems likely that this issue does indeed reach its final form in our question concerning *theōria* and *praxis*, it might seem reasonable to investigate each set of questions under the rubric of completeness, and see what light our investigations shed on the relation of *theōria* to *praxis*. For example, in looking at Aristotle's account of the various virtues, we might focus on those virtues that have some claim to being complete virtue, and then see whether the "most complete" among them, that is, the virtue with the strongest claim, issues in knowing for its own sake or action or both. Again, we might look at those places in the *Ethics* where Aristotle talks about external goods, and then see whether they suggest anything about the relative self-sufficiency of the theoretical life and the life of action. The difficulty with this approach is that Aristotle weaves his accounts of virtue, pleasure, reason, and external goods so closely together that it is almost impossible to separate them. To focus on each topic separately would be to distort the wholeness of Aristotle's own presentation.

This very complexity and the prominence given to virtue in the *Ethics* suggest an alternate route through Aristotle's inquiry. Four virtues stand out as possible candidates for complete virtue: 1) magnanimity or greatness of soul, which Aristotle twice associates with "all-complete virtue"; 2) justice or that form of it which he calls "complete virtue" and "whole virtue"; 3) prudence, which he claims in Book VI implies the presence of all the ethical virtues; and 4) wisdom, which he appears to call complete virtue in Book X. The question of external goods and their relation to happiness reaches its first peak in the course of Aristotle's discussion of the ethical virtues of magnanimity and justice. Likewise, the question of reason's relation to the ethical virtues culminates, or first culminates, as Aristotle discusses the intellectual virtues of prudence and wisdom. Thus we can treat the question of external goods and the question of reason each within their "natural" context if we discuss them as we weigh, in turn, the claims of magnanimity, justice, prudence, and wisdom to be complete virtue.

The issue of pleasure is somewhat more difficult to treat—it comes up in virtually every book of the *Ethics*. On the other hand, Aristotle does devote two sections of the *Ethics* to pleasure, and the very placement of these sections—both fall within the second half of his inquiry, and the second section immediately precedes Aristotle's defense of *theōria* in Book X—suggests that we should take up the issue of pleasure near the close of our own inquiry. Indeed, we shall find that every set of questions we have raised, and, above all, our questions concerning the relation of *theōria* to *praxis*, reach their final articulation only in the closing books of the *Ethics*, and will have to be considered anew in light of them.

One final point. Some time ago, as we were attempting to understand how virtue enters into Aristotle's definition of happiness, I suggested that Aristotle takes his bearings in the *Ethics* by the self-understanding of a certain class of men, those he calls the "cultivated and active." This hypothesis has already proven useful in a number of ways: it has helped us to understand Aristotle's willingness to identify "virtue" with the moral or ethical virtues in the early books of the *Ethics*—or what amounts to the same thing, his refusal to make *theōria* or even prudence an object of inquiry in those books. What we have not yet considered is how Aristotle's willingness to follow the lead of the "cultivated and active" shapes his account of the particular ethical virtues. This we must do now, as we begin our descent into the details of Aristotle's discussion of the ethical life. In particular, if we are to understand why Aristotle takes up magnanimity when he does— why it is first in the order of "complete" virtue, but not first in the order of virtue simply—we must consider the effects of Aristotle's preferred audience on the shape of his inquiry. To this end, I begin with a brief consideration of Aristotle's own reflections on his inquiry.

2

||||||||||||||||||||||||||||||||||||||||||||||||

MAGNANIMITY
AND JUSTICE

A T LEAST THREE TIMES in the course of Book I, Aristotle
pauses to reflect on what he is doing.[1] He stands back and
thinks about the character of his inquiry, its starting points, and
the kind of man most suited to take part in it. In chapter three,
for instance, he points out that "since the end is not cognition but
action (*praxis*)" the *Ethics* will be of no use to the "follower of his
passions," that is, those who "pursue each thing and live according to passion." At the same time, he notes that "for those who act
and fashion their appetites according to reason, to know about
such things may be of much use" (1095a4–11). Again, in chapter
four, where Aristotle wonders about the best starting points, the
appropriate *archai*, of his inquiry, he says that "it is necessary for
one who intends to hear in an adequate way about beautiful and
just and, in general, political things to have been led well in habits," because "the starting point is that something is so (*to hoti*),"
and where this is "sufficiently" clear, "there will be no further
need for the reason why (*to dioti*)" (1095b4–7).[2]

These passages make explicit what we earlier inferred from
Aristotle's way of proceeding in Book I: His inquiry has a specific audience. The first tells us that his inquiry is addressed not
to those who identify happiness with pleasure but to those who
put reason in the service of right action. The second tells us that,

in addition to being willing to follow the dictates of reason, "the fitting listener" must already possess certain habits or virtues—presumably the very ones Aristotle discusses in Books I through V (1095a1). But the second passage also tells us something else. It is not only that the proper understanding of ethical matters presupposes a certain cast of soul or that the *archai* of an ethical inquiry are accessible only to the "cultivated and active." Rather, there are things that Aristotle *could* explain but will not because they will be clear enough to his intended audience. The horizon of the cultivated and active will shape the inquiry in important ways: its character will be determined by theirs. What they take for granted—we might call them the moral facts—Aristotle, too, will take for granted; that is, he will not attempt to ground them, much less openly call them into question.[3]

These remarks cohere nicely with what Aristotle says about the character of his inquiry at the outset of chapter three: "The precise must not be sought [or insisted upon] in a similar fashion in all accounts" (1094b12–13). "To demand demonstrations of a man speaking rhetorically" would be as foolish as "to accept a mathematician who makes [only] persuasive arguments" (1094b25–27). The clarity and precision achievable in a given inquiry depends on "the underlying material" of that inquiry, "the nature of the business" at hand (1094b11–12; 25). There is no universal method, no universal *mathēsis* in Descartes' sense, that can guarantee the production of clear and distinct conclusions concerning any given subject matter.[4] The inquirer must instead take into account the nature of his subject matter—as Aristotle is doing right here—and then allow his vision and his path of inquiry (*methodos*) to be shaped by it.[5]

In the case of the *Ethics*, because "the beautiful and just things" admit of "much difference" and "much wandering"—so much so that they "seem to be by convention and not by nature" (what's just right in one situation may be dead wrong in another)—the inquirer, and his readers and listeners as well, "must be content" to accept a limited degree of precision in the inquiry (1094b14–16; 19–23). Better yet—since Aristotle doesn't quite say that his inquiry in the *Ethics* will *lack* precision, but only that "the precise must not be sought *in a similar fashion* in all accounts," and since the word we have translated as "one must be content" can also mean "one must find delight in"—those who participate in ethical inquiry must be capable of delighting in the *kind* of precision it can possess. The *Ethics* certainly lacks the kind of precision we associate with mathematical reasoning. But it has a subtle precision of its own—and the right reader of the *Ethics* is the person who can see and relish the subtleties inherent in its subject matter precisely because he is "at home" (*oikeios*) in it, that is, because he is not "without experience of the actions in life" (1095a2–3). Inquiry, object of inquiry, and inquirer have a natural coherence. Aristotle can shape his inquiry in the *Ethics* to fit the understanding of "the cultivated and active" because such men have themselves been shaped by its subject matter. Habituated in and by "the beautiful and just things," they are in a position to discern them and Aristotle's inquiry into them aright.

AFTER BOOK I, Aristotle spends far less time engaging in such reflection, but these judgments about the character of his inquiry and its participants inform it throughout.[6] At least through Book V, Aristotle's pursuit of the good remains what he calls it at the outset, "a sort of political inquiry," addressed primarily to the self-understanding of "the cultivated and active." His account of magnanimity makes this especially clear.

To begin with, Aristotle's account presupposes that we already recognize and value magnanimity, or greatness of soul; that is, we already know what sort of thing magnanimity is and know it to be a virtue. For instance, Aristotle tells us at the beginning of his discussion that "it makes no difference whether one considers the disposition or the man in accord with the disposition," and then goes on to consider the man, as if he expects us already to have a picture of him before our mind's eye, a picture summoned up by the very word *megalopsychia* (1231b7). A bit later he says that "even without argument great-souled men appear to be concerned with honor; for most of all they think themselves worthy of honor, and [of honor] according to worth" (1123b22–24). Here again Aristotle expects us to be so familiar with the magnanimous man that he can speak about him directly "from the things known to us" (1095b3–4). In general, Aristotle's discussion of magnanimity, more than his discussion of any other virtue, resembles a portrait of a man rather than an account of a disposition (*hexis*).[7] What allows Aristotle to proceed in this way? He can speak, for instance, of the magnanimous man's voice (never shrill) or his gait (never hurried)—details that clearly cannot be deduced from some higher principle—because he is convinced that we, his readers, share with him an understanding of the great-souled man. The magnanimous man belongs within our horizon: We "know the type," we have a "feel" for his character; we even have some sense of his inner life.

There is an even more important respect in which Aristotle's account of magnanimity has its source in the self-understanding of the cultivated and active. As we saw earlier, Aristotle's inclusion of virtue in his definition of happiness depends in part on that understanding. True, his working out of that definition in chapter seven of Book I supplies reasons for including virtue that are independent of it. But it is the self-understanding of such men, rather than of men who devote themselves to the pursuit of bodily pleasures, that allows him to locate and ground his definition of happiness within the everyday understanding of it. Insofar as Aristotle is serious about grounding his inquiry within "the things known to us," and insofar as virtue is to play a crucial part in that inquiry, "us" in this phrase must refer to the cultivated and active, and by "the things known," Aristotle must mean the common understanding of what is beautiful and just shared by such men (1095b3–4).

However, the cultivated and active do not, in the first instance, associate virtue with happiness. In chapter five of Book I, Aristotle may show them, and us, that virtue (or, rather, activity in accordance with virtue) is the true end of their way of life. But when he first characterizes their understanding of the good, he makes it clear that such men are inclined to identify happiness not with virtue but with honor. The cultivated and active aim not at virtuous activity as such but at the glory and recognition that accompany the performance of beautiful deeds; they aim to become *kaloi*, to achieve a kind of splendor in the eyes of the world. Since the men most clearly allied with Aristotle's own understanding of happiness tend to regard honor as the good, and perhaps tend to identify virtuous activity with the active pursuit of honor, wouldn't one expect him to take up these tendencies in his own account of virtue? In fact, if Aristotle is serious about having his inquiry ascend "from the things known to us" to "the things known simply," that is, from the familiar understanding of the good to the true understanding, wouldn't one expect him to make the relation between honor and virtue a vital part of his inquiry?

Aristotle does just this in his discussion of magnanimity. Here, through reflection on the great-souled man, he seriously considers the possibility that the man who possesses complete virtue, the man at the apex of human life, might necessarily engage in the pursuit of great honors—or at any rate, through reflection on such a man he considers and re-considers the connection between virtue and honor. I do not mean to suggest that Aristotle "invents" the great-souled man in order to give himself the opportunity to address the paramount question of his closest allies. Insofar as the magnanimous man is a type that he expects his readers to recognize and admire "*a priori*," we cannot regard him as Aristotle's invention. But I do think it's possible that Aristotle chooses to treat magnanimity as a major virtue, and chooses to treat it first among the possible complete virtues, because the relation of virtue to honor is uppermost in the minds of the readers he cares about most.[8]

IF IT IS FITTING for Aristotle to consider magnanimity first among the possible complete virtues, one might think it would be still more fitting if he considered it first in his treatment of the virtues as a whole, if, that is, he made the relation of virtue to honor an issue at the very outset of his account of the virtues. He does not. Instead he treats courage and moderation first and takes up magnanimity only after he has also discussed generosity and magnificence. Why? There are several possible answers.

In the first place, courage and moderation—and Aristotle's very separation of them from the remaining moral virtues suggests that he regards them as a natural pair—are clearly dispositions of the most elemental, and in some sense the most natural, human actions and passions. All living things strive by nature to preserve and maintain themselves by reproducing, by nourishing themselves, by fleeing danger, and by defending themselves and their progeny when flight is no longer possible. And nature provides most living things with the particular desires and passions needed to perform these activities well: the desire for pleasure that moves them toward reproduction and nourishment, the fear of pain that moves them away from danger, the spirit or *thumos* that moves them back into the fray and allows them to endure pain and fear when danger must be faced.[9] But human beings are distinguished from all other living beings by their "natural" need for dispositions of the soul beyond those provided by nature.[10] This holds true even in the case of these most elemental motions and passions. Human beings by nature desire to reproduce and nourish themselves, but left in "the state of nature," the desire for the pleasures that accompany these activities may exceed or, in rare cases, fall short of what is needed: Moderation is needed if our natural capacity for "right" reproduction and "right" nourishment is to reach completion. By nature, human beings fear danger and death, and sometimes show themselves spirited in the face of danger. But fear and spiritedness, too, can exist in the wrong proportions in the soul: In this case, courage is needed if our capacity for the "right" balance of fear and confidence is to reach completion.[11]

My point is this: Aristotle takes up courage and moderation before magnanimity because these virtues are in important ways prior to magnanimity and indeed all the other virtues. Courage and moderation settle, put in order, the part of the soul that we share with other animals—a part that has to be disposed properly before the distinctively human passions and activities can be settled.[12] Or to approach the issue from a somewhat different angle, courage and moderation precede magnanimity and all the other virtues because they are *pre-political* virtues. At any rate, in Book I of the *Politics* Aristotle suggests that the household, as opposed to the city, comes into being, and comes into being by nature, for the sake of reproduction and security (1252a26–35). Courage and moderation seem able to exist in some form outside of and prior to the city, but the remaining moral virtues are not likely to do so. Generosity presupposes the existence of a community of distinct families that do not share all things in common. Magnificence is displayed, above all, in the use of great wealth to lend a kind of splendor or beauty to the life of a city. And the very possibility of giving and receiving honor depends on the existence of a sizeable community of men who are equal enough to be worthy of honoring one another and unequal enough for their differences in rank to be apparent.

To say that courage and moderation can exist in some form outside of cities is not to say that cities can do without them. Courage and moderation may also be the most fundamental *political* virtues in the sense that they ground, and so make possible, the external and internal life of the city. A city that lacks men willing to risk their lives in its defense cannot be long for this world. And a city of "Sardanapollists" who cannot keep their hands off the goods and wives of their fellow citizens would likewise be short lived.

That courage and moderation are in fact key to the life of *any* healthy community is, indeed, evidenced by that greatest of authorities on the natural understanding of human affairs, Homer himself. The immediate and indirect cause of the action of the *Iliad* is immoderation, the inability of Paris (in the past) and Agamemnon (in the present) to control their appetites for women who are not theirs. And the virtue displayed on almost every page of the *Iliad* is courage: Goodness in the *Iliad* is almost synonymous with courage.[13] Courage, moderation, and their opposites also seem to be the ruling causes of the action of the *Odyssey*.[14] The monsters Odysseus encounters in the course of his travels are, above all, monsters of immoderation.[15] Odysseus is often saved by some combination of courage and moderation, and the community he has formed with his companions is gradually eroded and destroyed by their lack of moderation.[16] Once Odysseus arrives in Ithaca, he must face a crisis brought on by the desire of the suitors to devour his household, his kingdom, and his wife, and he can only resolve that crisis and re-found his community by exercising courage in the company of his son, his father, and his friends. To the degree, then, that Homer represents the everyday understanding of "the cultivated and active"—and it seems reasonable to suppose that Homer's books would stand high on the reading lists of such men—it seems appropriate for Aristotle to begin his account of the virtues with discussions of courage and moderation.[17]

Yet anyone who has read Homer knows that honor is as central to his books as courage and moderation. Achilles' demand for honor is as central a cause of the action of the *Iliad* as the immoderation of Agamemnon and Paris. Honor and virtue are as closely connected to one another in the minds of Homer's heroes as they are in the minds of Aristotle's preferred readers. Nor is Aristotle unaware that honor and courage are topics that naturally arise together. A closer look at his account of courage suggests that the question we have been trying to answer—why Aristotle chooses to discuss courage and moderation before taking up the issue of virtue's relation to honor—is somewhat misleading, for Aristotle *does* begin to address this issue at the outset of his inquiry into the particular virtues. At any rate, he draws a distinction there between true courage and "political" courage, that is, courage exercised for the sake of honor (1116a15–21). His discussion of honor reaches a peak in his account of magnanimity. But that discussion has already begun in his account of courage.

Aristotle places magnanimity where he does because he wants the very structure of his inquiry to imitate, and thus preserve, the natural order of human things. Because courage and moderation are first for us in a variety of senses, Aristotle places them at the beginning of his inquiry into the particular virtues. Because honor is, above all, an issue for men who must risk their lives in battle, he first mentions honor within this, its natural context. But because honor or love of honor is an issue that extends beyond courage alone, because it permeates the whole of political life—so thoroughly that serious men who engage in politics tend to regard it as the end of political life—Aristotle's examination of courage only lays the groundwork for his fuller treatment of honor within the context of magnanimity.[18]

I. MAGNANIMITY

What, then, does Aristotle's portrait of the great-souled man tell us about the proper relation of virtue to honor? Should the man who possesses complete virtue pursue honor? Is happiness, that is, activity in accordance with complete virtue, compatible with the active pursuit of honor? Or does the distinction between true courage and "political" courage imply that honor and the pursuit of honor have no place in the life of the truly happy man? Is Aristotle's presentation of magnanimity meant to confirm or undermine the self-understanding—and the lives—of his most serious readers?

It's hard to know. Several times, Aristotle tells us that the magnanimous man is "concerned about honor" or "concerned about honor and dishonor" (1123b21; 1124a5; 1124a12). And he arrives at this conclusion "by reason," that is, he infers it from the distinguishing characteristic of the magnanimous man, namely, that he "thinks himself worthy of great things, being worthy [of them]" (1123b1). Moreover, it is not difficult to find features in Aristotle's portrait that suggest that the magnanimous man is indeed concerned with honor. For example, he tells us that the great-souled man tends to be "lazy and hesitant except where a great honor or work [is possible]" and that he is a "doer of few things but of great and glorious ones" (1124b24–26).

Yet it seems equally easy to argue from Aristotle's presentation that the magnanimous man is *not* particularly concerned about honor. For instance, Aristotle tells us that the magnanimous man "will altogether belittle" the honor he receives "from chance men" and "will be [only] moderately pleased" by the honor he receives "from serious men" (1124a5–11). Is it conceivable that a man who cares much for honor could be disposed in this way toward it? Furthermore, to say that the magnanimous man is "*concerned about* honor" (*peri timas*) need not mean that he *cares for* it. *Peri* in this phrase may simply mean "about," and Aristotle may intend to say only that magnanimity is "about" honor just as generosity is "about" wealth and courage is "about" frightening things. In short, Aristotle's portrait of the magnanimous man puts us in much the same quandary as his discussion of external goods in the latter part of Book I. There we had difficulty deciding exactly what Aristotle meant to say about the place of external goods in the happy life; here it is difficult to know exactly what place Aristotle means to accord to honor—*the* external good from the point of view of his readers—within the magnanimous man's life.

It might be tempting to regard those features of Aristotle's portrait that seem to support the view that the magnanimous man cares for honor as concessions to his readers. The picture called up in their minds by the word *megalopsychia* is a picture of a man who cares about honor. They themselves regard honor as a great good, perhaps the greatest good of all. And so Aristotle must on occasion appear to agree with them about the importance of honor and the legitimacy of its pursuit. But in truth—so the argument might run—*Aristotle's* magnanimous man is above honor, as unconcerned about it as he is about wealth and other external goods.

There is something to be said for this reading of Aristotle's discussion of magnanimity. Competent readers have claimed that there is a kind of doubleness in his presentation of magnanimity and that if we look closely at it we find a popular or political form of magnanimity and a "higher" form as well—a form in light of which the popular form appears almost comic.[19] Moreover, the whole drift of Aristotle's discussion seems to be in the direction of self-sufficiency: The magnanimous man ultimately seems to preserve an almost god-like distance from ordinary human concerns, including honor. Finally, Aristotle seems to hint at the true character of magnanimity as early as Book I. In a passage I quoted earlier from the middle of his discussion of external goods—the first, incidentally, in which the word "magnanimous" appears in the *Ethics*—he tells us that the nobility of the virtuous man "shines out" even in the midst of great misfortune, namely, "whenever someone bears with good temper many and great misfortunes, not on account of insensitivity to suffering, but because he is noble and great-souled (*megalopsychos*)" (1100b30–33). We can learn at least two things from this passage. Because the word magnanimity is later used in connection with honor, it strongly suggests that the general problem of external goods resolves itself, in the *Ethics*, into the particular problem of honor: given what we later learn in Book IV about greatness of soul, we can infer that dishonor is the greatest of the misfortunes that Aristotle is thinking about in Book I. But the passage also suggests that magnanimity shows itself, above all, in a certain distance from honor: The great-souled man is someone who can endure even the loss of honor without flinching.

Still, there is something dissatisfying about a reading that draws so sharp a distinction between a "vulgar" and a "true" magnanimity, between the surface and the core of greatness of soul. Among other things, it implies that Aristotle does not take the political understanding of things very seriously, that is, it implies that he is not as serious as he says he is about beginning with "the things known to us." It would be more satisfactory, because closer to Aristotle's own stated principles, to try to see how the *whole* of Aristotle's discussion might arise from the self-understanding of the cultivated and active. Could Aristotle's portrait of the magnanimous man, complete with its apparent contradictions, be an attempt to re-present, to bring to light and to life, a sort of natural "dialectic" between virtue and honor that is *already* at work within the soul of his intended reader?

There are grounds for this view. In chapter five of Book I, Aristotle represents the "cultivated and active" as men who understand honor to be the good, that is, the end of political life. But he also concludes that "according to these men, at least, virtue is better [than honor]" (1095b29–30). According to Aristotle's own presentation of them, the cultivated and active are of two minds about the relative status of virtue and honor. Moreover, if we attend closely to the way in which Aristotle unfolds their understanding in chapter five, we can see that it corresponds rather closely to several of his observations about the magnanimous man.

Aristotle begins by reminding "us," that is, the cultivated and active, that "honor lies in those who honor rather than those who are honored." In effect, he reminds us that to regard honor, all honor, as the good would be to put our happiness in the hands of any chance comer (1095b24–25). Then, as if in response to "our" objection that "we" in fact seek honor only at the hands of those worthy to bestow it—the sound-minded who know us and our virtue—he points out that this implies that according to "our" understanding of things, virtue is better than honor. Clearly the first "moment" in this unfolding corresponds to the magnanimous man's "thinking little" of honors that come from "chance men," while the second corresponds—or *almost* corresponds—to his acceptance of honor from "serious men."

Aristotle tells us that the magnanimous man is only "moderately pleased" by the honors he receives even from "serious men." Here's where the correspondence breaks down: Aristotle says nothing resembling this in chapter five. No doubt, given their tendency to identify honor from any source with the good, the cultivated and active as a rule cherish deeply the good opinion of their equals. Nevertheless, both extremes of the magnanimous man's view of honor—his detachment as well as his attachment—can be seen as extensions of their self-understanding. For if we remember Aristotle's *reason* for saying that the cultivated and active think virtue is better than honor—"they seem to pursue honor in order that they might be sure they are good"—and then imagine a man who both *is* good and *knows* himself to be good, we arrive at just that god-like detachment from honor that led us a moment ago to posit a sharp distinction between a "true" and a "political" form of magnanimity (1095b26–28).

Aristotle's portrait of the great-souled man is chapter five writ large. It deliberately embodies the ambivalence of his readers toward honor and virtue, but it also draws out their self-understanding in the direction of self-sufficiency, that is, of complete detachment from any concern for honor, and it does so precisely in terms that such men can understand. The magnanimous man is, at one level of description, still concerned about honor, as are the cultivated and active, but he knows enough about the limits of honor to think little of the honor he receives from "chance men"—as do the cultivated and active, with a little prompting from Aristotle. Again, the magnanimous man, like the cultivated and active, accepts honor from "serious men," yet he differs from them in taking only moderate pleasure in such honors. But again, this difference is one that just such men can understand and appreciate, for the cultivated and active seek honor from others only in order that they might know or rather trust (*pisteuein*) that they are good. Their need for honor is grounded in ignorance of themselves; they love honor because they desire—and lack—self-knowledge. But the magnanimous man *already* knows he is good. He "thinks himself worthy of great things, being worthy of them." In other words, the great-souled man contains within himself the self-knowledge that the cultivated and active seek from others in the form of "recognition," and this self-knowledge or self-recognition renders the recognition of others unnecessary.

The magnanimous man's self-containment or self-sufficiency, grounded in a self-confidence that springs from genuine self-knowledge, is thus the very end that Aristotle's readers implicitly seek through their pursuit of honor as *the* good. In the person of the magnanimous man, Aristotle represents to his readers the possible completion of their highest longing: a man who can dispense with honor because he knows his own worth, a man who, knowing his own worth, knows there can be no honor worthy of it (1124a8).[20]

Homer's works, which, as I suggested earlier, exemplify the way of looking at the world that Aristotle addresses in the *Ethics*, offer further evidence for this view of magnanimity. In the

Iliad and especially in the character of Achilles, we see the "dialectic" between virtue and honor displayed with great intensity. In reading the *Iliad*, we enter a world where men at once possess great virtue and care deeply for great honors. The Achilles we see throughout most of the *Iliad* stands at the peak in both respects. He is the most great-souled of the great-souled Achaians in that he both possesses the greatest virtue and has the greatest hunger for great honors.[21] Indeed, this hunger for honors befitting his great virtue lies at the root of his quarrel with Agamemnon and his decision to make his fellow-Achaians suffer for their unwillingness to defend him in that quarrel. But as the action of the *Iliad* unfolds, Achilles becomes increasingly aware that no honor, however great, can match his virtue. In effect, we see Achilles *becoming* magnanimous in the higher sense of the term. This "motion" in Achilles' soul reaches a first peak in Book IX, where the hero refuses the gifts and pleas of the Achaians. It is beautifully represented by his sitting, the next day, perched on his ship as if ready to leave the world of battle and honors, yet eager to witness, from this vantage point, the actions that still matter so much to him.[22]

Of course, Achilles' attempt to adopt a Zeus-like (*dios*) posture toward human affairs is forgotten once his friend Patroklos falls in battle. He must become *dios*, radiantly active, after all. But it is just here, once his deep-seated rage—at the world that did not, and could not, honor him as he wished—begins to subside, that we see him approach something like the upper limit of magnanimity. His extraordinary behavior toward his former companions at the funeral games, where he exhibits an almost divine unconcern for their quibbling over honors, and his still more extraordinary behavior toward Priam, to whom he both returns the body of the man who felled his beloved friend and grants the respite needed for the burial that concludes the *Iliad*, point to, if they do not fully represent, magnanimity in its highest form.[23]

HAVING SEEN THE COMPLEXITY of Aristotle's presentation of magnanimity, we are now in a position both to understand the sense in which it is a complete virtue and to assess its claim to be *the* complete virtue: we can now begin to answer the questions that led us to magnanimity in the first place. Clearly, it is not complete in the sense that it alone could bring a man happiness. As Aristotle points out repeatedly, magnanimity cannot even exist without the other moral virtues. In the absence of other virtues, a magnanimity-like disposition is empty (*chaunos*)—so much so that Aristotle calls this vice simply "emptiness" (or vanity) (*chaunotēs*) (1123b9; 1124a1–3, 28–29; 1126a32–33).[24] The magnanimous man "thinks himself worthy of great things, being worthy of them," and he cannot be worthy unless he is also a man of extraordinary character; the remaining moral virtues form, as it were, the content of magnanimity.

What about the reverse? Can the other moral virtues exist without magnanimity? Or does magnanimity somehow bring those other virtues to completion—and perhaps complete the man who possesses them as well? Is magnanimity complete virtue in this sense? The answers to these questions are not immediately clear. At times Aristotle seems to imply that the remaining moral virtues, if not the man who possesses them, can be complete in the absence of magnanimity. For instance, smallness of soul, the vice that lies at the opposite extreme from emptiness or vanity, characterizes (or can characterize) someone who thinks himself unworthy of great things while being worthy of them (1123b9–11). Since to be worthy is to be virtuous, and since the magnanimous man must both be worthy, and think himself worthy, of great things, the very existence of this vice seems to imply that the virtues can exist apart from magnanimity. The same conclusion seems to follow from Aristotle's calling magnanimity "a sort of ornament of the virtues": ornaments may lend a certain beauty and grace to the things they adorn, but they can scarcely be said to complete them (1124a1–3).

Nevertheless, Aristotle does call magnanimity complete virtue. If magnanimity is not by itself the "best and most complete virtue" but still merits the name "complete," one would think that it must, in some sense, complete or make whole the remaining moral virtues. That it serves just this purpose is in fact implied both by the line "for it [magnanimity] makes them [the virtues] greater" and by the very word Aristotle twice uses to denote the kind of completeness magnanimity provides: *pan-telos* (1124a2–3; 7–9; 28–29). *Pan* tells us that magnanimity depends on the presence of all (*pasai*) the remaining virtues, but *telos* suggests that all these other virtues reach their end or completion through the presence of magnanimity.[25] Moreover, we must perhaps beware of making too much of Aristotle's calling the small-souled man worthy and magnanimity an ornament. As his discussion of the five "courages" makes clear, Aristotle is at times willing to participate in the ambiguity of ordinary speech about the virtues; he is willing to assume that some virtue-like dispositions bear a close enough resemblance to genuine virtues to merit their names (1116a15–1117a28). Thus it is possible to argue that, when Aristotle calls the small-souled man worthy, he only means to say that he *somehow* possesses the remaining moral virtues but not those virtues in their complete forms. Likewise, while ornaments for the most part merely adorn things without completing them, it is possible to imagine forms of adornment without which the thing adorned would not be what it is. Aristotle uses the word *kosmos* to characterize magnanimity rather than, say, *periaptos*, which would have implied that magnanimity was something merely attached to or fastened about the remaining moral virtues.[26] To call magnanimity "a sort of *kosmos* of the virtues" is to suggest that it somehow brings the other virtues to order, perhaps orders them toward their end, perhaps even *is* the order toward which the remaining virtues are ordered.[27]

Clearly we must ask ourselves how the ordering of soul that Aristotle calls magnanimity might complete the remaining moral virtues and their possessor. Let us begin by reminding ourselves why Aristotle chooses to discuss the individual virtues in the first place: The end of human life is happiness, and happiness turns out to be an activity in accordance with virtue. But this means that the virtues are not ends in themselves. They reach their end or completion only in the activities that take place in accordance with them and the man who has them reaches his end, not by possessing them but by exercising them. Now, what if—to take the

case of the small-souled man first—there were a man who possessed the virtues, who was in this sense capable of noble actions,
but who, out of a kind of ignorance of himself, thought himself
unworthy to perform them. Such a man might be *called* virtuous or worthy, but neither he nor his virtues could be said to exist
in completion (*entelecheia*). His lack of confidence in himself,
his lack of trust in his own goodness, would render both his virtues and his happiness dormant, for as Aristotle observes, no one
would call this sleep-like state happiness: Happiness is a form of
activity (*energeia*), a matter of *acting* and thus faring well (*eu prattein*) (1095b31–1096a2; 1098b31–1099a2). Obviously one remedy
for this problem is greatness of soul, that is, the self-knowledge
and well-founded self-confidence that enable a man to be *active* in
accordance with virtue, to "*be* all he can be."

Yet someone might argue that what such a man needs is not
magnanimity but a healthy dose of honor. In other words, greatness of soul might be useful to him but not necessary—what the
worthy but diffident man needs is, not an additional disposition
of soul, but sound-minded comrades who will honor his virtues.
For honor, as Aristotle points out, is what men seek "in order that
they might trust in their own goodness." This objection forces us
to ask whether honor and the desire for honor can perform the
same service for the virtues and their possessor as magnanimity
does. According to the terms of Aristotle's definition of happiness,
they clearly cannot: When men do courageous or generous or just
things for the sake of honor, they do not, in principle, do them for
their own sake. But the good, that is, activity in accordance with
virtue, must be chosen for its own sake if the terms of Aristotle's
definition are to be fulfilled. Magnanimity, that disposition of
soul which allows a man to see that nothing external to his excellence—not honor, not dishonor, not even death—is great, opens
up the possibility that beautiful actions might be chosen freely,
that is, chosen simply for their own sake; honor or the desire for
honor does not.

Why is this difference so important? To answer this question
let us turn our attention to the cultivated and active and ask our-

selves why Aristotle is intent on using his portrait of the great-souled man to shift their focus away from honor and toward virtue. If human happiness lies in courageous or generous or just actions, what difference does it make whether those actions are chosen for their own sake or for the sake of honor? Let us recall, once again, Aristotle's common-sense observation about the character of most men: most are informed less by longing and admiration for the beautiful than they are by a longing for bodily pleasures. In an average community, therefore, one is likely to find a much higher proportion of "Sardanapollists" than "sound-minded" men. Suppose, then, that a worthy man who cared greatly for honor were to find himself in a community dominated by Sardanapollists, that is, a community where men less worthy than he bestowed most honors on less-than-worthy objects. In these circumstances, how likely would such a man be to stay on the path of virtue? Even if this community were to contain a sizable proportion of sound-minded men, willing to recognize and honor virtue over pleasure—a hypothesis that Aristotle, for one, would perhaps not wish to have the cause of virtue and happiness rest upon—what, if not magnanimity, what, if not a disposition to recognize and affirm the worth of virtue over honor, would give him the distance needed to distinguish between honors to be pursued and honors to be rejected?

To look at the same problem from another angle, suppose the community we have described did not honor our virtuous yet honor-loving man as he wished or did not honor him at all or even positively dishonored him. Would he not be likely to withdraw all support for it, that is, to become inactive, *a-praktein*, with respect to virtue? Worse still, might he not fall into a rage and do his best to make his community suffer? Let us remember, after all, the "passive" revenge that Achilles wreaks on his fellow Achaians. In that case we see the refusal to act and the act of taking revenge united in their most terrible form, a man who makes the community that has not honored him as he wishes suffer terribly precisely through his inaction.

Indeed, the case of Achilles suggests that even in the best of communities, that is, even in a community dominated by virtuous lovers of honor rather than lovers of pleasure, love of honor can be problematic. It suggests that the problem does not lie simply in the preponderance of the "wrong" men in a community but in love of honor itself. Honor is an external good, and as such it is limited in quantity. Great honors are presumably still more limited in quantity. Thus in a community where great men pursue great honors, there will simply not be enough honor to go around, and the very combination of great abilities and great longing for honor is likely to be lethal. Even in situations where the results are less deadly than those we witness in the *Iliad*, the cause of good is more likely to be harmed than helped by excessive love of honor. The man who withdraws his support from the community and becomes inactive is not happy, that is, active in accordance with his virtues. Nor does he contribute to the well-being of his community through the active presence of his virtues—and we must remember that, although the focus in the *Ethics* is on individual happiness, Aristotle remains deeply concerned about the "seizing and securing" of the common good (1094b7–9).

We can see, then, why Aristotle insists that virtuous actions be chosen for their own sake. His insistence is not simply grounded in a desire to model his discussions of the individual virtues on the "abstract" prescription for happiness he lights on in Book I. If the happiness of the individual and the happiness of the community to which he belongs are to be secured, something resembling moderation with respect to honor is needed. Men who are worthy of great deeds but lacking in self-confidence and self-knowledge may need to be drawn out of themselves. But still more, Aristotle must shift the attention of men who are capable of worthy actions but likely to perform them only when honor is forthcoming, men who are at once *praktikoi* and *philotimoi*, away from honor and toward virtue. And this, in part, is what Aristotle means to do through his discussion of magnanimity. He brings to light an ordering of the soul that makes virtue rather than honor the central feature of a "complete life." Indeed, Aristotle may present magnanimity in the form of a *portrait* precisely in order to show his readers that to regard honor as at best an external measure of the truly important thing, virtue, is a genuine human possibility. By picturing or portraying this possibility, he makes it believable; he brings it to life. In any case, some features of Aristotle's presentation as well as his first mention of magnanimity in the *Ethics* point to the possibility of a well-tempered disposition toward honor. They remind us that even in the midst of great misfortune, for example, even in the face of great dishonor, "the beautiful shines through whenever someone bears [it] with good temper" (1100b30–31).

YET WE MUST ALSO remember the ambiguities in Aristotle's portrait of the magnanimous man. We have been supposing, for the last several pages, that magnanimity represents an alternative to love of honor, an almost divine, almost Zeus-like (*dios*) disdain for the mortal concern with honor, but as we saw earlier, at least some features of Aristotle's presentation suggest that the magnanimous man *is* concerned about honor. In fact, when Aristotle brings Zeus forward as an instance of magnanimity, he means to illustrate, not detached disdain for honor, but the "touchiness" of great men with regard to the debts they might owe others: From the point of view of magnanimity, even the gods seem capable of jealousy (1124b12–17).[28] Moreover, we see the magnanimous man display those very "Achillean" traits that a moment ago we were suggesting magnanimity might provide an alternative to. Aristotle tells us that he "does not enter into the things commonly held in honor (*ta entima*) or where others are first" (1124b23–24). The first phrase here could be taken to mean that the magnanimous man has no interest in honor, at least paltry honors, but the second certainly suggests that the likelihood of honorable success will inform his decisions about whether or not to enter the fray. And Aristotle goes on to say immediately that the magnanimous man is "lazy (*argon*) and hesitant [to act] except where [there is] a great honor or deed; and he is a doer [*praktikon*] of few things, but great and nameworthy ones" (1124b24–26). Here again we see the magnanimous man's actions apparently being shaped by his desire for great honor—so much so that although capable of action (*praktikon*), he will for the most part fail to act (*apraktein*) or remain deedless (*a-ergon*).

As was mentioned earlier, this passage and others like it could be the residue of "vulgar" magnanimity, the result of Aristotle's attempt to paint a portrait of the magnanimous man that at some points remains true to the average understanding of his honor-loving readers. On the other hand, it is equally possible to argue that this portrait of a largely inactive man, only willing to perform great deeds, is consistent with the higher form of magnanimity as well. For while the whole drift of Aristotle's discussion of magnanimity seems to be away from honor and toward virtue, it does not necessarily move in the direction of virtuous *activity*. The magnanimous man is so lofty in character, so above ordinary concerns, that it is easy to imagine him refusing to take part in the kind of everyday actions that make up the daily life of a community. Magnanimity might release a man from the constraints of honor, might free him to act in accordance with virtue for its own sake. But it need not. Disdaining everything outward and external, the magnanimous man might turn in on himself, acting only in moments of great crisis or to avoid the appearance of indebtedness. His possession of virtue might become an end in itself for him, his magnanimity a *kosmos* in the sense of an end toward which his other virtues are ordered. In such a case, resting content in the contemplation of his own goodness, a world unto himself, the magnanimous man would be of service neither to himself nor his community. Largely inactive with respect to virtue, he would fail to secure both his own happiness and the happiness of his community.

That there is no specific activity, no *energeia*, directly connected with magnanimity lends support to this conclusion. In the case of all the other moral virtues it is possible to say that as possessor of this or that virtue a man will typically act in a certain way in certain situations: *as* courageous he will perform brave deeds in battle, *as* generous he will give freely of his wealth, *as* moderate he will eat, drink, and be merry in due measure. But the actions of the magnanimous man *as* magnanimous seem to be limited to walking without hurrying and speaking without shrillness.

Now there is surely something to be said for such "deeds." Just as the magnificent man adorns his city by means of his wealth, so the magnanimous man lends a certain grace and beauty to his city through his presence within it. What is more, his very manner of walking and speaking could have a beneficial effect on his fellow citizens. His *gravitas* might remind them of the superiority of virtue, even the mere possession of virtue, to the external goods they so frantically pursue. But can Aristotle be satisfied, and can we be satisfied, by a "complete" virtue with so limited an *energeia*—an *energeia a-ergos*, as it were? To give the question a more general form: If magnanimity does not lead directly to the practice of other virtues for their own sake and does not itself have a persuasively complete activity associated with it, can it be the complete virtue Aristotle is looking for?

The answer seems to be "no." In particular, we have not found in magnanimity a satisfactory resolution of the tension between honor and virtue. Through his portrait of magnanimity, Aristotle may point to the possibility of a man who regularly exercises the virtues without being particularly concerned about honors and dishonors. Thus Aristotle tells us at one point that the great-souled man will speak and act "ironically," that is, with a certain self-deprecating gentleness, toward the many (1124b26–31). But it is difficult to see how this possibility can be derived from the defining characteristic of the magnanimous man: *ho megalōn hauton axiōn, axios ōn*. If *axiōn* here means "demand," the magnanimous man is "he who *demands* great honors for himself, being worthy of them"; we get "vulgar" magnanimity. If *axiōn* simply means "think oneself worthy," the magnanimous man is "he who knows or thinks himself worthy of great things, being worthy of them"; we reach a higher form of magnanimity but one that is as likely to issue in inactivity as activity.

I repeat: There is something praiseworthy about each form of magnanimity. Ignorance of one's own goodness or virtue may not be a vice, a *kakia*, in the precise sense of the term (1125a18–19), but the great-souled man's self-recognition and recognition of the superiority of internal goodness to any external good surely deserve emulation (1125a16–24). Moreover, there is a cost associated with giving up on the demand for honor. It may be true— Aristotle certainly insists that it is true—that there can be no honor worthy of complete virtue, no honor that measures up to virtue at its peak (1124a7–9). Yet there is something noble about the *wish* for a correspondence between virtue and the appearance of virtue. Insofar as the man who demands honor seeks to have his virtue recognized for what it is, insofar as he seeks truth or unconcealment in this sense, there is something noble about him.[29]

What seems to be lacking in each form of magnanimity, then, is not worthiness—magnanimity is not a failure in the sense that it "really" turns out to be a vice—but a principle that would connect great virtue directly with action or *energeia*. Nevertheless, were magnanimity the only "complete" virtue among the moral virtues, we might be tempted to conclude that no such principle exists on the level of moral virtue—and that the problem of honor cannot be resolved within the understanding of virtue and activity possessed by the cultivated and active. In other words, we might be tempted to conclude that the full meaning of happiness, of being at work in accordance with virtue, lies beyond the ken of the cultivated and active. But Aristotle does, in fact, discuss another "complete" moral virtue—justice—and before we draw this conclusion, we must consider his account of it at some length.

II. JUSTICE

Near the beginning of Book V, Aristotle tells us—warns us—that justice is "meant in various ways" (1129a26). Justice is a homonym, a word applied indiscriminately to things different in kind.[30] What's worse, it is not a homonym in the way that, say, *kleis* is (1129a27–30). *Kleis* can mean either collarbone or key; it is "meant in various ways," yet it is difficult to imagine a situation where context would not tell which meaning was intended. Justice is a homonym of a different color. Its meanings are so "close" to one another that differences between them are liable to "escape our notice" (1129a27–28). "Justice" is unavoidably ambiguous.

Aristotle's account of justice in Book V reflects this ambiguity, even as it attempts to sort out the various meanings of the word. Book V is easily the most confusing book in the *Ethics*. Aristotle's maddeningly brief discussion of natural justice and the distinction between natural and conventional justice is a case in point. It is enough to try the intellect—and patience—of even the most serious reader of the *Ethics*.[31] His somewhat longer account of the fine distinctions between being unjust and acting unjustly, between unjust acts and unjust effects, also serves to remind us of the subtle sort of precision peculiar to ethical inquiries. Aristotle's inquiry into justice remains so true to the phenomena that at times it is even difficult to know *which* type of justice he is discussing. For instance, it is not easy to tell whether he regards reciprocity, the kind of justice that obtains between, say, shoemaker and house builder, as a form of distributive or a form of corrective justice. Reciprocity resembles corrective justice insofar as it has to do with exchanges between two or more persons. But it resembles distributive justice, and differs from corrective justice, inasmuch as a reciprocal exchange takes into account differences between the contributions and persons involved in the exchange (1133a5–1133b28).

This much, at any rate, seems clear about Book V: The two fundamental forms (*eidē*) of justice that Aristotle intends to focus on are distributive and corrective justice. Both forms have to do with equality, but each aims at producing a very different kind of equality.

Distributive (*dia-nemētikē*) justice, as its name suggests, has to do with the distribution (*dianomē*) "according to merit" of goods held in common by a political community (1120b30–35). As Aristotle points out, although men may disagree about what constitutes merit, all would agree that common goods, such as wealth and honor, should be distributed according to it (1131a25–29). But since the very notion of a distribution according to merit implies that men are unequal in worth, a just distribution will necessarily give more to the more worthy and less to the less worthy. Distributive justice aims, then, at a kind of proportionate equality, a meting out of goods proportioned to the differences in merit of members of a community (1131a29). It aims at what Aristotle calls geometric equality, an equality or sameness of ratios: as person A is to person B so, according to distributive justice, are the goods received by A to the goods received by B (1131a31–1131b13).[32]

Corrective justice, by contrast, aims what Aristotle calls arithmetical equality (1131b32–1132a2). Person A wrongs person B in the course of a voluntary or involuntary exchange, for example, a purchase of land or a robbery (1131b25–26). As a result, A ends up with more than he should and B with less. Corrective (di-orthōtikē) justice seeks to "rectify," to put right (orthos), this situation by returning to B what he has lost and taking from A what he has gained (1132b1–6). In other words, corrective justice seeks a return to the state of simple equality between persons that existed before the act it corrects took place. It does not attend, as distributive justice does, to possible differences in merit between A and B (1132a1–6). It simply looks to the act committed and the gain and loss on either side, while regarding A and B as numerically equal, as indistinguishable units or quantities. Of course, this simple equality may not be simple to obtain. Aristotle is far from advocating an eye-for-an-eye approach to justice.[33] In Aristotle's view, it is not easy to decide exactly what is due to a man wrongfully maimed and what is due from the man who maimed him (1132b21–30). Still, the distinction between distributive and corrective justice remains: both aim at "the equal" (to ison), but each aims at a different sort of equalization (isazein).

THESE, THEN, ARE the two basic forms of justice that Aristotle discusses in Book V, and neither, at first glance, seems likely to shed light on the questions raised by Aristotle's account of magnanimity. Although Aristotle uses some of the same language to discuss magnanimity and distributive justice—worth or merit (*axia*) and its cognates are key terms in both accounts—and although honor is both central to magnanimity and one of the external goods with which distributive justice deals, it is difficult to see a significant connection between the right *distribution* of honor (one of the concerns of distributive justice) and the right *reception* of it (the concern of magnanimity). The chief problem posed by magnanimity is not whether the great-souled man will justly distribute honors due to others—at any rate, Aristotle does not allude to this problem directly in his discussion of magnanimity—but whether he will be willing to be at work according to virtue in the absence of honors that befit his great virtue.

Are we to conclude that Aristotle's discussion of justice does not go any way toward answering the questions we have raised? Perhaps not. His brief account of natural justice and his somewhat more ample account of right relations between shoemakers and builders seem likely to be of no more service to us than his discussions of corrective and distributive justice, but Aristotle prefaces his account of all these "justices" with a brief discussion of another justice, to which they stand in the relation of part to whole. This "whole" (*holē*) justice is the form of justice that Aristotle names "complete (*teleia*) virtue," and indeed, it is his awareness of this justice that first leads him to claim at the beginning of Book V that justice is "meant in various ways." It is here, then, in his remarks about that justice in which "every virtue is gathered" and than which "neither morning nor evening star is so wondrous," that we might expect to find answers to our questions (1129b27–30).

Nevertheless, someone might argue on structural, as well as other, grounds that Aristotle cannot have intended his remarks on "whole" justice to contribute significantly to the *logos* of the *Ethics*. In terms of structure, they serve as a preemptive digression, dictated by the vagaries of everyday speech about justice—a digression that Aristotle must go through in order to make it clear that he intends to focus on "real" justice, that is, distributive and corrective justice.[34] In terms of content, the complete virtue that Aristotle discusses is not, after all, so remarkable. In spite of Aristotle's accolades to it (which all take the form of citations from others), whole justice seems to amount to nothing more than law-abidingness. Could the mere tendency or disposition to obey the law—something any decent citizen does "as a rule"—have anything to do with the completeness and worthiness exemplified by the great-souled man?

Yet—to begin with the objection from structure first—we must beware of making hasty judgments based on the style or form of the *Ethics*. We have already seen cases where apparent digressions—for instance, Aristotle's reflections on inquiry in Book I—turn out to contribute significantly to his *logos*. In addition we have seen that in Aristotle's view mere vagaries of ordinary usage can often open up paths of inquiry that are worthy of serious consideration. Moreover, there is something curious about Aristotle's "digression" on whole justice. If his only concern had been to establish the distinction between this justice and justice in the strict sense, he could presumably have done so quickly and efficiently. Instead, he discusses whole justice at some length in chapter one and then returns to the topic twice in chapter two. If anything, Aristotle's "style," his repeated approaches to the theme of whole justice, serve to underscore its importance. That whole justice amounts to nothing but obedience to the law seems open to question as well. It is true that Aristotle praises it through the mouths of others, but he says nothing to qualify that praise. If we are to understand what he means by whole justice, we may need to deepen our understanding of law and law-abidingness.

What is it about whole justice that leads Aristotle to call it complete virtue? What is whole justice, and what is its connection with obedience to the law? Let us consider for a moment the way that we ordinarily use words like *right* and *wrong, just* and *unjust, fair* and *unfair*. When a man takes more that his share of something good or shoulders less than he should of some evil, or when a man robs or otherwise harms another, we say he has done something unfair or wrong or unjust. Similarly, when a man accepts from others and metes out to himself his share of goods and evils, or when he refrains from doing harm to others, we say that he has done something just or fair or right. These are the sort of just and unjust actions that Aristotle treats in the body of Book V. The settled tendency toward such acts, toward fairness or unfairness, equality or inequality, is what he means by justice and injustice in the partial or narrow sense.

But our use of the language of justice and injustice, right and wrong, clearly has a wider application as well. If a man deserts his comrades in battle, we not only say that he has acted like a coward; we also say that he has done his fellow soldiers an injustice. Likewise, if a man commits adultery, we say he has wronged his wife as well as behaved immoderately. On the other hand, if a man gives money to someone in need, we say he has acted generously and "done the right thing." In other words, we apply the language of right and wrong, justice and injustice, across a very wide spectrum of acts. Right and wrong, in particular, seem almost coextensive in range with the moral virtues and vices: To act virtuously is to do what is right; to act viciously is to do what is wrong.

The Greek language resembles English in this, and it is Aristotle's finely-tuned awareness of the nuances of Greek that leads him to claim that *dikaiosynē* has a broad as well as a narrow sense, that justice in some sense of the term includes all the moral virtues, indeed, *is* the moral virtues taken as a whole. But Aristotle takes this observation a step further than we are accustomed to. He associates this broad sense of justice with law-abidingness; at any rate, he implies that in a well-ordered political regime, to be law-abiding is to be virtuous (1129b19–25). Now, while most of us are willing to say that it is just or right to obey the law, the notion that obedience to the law coincides or could in some circumstances coincide with justice as whole virtue is likely to strike us as strange, or even offensive (1129b25–27). For it implies that law is intended to "legislate morality" and that people become good, or at any rate begin to become good, by following the law. This is why I suggested earlier that Aristotle's discussion of whole virtue might oblige us to deepen our understanding of law and law-abidingness. When we think of the law as a series of hedges, a tool intended merely to keep men from doing harm to one another, we regard it in a distinctly modern light.[35] If we wish to understand whole justice as Aristotle does, we must attempt to imagine the law—as Aristotle attempts to do—as the source of all the moral virtues.[36]

One further point needs to be made about whole justice. Whole justice is not, according to Aristotle, simply identical with "virtue" or the sum of the virtues. It is "the same," but its "being" is not the same as that of virtue taken simply (1130a12–13). Aristotle means two things by this. In the first place, whole justice "is most of all complete virtue because it is the employment (*chrēsis*) of complete virtue" (1129b30–31). In other words, the notion of whole justice is inseparable from the notion of its use or activity; the being of whole justice, as opposed to the being of courage, moderation, etc., lies in activity. In the second place—and Aristotle connects this point directly with the first—whole justice "is complete, because the one having it is capable of employing virtue toward another (*pros heteron*)" (1129b31–33). That is, the very notion of whole justice is inseparable from the notion of acting for or in relation to (*pros*) the good of others. Whole justice and virtue are the same thing, but "insofar as it is in relation to another, it is justice, while insofar as it is such a disposition simply, it is virtue" (1130a12–13).

Here the connection between law-abidingness and whole justice becomes especially clear. Insofar as the law ordains the virtues, it ordains them for the common good, that is, it orders them "toward" others. Insofar as whole justice consists in *obeying* the law, it is inseparable from the practice or exercise of the virtues. Indeed it seems to be just these features of whole justice that make its confusion with justice in the narrow sense seem reasonable, for distributive and corrective justice, too, seem inseparable from an active relation toward others. It takes two to be just or unjust in *every* sense of these terms: To take or not to take more than one's share of what is common implies the existence of a community;

to gain or not to gain more than one's due implies the existence of some other who loses or does not lose what is due to him. In short, courage or moderation can be imagined in the absence of some other toward whom those virtues are exercised; justice, whether in the broad or narrow sense, cannot.

A VIRTUE THE VERY BEING of which involves being at work and being at work in relation to others; which sets the other virtues to work in relation to the common good; which therefore makes possible the happiness of the community as well as the happiness of its possessor—this seems to be just what we have been looking for. Our search for complete virtue, for the disposition of soul that makes happiness possible, began with magnanimity. The magnanimous man possesses all the virtues, knows it, and knows the superiority of virtue to external goods. This knowledge grants him a kind of completeness or self-sufficiency with respect to external goods, and in this he seems to possess one of the basic features of happiness (1097b6–21). But as we saw earlier, his very immunity, his "a-pathy," with respect to external goods is likely to lead to his withdrawal from the sphere of action in all but the rarest of circumstances. The magnanimous man is likely to become "apathetic," lazy, workless (*argon*). At any rate, there is no *reason* why this should not happen, and if it does, the magnanimous man will achieve neither his own good, that is, activity in accordance with virtue, nor the good of the community to which he belongs.

With whole justice this is not the case. The wholly just man *of necessity* exercises his virtues and exercises them in relation to others. Precisely insofar as he is just, he works in relation to or for (*pros*) the common good, and precisely by this means he secures his own happiness. In the case of magnanimity, Aristotle's attempt to ascend from the political understanding of the good, that is, the desire for honor, to an understanding consistent with the terms of his definition of happiness ends in failure: it magnifies self-sufficiency at the expense of *energeia* and the common good. But this does not mean that the political understanding of the good as such must be abandoned. For in his account of justice, which certainly has as much claim as magnanimity to be rooted in the political understanding of the good, Aristotle shows us the possibility of a complete virtue that both fulfills the requirements of his definition *and* remains firmly embedded in the political understanding of virtue and happiness. In short, whole justice is Aristotle's alternative to magnanimity: it supplies what is missing in magnanimity, what magnanimity points to but does not provide.

Yet there is something curious about Aristotle's account of justice, something that can best be seen by considering the relation of whole justice to distributive justice. The "wholly" just man must obviously possess and exercise each of the partial or particular forms of justice. Indeed, it seems reasonable to suppose that he, more than anyone else, would be likely to distribute well the common goods of his community according to the principle of distributive justice, that is, according to merit (*kat' axian*). At first glance there appears to be nothing problematic about this: Aristotle's suggestion that the wholly just man would make the best ruler in his community makes perfect sense (1129b31–1130a1). And as long as the just man limits himself to apportioning goods among his fellow citizens, no problem need arise.[37] But what if he brings himself into the equation? We must remember what Aristotle says about the relation between virtue and external goods in his discussion of magnanimity: Honor is the greatest of external goods, and even honor fails to be an adequate measure of complete virtue (1123b20–21; 1124a7–9). This means, if we take it seriously, that the efforts of a community to give the wholly just man his due, that is, his share of external goods, are doomed to failure. What is more, it means that the wholly just man cannot do justice to himself. Were he to honor himself according to his merit, he would have to apportion to himself *all* the honors his community had to give, and even this would fail to reveal his full worth. His very attempt to exercise justice would necessarily result in injustice to himself.

Roughly the same problem emerges when we consider complete virtue in light of reciprocal justice. According to the model of reciprocity that Aristotle presents, in a given exchange various members of a community, say, a shoemaker and a house builder, receive goods proportionate to their contributions. If a house is worth ten pairs of shoes, the exchange should result in the house builder possessing ten pairs of shoes and the shoemaker possessing one house. According to Aristotle, money (*nomisma*) has come into being precisely in order to provide a common measure (*metron*) for such exchanges; it *can* serve as a measure because such exchanges already presuppose that the goods exchanged, though different in kind, are somehow commensurable (*summetra*) (1133a16–22; 1133b16–18). The dealings of shoemakers and builders are unproblematic: no home can be built that is not the equivalent of some number of shoes or their equivalent in money.[38] But now consider the case of complete virtue. What contribution on the part of his fellow citizens, even all of them taken together, can be equivalent to the wholly just man's contribution of his superior excellence to the community? The answer seems to be "none." Complete virtue is "incommensurable" with the other goods a community has to offer; there can be no ratio or set of ratios that "equalizes" the contributions of the just man and others because no common unit of measure exists—not wealth, not even honor—that could serve as a mean (*meson*) between them (1133a19–20).[39]

WE SEEM TO HAVE made no progress at all toward resolving the problem posed by magnanimity. The problem has simply been brought into sharper focus. The law (*nomos*) may be the ultimate source of the virtues and its highest function may be to produce a man who possesses all the virtues in completion, but having produced such a man, it cannot reward him as it ought, in a coin (*nomisma*) that measures up to his goodness. Again, the man who possesses complete virtue may seek to exercise it within his community; he may even be given the chance to distribute its goods. But even given this opportunity and precisely *because* he is so good, he cannot do justice to at least one member of the community. The man who possesses whole justice cannot be wholly just.

Are we to conclude, then, that the tensions between the possessor of complete virtue and the political community—between the common good and the good of the best man—are simply too great to be overcome? Is Aristotle at once concealing and revealing a fundamental difficulty when he tells us, as the *Ethics* begins, that even if the good "is the same for one man and for the city, to seize and preserve the good of the city appears greater at least and more complete" (1194b7–9)? Are the human good and the political good different in kind, and can one be secured and maintained only at the expense of the other?

To address these questions we need to reflect further on law and distributive justice. Suppose the end or intent of the law (*nomos*) were not, strictly speaking, the distribution (*nemein*) of goods in accordance with merit. Instead, suppose its end were the cultivation of virtue in those who can possess it, and the prevention of wrongdoing on the part of those who cannot. Suppose, that is, that justice, in the highest sense of the term, did not depend on the strict application of the rules and ratios, the *logoi*, of distributive justice. Seen in this light, laws that nudged ordinary men in the direction of virtue, even at the expense of those who most deserved its rewards, would not have to be regarded as unjust. And the man who acquiesced in or even applied such laws would not have to be regarded as either a willing or unwilling participant in injustice.

Aristotle signals his awareness of this solution in the closing sections of Book V, in his discussion of equity and the equitable man. But he also acknowledges the problem it addresses. In the opening pages of Book V, whole virtue or justice is virtually identified with law-abidingness, but by its end, Aristotle is taking issue with those who suppose that doing justice (and injustice) are "easy and in our power"—are, that is, simply a matter of obeying or disobeying the law (1137a4–17). By the end of Book V, what constitutes a just action has become a question. How does Aristotle's discussion of equity address it?

As Aristotle presents it, equity comes into play when the law, which is of necessity universal, fails to take into account extraordinary circumstances (1137b13–14). Equity does not negate the law, which is for the most part just, but completes it by "setting it right" with respect to particulars (1137b11–13; 14–19). In equity, in other words, we glimpse an understanding of justice within which the laws, and hence the rules and ratios of distributive justice, are no longer seen—as they must be seen in the daily course of political life—as fixed and immutable. Flexibility is all (1137b29–32).[40]

The equitable man, in turn, is he who is "capable of choosing and acting" (*proairetikos kai praktikos*) in accordance with what the legislator of a law *would* ordain were he present and aware of the particular case at hand (1137b21–24; 35). He is a man whose understanding of justice and just action is not strictly determined by the law; he follows a "higher law," the original intent of the legislator. The closing lines of the chapter, where Aristotle shows us the characteristic behavior of the equitable man, indicate what this means in practice. The equitable man is not "overprecise about justice" (*akribo-dikaios*) but rather is "content with less than his share" (*elattōtikos*) even though he has the law on his side (1137b34–1138a3). These lines point to just the sort of man who is needed, a man who, while possessing complete virtue, is nevertheless willing to be satisfied—and *justly* satisfied—with less than his share of goods, including honor.

III. CONCLUSION

The closing pages of Book V do, then, provide a sort of answer to the questions raised by Aristotle's discussions of magnanimity and whole justice. At any rate, it has become clear that equity, as well as magnanimity and whole justice, is needed if the man who possesses complete virtue is to find happiness within the active life, the life of participation in his political community. Something resembling magnanimity is needed to curb and restrain the somehow virtuous man's "natural" appetite for honor, to allow him to choose and exercise the virtues for their own sake, independently of external demands and pressures. Something resembling whole justice is needed to keep the good man "at work" within the sphere of political action and public life. But something like equity or the understanding of justice implicit in equity is necessary, too, if there is to be a just and lasting solution to the best man's transcendence of honor and the rules of distributive justice.

This is not to say that magnanimity, whole justice, and equity, taken together, are sufficient conditions. Aristotle's account of equity leaves serious questions unanswered. As yet we still do not know *why* the man who possesses complete virtue should choose to be equitable, why, that is, he should be *praktikos* if he must also be *elattōtikos*. In other words, Aristotle's brief sketch of equity still leaves open the question, which began to haunt us even as we looked at his account of magnanimity, whether the sphere of *praxis*, that is, the sphere of moral virtue, can provide the truly virtuous man with a space large enough for the activity proper to his virtue. Why should he bother with those who cannot, in principle, see him for what he is? Perhaps what looks like mere "laziness," like an *energeia a-ergos*, from the point of view of politics conceals what is in fact the highest form of activity, the form in which the best man is at work in completion (*entelecheia*).

Again, Aristotle's "solution" to the problem posed by distributive justice comes, as solutions often do, at a cost. In this case, the cost can be measured by the distance between the starting point of Aristotle's *meth-odos* and his account of equity. His inquiry begins with the cultivated and active, who understand honor to be the good and the end of political life, and who presumably enter political life on the understanding that virtuous deeds will be—and can be—rewarded in full by honor. But by the end of Book V, that is, by the end of his account of the moral virtues and at the precise mid-point of the *Ethics*, Aristotle is suggesting that the good man is precisely the man who must be *elattōtikos*, ready and able to put up with less than his full measure of honor. Aristotle's attempt to find a meaning for complete virtue that is compatible with the everyday understanding of activity as *praxis* ends in the discovery that no such compatibility is possible. Once again the question of a principle or reason for participating in public life, for contributing to the common good, arises—this time from the point of view of ordinary virtue and ordinary men. Can such a reason be found within the everyday understanding of things? Is it enough to say that virtuous actions must be chosen for the sake of the noble—when the nobler the man, the less possible it is that his virtue can be recognized?

These questions cannot be answered within the terms of the first half of the *Ethics*. If answers are to be found anywhere, they are to be found in Aristotle's account of friendship in Books VIII and IX. But before we turn to those books, we must examine in some detail Aristotle's discussion of the intellectual virtues in Book VI, for wisdom and prudence are the remaining virtues that, by Aristotle's own account, can lay some claim to being "complete," that is, sufficient conditions for happiness. As we begin to examine them, we must remember that the question we are asking—the question any serious reader of the *Ethics* must ever keep before him—is not whether this or that disposition of soul is a condition for virtuous *action* (*praxis*) but rather what disposition of soul makes possible the fully human activity, whatever that activity (*energeia*) turns out to be.

3

||||||||||||||||||||||||||||||||||||||||||||

PRUDENCE
AND WISDOM

A RISTOTLE'S INQUIRY INTO the good takes a sudden turn
in Book VI. As we observed earlier, thought or reason, *logos*,
is largely absent from his account of the good life in the first half
of the *Ethics*. Book I is a case in point. Aristotle leaves reason out
of his definition of happiness, and when he turns to the defense
of that definition, he lists a number of candidates for human happiness, including prudence and wisdom, and then proceeds to
ignore them and discuss all the rest.[1] In the four books that follow, we see more of the same. Aristotle not only concentrates on
defining the ethical virtues in these books; he also claims repeatedly that they arise from deeds rather than words, and even goes
so far as to suggest that knowledge is of no great moment in the
ethical life (1103b13–23; 1104a18–b3; 1105a26–b5). No passage
better captures the tone of the first half of the *Ethics* than Aristotle's denunciation, in Book II, of those who "taking refuge in
logos, imagine they philosophize and that in this way they will be
serious men" (1105b12–14).[2]

There are, to be sure, moments in the first half of the *Ethics* when Aristotle looks ahead to Book VI. Close to the beginning of Book II, he observes that "to act in accordance with right
reason is common [to the ethical virtues] and let it be supposed
(*hypokeisthō*)—there will be talk about it later, both what right

reason is and how it stands in relation to the remaining virtues" (1103b31–35). Somewhat later, and somewhat surprisingly, given the course of the argument, he defines [ethical] virtue as a "disposition to choose, being in the mean relative to us, [a mean] determined *by reason*, indeed the reason through which the prudent man would determine it" (1106b36–1107a2). Again, Aristotle considers deliberation, certainly a form of reasoning, at some length in Book III (1112a18–1113a14). But in all such cases—and they are rare—he merely alludes to the possibility that reason might play a vital role in the good life or lets reason enter the picture only indirectly, as an adjunct to the discussion of ethical virtue.[3]

This is emphatically not the case in Book VI. Here reason and the part of the soul that "possesses reason" (*to logon echon*) occupy the foreground of the argument and are for the first time given their due. Right reason is no longer merely "supposed" to "underlie"—*hypokeisthai* means both—the activity of the ethical virtues. Aristotle brings its nature to the surface; he makes the being of prudence an object of inquiry. The reasoning part of the soul likewise gets considered from all sides; Aristotle brings to light the fundamental forms of thinking and marks them off from one another.

The import of these inquiries for Aristotle's own *logos* is very great. In the first place, his examination of prudence leads him to the conclusion that right reason is more than a perhaps essential, yet subordinate, feature of the ethical life: In the final chapters of Book VI prudence emerges as the unifying ground of the ethical virtues (1144b30–1145a2). What is more, Book VI calls into question, at least implicitly, the ruling assumption of the first half of the *Ethics*—the assumption that the good life and the ethical life are synonymous. That is, the possibility that happiness might lie elsewhere than in action, might be found in *theōria* rather than *praxis*, comes to light for the first time in Book VI. No wonder Aristotle "makes another beginning" at the outset of Book VII (1145a15–17). A new beginning (*archē*) is in order because the old order and old starting-points (*archai*), which reigned supreme in Books I through V, are no longer sufficient to account for what emerges in Book VI. Book VI casts the sources or springs (*archai*) of the human good in a new light.

WHY DOES THE INQUIRY take this turn, and take it when it does? Somewhere in the *Ethics* Aristotle must give an account of the reasoning part of the soul and the part that reason plays in the ethical life. In the first place, as we saw earlier, his initial working out of the definition of happiness in Book I rests on the observation that man is the "talking animal," the animal that alone "possesses reason." Moreover, the division of the soul at the end of Book I into a part that possesses reason "primarily and in itself," and a part that possesses reason in the sense that it "listens" or "can listen" to reason, also implies that some discussion of reason is in order (1102b13–14; 1103a1–3). Any full account of the ethical virtues, which are modes or dispositions of the listening part of the soul, must include an account of what the soul listens to. In short, once Aristotle assumes, as he does at the beginning of Book II, that actions must be in accordance with right reason, the questions "What is right reason?" and "How is it related to the remaining virtues?"—the questions with which Aristotle opens and closes Book VI—become questions that he must address at some point in his inquiry (1103b31–34). As for the emergence of *theōria* in Book VI, one can argue that this is largely accidental; *epistēmē, nous,* and their union in *sophia* become topics of discussion only because the task of defining right reason obliges Aristotle to specify the ways in which it differs from other intellectual activities and dispositions.

There is something to be said for these arguments. The opening lines of Book VI—"But since we happen to have said earlier that it is necessary to choose the mean, and neither the excess nor the deficiency, and [since] the mean is as right reason says, let us define this"—recall Book II and suggest that Aristotle's intent, his only intent, in Book VI is to define right reason and thus fill in the gap left in his discussion of the life of action (1138b18–20). Moreover, in light of these lines, Aristotle's discussion of *epistēmē, nous,* and *sophia* indeed appears incidental to his discussion of "practical reason." And yet, I think it is possible to give a more satisfying account of the character and content of Book VI, one that more fully explains the dramatic shift of focus we find there.[4] We need only consider what we have learned from our investigations of magnanimity, justice, and equity.

In the first place, we have seen that the man with complete virtue cannot look exclusively to the law for an account of what is just: Since the law cannot honor him adequately, in order to take himself into account, he must be able to take a legislator's-eye view of the law and its way of distributing the community's goods. But to say this is to say that such a man must be able to look beyond the *logoi* and *analogiai*, the ratios and proportions, that constitute and reveal his city's understanding of the just and the good. This, in turn, seems to mean, if equity is to be more than a disposition to acquiesce in his city's apparent injustice, that the good man *qua* equitable must possess *within himself* the *logos* and the kind of *logos* that his city lacks. If he is to come to terms with his community and himself, he must possess the capacity of a legislator—he must be a sort of law unto himself—whether or not his city provides him with the opportunity to exercise that capacity in a public fashion.[5] The great-souled man is simply too big for his city, and because he is, he must become a master of proportion, a source of due measure. The very existence of equity seems to presuppose and point to something like *phronēsis*, a highly developed capacity to sort out for oneself what is good or bad—for oneself and for others. Hence, I suggest, Aristotle's turn to the consideration of right reason at the beginning of Book VI.[6]

The *manner* in which Aristotle discusses equity invites us to take this argument a step further. As I noted earlier, his account of equity does not explicitly allude to the peculiar predicament of the simply good man, his transcendence of any city's capacity to honor. Indeed, Aristotle makes no effort at all to specify those occasions upon which equity might appropriately come into play. Instead he prefaces his discussion of equity with the observation that men are wrong to assume that justice is easy to understand because the law is easy to understand—he quietly introduces a distinction between the just and the lawful—while in that discussion he both emphasizes the flexibility of equity and virtually identifies it with goodness (1137a4–17; 1137a31–1137b2; 1137b29–32).

This way of treating equity may be significant, for Aristotle may be implying that the good man's peculiar predicament with regard to honor is simply a special case of a larger problem with the law. Contrary to the common understanding of such matters, the law—even law (*nomos*) broadly conceived as the customary understanding of what should and should not be done—may fail to provide the virtuous man with sufficient guidance in almost every realm of human affairs. His actions may for the most part be *in accordance with* the law: nothing in Aristotle's account of equity suggests that he will routinely "break" the law. But it is one thing to say this and another to say that his actions are sufficiently *defined* or *determined* by law, that is, by the *nomoi* or commonly held opinions about what is just and good. And if the good man's actions are not "as a rule" defined by law, we must ask what rule or principle does define them. Seen aright, the ultimate source of *all* the good man's deeds may lie within him, in *his logos* rather than the *logos* of the law. In appearance his deeds may be *kata nomon*, in accord with law; in truth they may be *kata logon*, in accordance with reason. Here again, the conclusion of Book V points directly to Book VI. Here again, the search for complete virtue, for the inner condition or set of inner conditions of the soul for the attainment of the human good, demands an investigation of that part of the soul that is "able to speak" rather than just listen.

This is not all. The complications that arise in the course of Aristotle's search for complete virtue in Books I through V not only compel him to investigate the nature of practical reason; they also compel him to investigate the nature of theoretical reason. As we saw earlier, Aristotle's discussions of magnanimity, whole justice, and equity force out into the open the question of whether there is any link *at all* between the everyday understanding of virtue and happiness and the true understanding of virtue and happiness. No doubt the attainment of happiness requires the exercise of virtue, and no doubt this *appears* to mean that happiness is to be found in *praxis*, in acts of courage, generosity, justice, and so on. But by the end of Book V what complete virtue is and what its activity will "look like" have become open questions. For the assumption that virtuous activity (*energeia*) and virtuous action (*praxis*) are synonyms may be no more sound than the assumption that every virtuous activity is honor-able, that is, able to appear as it is in the eyes of most men. Both assumptions in fact seem to be elements of that very everyday understanding of things quietly called into question by Aristotle's investigations of magnanimity, whole justice, and equity.

But if happiness is not to be found in a life of action, where is it to be found? Aristotle's working out of his definition of happiness in Book I—and any reader discerning enough to be troubled by the end of Book V might well turn back to Book I for a second look—at least suggests that it might lie in *theōria*, in the exercise of understanding for its own sake. The linchpin of that working out is Aristotle's observation that the activity of thinking or reasoning is the distinctively human work (*ergon*) or activity (*energeia*). But if the human good is present "in" the work of man, if human happiness—the most choiceworthy of all activities—is nothing but the being at work well of the distinctively human part of us, then reason would seem to dictate that it lies in the exercise of reason for its own sake. In other words, once everyday assumptions about virtue and happiness no longer bear the mark of self-evident truths—and they do not by the end of Book V—the way lies open for the serious consideration of the possibility that happiness may lie in *theōria*.

SEEN ARIGHT, THEN, Books I through V do provide grounds for Aristotle's inquiries in Book VI, and not only in the sense that Book VI fills in a gap in the structure of his earlier argument. Book VI has *dramatic* significance—it addresses questions that *can* be asked and that *must* be asked because of difficulties that emerge over the course of Books I through V. Thus Aristotle's inquiry in Book VI can and must become an inquiry into the reasoning part of the soul—and into prudence and wisdom in particular—because by the end of Book V two apparently distinct possibilities have opened up in his pursuit of the human good, one less radical than the other. Either we are to continue to think that happiness lies in right action, but are now to understand reason—a reason located *within* the soul of the virtuous man—to be in some significant measure responsible for the rightness of those actions. Or we are to shift our attention away from actions or deeds to the activity of thought itself, and are to understand happiness to lie in thinking, in seeing, for its own sake. To arrive at a clear understanding of the first possibility, we need an account of prudence or right reason, that is, the disposition of reason that makes right *praxis* possible. To arrive at a clear understanding of the second, we need an account of wisdom, that is, the disposition of reason that makes *theōria* possible. What we need, in fact, is a full-fledged account of the part of the soul that reasons. Hence, I suggest, Aristotle's inquiries in Book VI.

I. THE OBJECTS OF THOUGHT

What, then, are wisdom and prudence? And what relation do they bear to one another and to the remaining intellectual dispositions—for Aristotle's inquiries in Book VI are not limited to *phronēsis* and *sophia*. Art (*technē*), science (*epistēmē*), intellect (*nous*), judgment (*gnomē*), and understanding (*synesis*): Aristotle makes the whole realm of intellectual activities and dispositions the object of inquiry in Book VI.[7] Even if we remove science and intellect from this list, on the grounds that they are "elements" of wisdom, and even if we suppose, as seems probable, that Aristotle only considers art, judgment, and understanding in order to clarify the meaning of prudence, we are still left with the question: just what does Aristotle's consideration of these elements and alternative dispositions contribute to our understanding of wisdom and prudence? In short, we must ask: On what grounds are wisdom and prudence singled out as *the* virtues of the intellect?

Before we can answer any of these questions, we must face another. We have been supposing for the last several pages that a fundamental division exists among the various forms of reasoning and that, accordingly, there must be at least two virtues of the intellect—prudence and wisdom—one associated with each basic form of reasoning. Aristotle makes this same assumption at the outset of Book VI. He supposes (*hypokeisthai*) that, just as the soul as a whole is divided into two parts, so, too, the "half" of the soul that reasons is itself divided into two parts; and he proposes to seek out "what is the best condition of each part," on the grounds that "this is the virtue of each" (1139a2–6; 15–16).

This "hypothesis" at once underlies everything else Aristotle says in Book VI and paves the way for his later claims in Book X about the fundamental distinction between *theōria* and *praxis*. But how sound is it? Surely everyone would admit that in some sense carpenters and physicians, mathematicians and statesmen reason differently. But what grounds are there for saying that reason is not, in a still stronger sense, one and the same in each case; that, on the contrary, there are such sharp differences between some types of reasoning that it is necessary to suppose that more than one excellence or virtue of reason exists? To put the question in terms of our earlier argument, does it make sense to say that the one who reasons prudently and the one who reasons wisely are not, in the most decisive sense, the *same*, that is, engaged in the same activity and characterized by the same virtue insofar as they reason well?

LET US CONSIDER FOR a moment the things about which we think, the *noēta* or objects of our thought. Sometimes, perhaps most of the time, our thinking is directed toward changeable objects. The carpenter thinks about wood, *hylē*, which he plans to turn into a chair or a table; the physician thinks about the patient who sits before him, whom he hopes to make well by means of his art; the generous man thinks about the poor man, whose lot he intends to improve through a change in his own stock of available goods; the statesman thinks about his people, whose character he looks to improve by judicious changes in the law. In all such cases, thought is focused on what is changeable, indeed, is inseparable from the possibility of change: no carpenter would give wood a second thought were it not capable of becoming a chair or table.

The case of the mathematician is quite different. He reasons about objects—numbers, say, or geometrical figures—which he supposes do not change and which he certainly does not expect to see change as a consequence of his thinking about them. If the equality of the angles of a triangle to two right angles were to depend on his thinking about them, were six now a perfect and even number, but yesterday or tomorrow an odd or imperfect number, he would not give them a second thought. And the mathematician is not alone in this. The astronomer supposes, of necessity, that there is something unchanging in the changing appearances of the heavenly bodies: these may move from place to place, even move differently at different times as a consequence of his position with respect to them, but were he unable to discover the unchanging patterns that in-form their motions, he would consider them unworthy of his attentions. This list can be extended to include the "sublunary" sphere. For example, the zoologist and botanist attend not so much to the multitude of changes that plant and animal life exhibit as to the underlying forms that manifest themselves in the midst of those changes. If they pay attention to change, it is because the different natures of living things are revealed in their peculiar motions: the "whatness" of a dog shows itself over time, in its distinctive walk and its manner of growth, as well as in its mature bodily structure.[8]

The point is this: If we take into account the *objects* of thought, we cannot fail to notice that a fundamental distinction exists among them and that at times our thinking aims at changing what is changeable, while at other times it is directed either toward what is unchanging in the midst of the changeable or, as in the case of mathematics, what is simply unchanging. Nor, it should be noted, is the latter sort of reasoning the peculiar province of "specialists": the distinction we are making does not presuppose a distinction between *theōria* and *praxis*. If anything, our everyday understanding of the world presupposes an awareness of what is unchanging and thus points to the possibility of the "special sciences." We count, measure, and compare things every day, and would no doubt be appalled to discover that two plus two only occasionally equals four: the mathematician simply makes explicit what we presuppose and somehow already know about shapes and numbers, ratios and magnitudes. Similarly, while an awareness of what takes place in the "circling heavens" may be sadly lacking among city dwellers in our day, anyone who raises, say, roses would be surprised to discover that roses do not produce roses that do not produce roses: the botanist simply makes explicit what the good gardener already knows. In short, if we take our bearings by the possible objects of our thought, if we think about thinking by thinking first about what we think *about*, it makes sense to suppose that reason is by nature twofold and that there are not one but two virtues of the intellect.

Aristotle does precisely this at the outset of Book VI. He does more than assert that the part of the soul which reasons has two parts and then propose to seek out the "best disposition" or virtue of each part. His "hypothesis" is based on the claim that there are two fundamentally different kinds of beings and hence two fundamentally different kinds of thinking: "And let two parts having reason be supposed (*hypokeisthō*), one by which we observe those sorts of beings the principles of which do not admit of being otherwise [than they are], and another by which [we observe] the beings which admit [of being otherwise than they are]" (1139a6–8). The "middle term" that allows Aristotle to conclude that a distinction among beings implies a distinction in the soul he puts as follows: "for of the parts of the soul, different in kind is the part natured (*pephukos*) in relation to each of the beings different in kind, if indeed knowledge belongs to them in virtue of a certain similarity and kinship" (1139a8–11). Reason is not a free-floating power that can bring any object it encounters within its orbit. Knowing presupposes a natural connection, a natural kinship (*oikeiotēs*), between knower and known: knower and known must, as it were, belong to the same family. Accordingly, since there are objects of knowledge that differ in kind, there must be different cognitive powers in the soul, each of which has a "natural" relation to its "natural" object.[9]

WE HAVE ALREADY SEEN a version of this principle articulated in the opening chapters of Book I of the *Ethics*. There Aristotle had observed that the "nature of the business at hand," the "underlying material" of an inquiry, can affect its level and type of precision and that, in effect, different objects of inquiry dictate different modes of inquiry. In addition, Aristotle had argued that an inquiry must begin "from the things known [or familiar] to us," and that those things, in the case of the *Ethics*, are only accessible to a certain type of man, the "noble and good" man whose education and experience has prepared him to hear about "beautiful and just and generally political things."

The lingering effect of these observations and arguments on the shape of Aristotle's inquiry in Books I through V has gradually become apparent. The principle that different objects of knowledge require different types of inquiry and different dispositions of the soul shows itself, for instance, in Aristotle's continual attentiveness to the self-understanding of "the cultivated and active." As much as possible, he makes their understanding of the virtues and happiness, for example, their attachment to honor and action, the starting point of his own inquiry into the good. Now, however—and this is crucial—the application of the *same* principle at the beginning of Book VI helps to prepare the way for Aristotle's abandonment of his hitherto unquestioned acceptance of their understanding of things. For his claim that there must be some part of the soul "by which we observe those sorts of beings whose principles do not admit of being otherwise [than they are]" and his insistence that we investigate the "best disposition" or virtue of this part leads more or less directly to the claim that there is a *trans-practical* virtue, *sophia*, the being at work of which may constitute true happiness. The very principle of inquiry that compels Aristotle to focus on *praxis* and neglect *theōria* in the first half of the *Ethics* now compels him, as he begins the second half of his inquiry, to consider the possibility that happiness may lie in *theōria* rather than *praxis*.

In saying this, I have gone considerably beyond what Aristotle says in the first chapter of Book VI. He says nothing there about wisdom or prudence—for that matter, he says nothing there about a distinction between the theoretical and the practical. Aristotle merely divides the reasoning part of the soul in two according to the terms mentioned above, proposes that one part be called "the scientific" (*to epistēmonikon*) and the other "the calculative" (*to logistikon*), and further proposes that the best disposition of each be sought out (1139a11–14).[10] If we are to understand how wisdom and prudence come to occupy the place they do in Aristotle's discussion, we need an account of the dispositions that fall under the "scientific" and "calculative" divisions of the soul.

Aristotle proceeds to provide this account in chapters three through eight of Book VI. In the concluding lines of chapter two, he lays down a criterion for deciding which among the dispositions is best. "The work of both the *noetic* parts of the soul is truth;" accordingly, the virtue of each part will be that disposition in accordance with which each part "most of all discloses truth" (1139b12–13). He then discusses at length five possible candidates for intellectual virtue, that is, five dispositions "by which the soul discloses truth": *technē* (art), *epistēmē* (science), *phronēsis* (prudence), *nous* (intuition), and *sophia* (wisdom) (1139b15–17).[11]

II. SOPHIA

Let us begin where Aristotle begins, with science or *epistēmē*. As Aristotle opens the discussion by observing, the very name *epistēmē* places it within that part of the soul "by which we observe those sorts of beings the principles of which do not admit of being otherwise [than they are]." "If we are to speak precisely and not to pursue [mere] likenesses," if, that is, we think carefully about what we say, "we all understand what we know (*epistametha*) not to admit of being otherwise" (1139b18–21).[12] By common consent, *epistēmē* is knowledge of what exists "of necessity;" it is the science of "the eternal," "the ungenerated and indestructible things;" no doubt this is why Aristotle calls the part of the soul to which it belongs "the scientific (*to epistēmonikon*)" (1139b22–24). Indeed, given the first half of Aristotle's description, we might suppose *epistēmē* to be an obvious candidate for intellectual virtue. What more could one ask for—what better name than *epistēmē* for knowledge of what cannot be otherwise, what disposition of the soul closer to truth than knowledge of the eternal?

The answer lies in the second half of Aristotle's description. Every *epistēmē*, he says, is teachable, and every object of *epistēmē*, learnable. But all teaching proceeds "from things recognized beforehand": all teaching is either teaching "through induction" (from previously recognized particulars) or teaching "by syllogism" (from previously recognized universals) (1139b25–31).[13] Herein lies the problem: *epistēmē*, which clearly belongs in the latter class, must—being teachable—rest on principles or beginnings that are not known through *epistēmē* itself, that is, through syllogism.

Consider the mathematician. As someone with an *epistēmē*, he can demonstrate and thus teach others the various properties of, say, circles and squares. He cannot, however, demonstrate the principles upon which his demonstrations rest. Faced with a student who cannot "see" that the whole is greater than the part, or who cannot "see" what makes a circle a circle and not a square, he must shrug his shoulders or break his chalk in despair. Likewise, the mathematician himself does not know the first principles of his science through that science; otherwise he could demonstrate them, in which case they would not be first principles. This is not to say that the mathematician is ignorant of the starting points of his demonstrations. As Aristotle argues here and in the *Posterior Analytics*, to which he refers us in this passage, *epistēmē* must rest on principles that are better known than the demonstrations that flow from them: everyone who deserves the name of *epistēmōn* must know what he is talking about (1139b31–35). It simply means that the mathematician or any possessor of an *epistēmē* knows certain things, the first principles of his science, by means other than that science. *Epistēmē* is a "demonstrative disposition" (*hexis apodeiktikē*), and precisely because it is, it presupposes knowledge of that from (*apo*) which its demonstrations, its "displays" (*apodeixeis*), proceed.[14]

If *epistēmē* rests upon knowledge that it cannot itself provide, and if the knowledge upon which it depends is "true and primary and immediate and better known and prior and responsible for the conclusion," then it cannot, by itself, be the disposition we are looking for (*Post. Ana.* 71b20–23). *Epistēmē* cannot be one of those dispositions of the soul "in accordance with which each part discloses truth most of all." What must be added, if *epistēmē* is to be complete—what in fact gives *epistēmē* the "right" to be called *theōria*—is just that disposition with which we "see" (*theōrein*) the "first things," the *archai* upon which demonstrations depend. Aristotle fittingly calls this condition of soul *nous*. For *noein* means to see, to perceive, to be in immediate contact with an object of knowledge.[15]

THIS BRINGS US TO *nous*, the second disposition belonging to that part of the soul "by which we observe those sorts of beings whose principles do not admit of being otherwise," and in coming to it, we come face to face with a question about the third such disposition: *sophia*. By themselves, *nous* and *epistēmē* seem to exhaust the possibilities of the part of the soul with which we observe unchanging things. Either we think, or rather see, such things immediately (*a-mesōs*), in which case we exercise *nous*, or we think them mediately, by means of or by employing as middle terms (*mesa*) the insights provided by *nous*, in which case we exercise *epistēmē*. What place, then, is left for *sophia* in Aristotle's scheme? Is it only a blanket term for the conjunction of *nous* and *epistēmē*? Do *epistēmē* and *nous* together constitute, if not complete virtue, then at least the completed virtue or best disposition of the part of the soul to which they belong? Or is there something distinctive about *sophia*, something that makes it more than just the sum of *epistēmē* and *nous*, something that entitles it to be called a condition or disposition of the soul in its own right?

Before we go on to consider this question, we should note that a similar question arises in the case of *phronēsis* and *technē*. Both are dispositions of the part of the soul "by which we observe the things which admit of being otherwise [than they are]." Moreover, the activities of both conditions involve deliberation rather than observation or demonstration, and hence reach their completion in the changing of what is changeable. What Aristotle says holds true of "every *technē*," namely, that it is "concerned with generation and fashioning and seeing how some one of the things which admit of both being and not being might come into being . . . ," seems to hold true of *phronēsis* as well (1140a10–13). Likewise, what he says by way of distinguishing *phronēsis* from *epistēmē*, namely, that "no one deliberates about things which are incapable of being otherwise, nor about things which do not admit of being done by himself . . . ," seems to apply equally well to the "technician" (1140a31–33). It is true that Aristotle begins his account of *technē* by telling us that "making" (*poiēsis*) and "doing" (*praxis*) differ from one another, and then goes on to associate *technē* with making and *phronēsis* with doing (1140a1–6), but it is also true that Aristotle initially bases his distinction between making and doing on "the exoteric accounts" of them (1140a2–3). Given the similarities between *phronēsis* and *technē* that come to sight in the course of his discussion, we must wonder whether Aristotle's initial "trust" (*pisteuein*) in the everyday or exoteric accounts of making and doing is well founded. Do *phronēsis* and *technē* perhaps differ from one another only in name, and by convention, as it were? Could *phronēsis* in truth simply be a kind of *technē*? Or might *phronēsis* be present in varying degrees in all "technical" reasoning?

As similar questions concerning the relation of *sophia* to *epistēmē* and *nous* and the relation of *phronēsis* to *technē* arise in the course of a cursory reading of Aristotle's accounts of them, so similar answers emerge as we read those accounts more closely.

Let us begin with *sophia*. At first glance, it appears that Aristotle does in fact intend *sophia* to signify the simple conjunction of *nous* and *epistēmē*. He begins by observing that *sophia* is used in everyday speech to signify excellence or precision in the arts: the best and most subtle artisans are commonly called wise (1141a9–12). Applying these same criteria to the realm of *epistēmē*, supposing, that is, that *sophia* in its most proper sense constitutes the virtue of *epistēmē*, he concludes that "*sophia* would be the most precise of the sciences" (1141a16).[16] What this amounts to he tells us in the line which follows: "it is necessary, then, for the wise man not only to know the things that result from first principles (*ta ek tōn archōn*) but also to possess the truth (*alētheuein*) about the first principles" (1141a17–18). What makes *sophia* the most precise of the sciences, what makes it and not *epistēmē* alone a virtue, he seems to say, is simply the addition of *nous*: "So that *sophia* would be *nous* and *epistēmē*—*epistēmē*, as it were, in possession of a head . . ." (1141a18–20).

At any rate, this is how things look before we finish the sentence just quoted. Here is how Aristotle completes the sentence: *sophia* is "*epistēmē*, as it were, in possession of a head *of the most honorable things.*" He later repeats the phrase in the final form of his definition: "From these things it is clear that *sophia* is *epistēmē* and *nous* of the most honorable things by nature" (1141b2–3). *Nous* is clearly integral to *sophia*. But what elevates *sophia* above *epistēmē* and gives it the status of a virtue is not *simply* the directness of the wise man's gaze; the *objects* of his gaze make a difference as well. In other words, just as his recognition of the difference between changing and unchanging things earlier enabled Aristotle to distinguish between parts of the reasoning part of the soul, so here the recognition that there are differences among "epistemic" objects enables him to separate out *sophia* from the remaining *epistēmai*. Every *epistēmōn*, every possessor of a science, has "intuitive" knowledge of the first things in his science. But not every science is a science of "the most honorable things." What makes the wise man wise, and makes *sophia* the virtue of the "scientific" part of the soul, is the "kinship" of each with the best and most honorable things.

What are these "most honorable things"? Are the proper objects of the wise man's study to be found among the things that are by nature, for example, animals, plants, and the heavenly bodies? Such things move and change, but at least—in contrast to the things produced by art—they have the stable sources of their movement and change within themselves (*Physics* 192b8–32). What about the objects of mathematics? They are surely unchanging and, as their very name indicates, highly intelligible.[17] Aristotle's account of *sophia* does not give us much help in answering these questions. He excludes, or at least appears to exclude, one possibility—to which we shall return later—in the course of his discussion. He also suggests that *sophia* might have something to do with the study of "the most radiant things, out of which the cosmos is composed," by which he presumably means the objects of astronomy (1141b1–2). But perhaps more important is something he hints at right at the outset of his account: In the course of moving from the everyday understanding of *sophia*, as the virtue of *technē*, to his own understanding of it, as the virtue of *epistēmē*, he observes that "we imagine some men to be wise as a whole (*holōs*) [and] not in part (*kata meros*) or wise in something . . ." (1141a12–14). Aristotle *may* intend by this simply to show that *sophia* in its most proper sense has a place among the sciences: all the sciences are characterized by a certain focus on the universal, on the whole of things (*to kath-holou*). But he may also mean to suggest that *sophia*, in contrast to the remaining *epistēmai* as well as the *technai*, is somehow defined by the universality of its objects. The wise man, in other words, may be the man whose knowledge transcends every particular subject matter; and *sophia*, in the strict sense of the term, may be that disposition of the soul through which we contemplate the first things simply.[18]

SOPHIA THUS APPEARS TO have three characteristic features. In the first place, it is more closely tied to *nous* than any of the other *epistēmai*: *sophia* is inseparable from insight even "in speech." Moreover, *sophia* is distinguished from the remaining dispositions of the "scientific" part of the soul by the excellence of its objects: its status as the virtue or excellence of that part is derived, at least in part, from its being knowledge of the best and most honorable things. Finally, *as* knowledge of such things, it is "particularly" concerned with what is universal (*to kath-holou*), with what is as a whole.

III. *PHRONĒSIS*

A. *Poiēsis* and *Praxis*

Do these criteria, or something like them, also distinguish *phronēsis* from the *technai*? Is *phronēsis* the virtue of that part of the soul "by which we observe beings which are capable of being otherwise" because of its universality or the excellence of its objects or its close association with *nous*? Let us return to the distinction between *poiēsis* and *praxis*, that is, the distinction that Aristotle treats as the basis for the distinction between *phronēsis* and *technē*. Aristotle hints at his own reasons for accepting this "exoteric" distinction in the second chapter of Book VI. Not every kind of thought, he observes here, is responsible for change. "Thought itself moves nothing, but [thought which is] for the sake of something and *praktikē* [does]; for this is also the source (*archei*) of *poiētikē*; for everyone who makes, makes for the sake of something . . ." (1139a35–b1). What "poetic" and "practical" thought share, in other words, what differentiates both from "theoretical" thought and makes them both "causes" of motion is their deliberative character. Practical and poetic reasoners alike think with a view to attaining some end.

Yet it is just here that the difference between poetic and practical thought becomes apparent. For "what is made" (*to poiēton*) is not an "end simply"; it is "in relation to something and of something" (1139b1–2). What is done (*to prakton*), by contrast, is an end simply, "for acting well (*eupraxia*) is an end, and the desire is for this" (1139b2–3). Every maker aims at some end, but every such end, every made thing, points beyond itself: the house that the housebuilder aims to build is related to and belongs to a "higher" end, that is, shelter. But not every work (*ergon*)—to use a word that cuts across the distinction between *poiēsis* and *praxis*—exists for the sake of some further end. Otherwise, as Aristotle observes in the opening chapters of the *Ethics*, all desire would be in vain: To say that everything is pursued for the sake of something else would be equivalent to saying that nothing is pursued for the sake of anything else (1094a18–22). There must be an upper limit to the ends we pursue; some ends must be desired and pursued for their own sake. Such ends Aristotle calls—here, at any rate—*praxeis*, and the thought that "minds" them, practical thought. Thus, since poetic and practical thought are both defined by their relation to ends, and since the ends they aim at are different in kind, they must be different in kind as well.

We can now see not only why Aristotle distinguishes *phronēsis* from *technē* but also why he regards *phronēsis* as the virtue of the soul that calculates or deliberates (1139a11–14). For *phronēsis* and *technē* are simply the dispositions or best dispositions, respectively, of practical and poetic reason: If the ends of practical and poetic reason are distinct, the dispositions toward those ends must also be distinct. But the ends of practical and poetic reason are not only distinct; they differ in *goodness* as well as in kind. To say that practical reason, as opposed to poetic reason, considers and pursues things that are "ends simply" is to say that it is concerned with things that are simply good. In other words, practical reason concerns itself with the best of the objects that fall within the purview of deliberative reasoning, and *phronēsis*, as the best disposition of practical reason, is what allows us to deliberate about such objects well. Once again it is Aristotle's consideration of differences among the *objects* of knowledge that leads him to posit distinctions between the intellectual dispositions and permits him to regard one of those dispositions as a virtue. *Phronēsis*, like *sophia*, is a virtue in virtue of the excellence of its objects.

B. Universals and Particulars

What, then, of the criteria of universality and of inseparability from *nous*? Do these criteria, too, serve to define *phronēsis* as well as *sophia*? The opening lines of Aristotle's treatment of *phronēsis* suggest that universality, or something like it, is a distinguishing feature. As in the case of *sophia*, Aristotle begins with common usage: he takes a look at those "whom we say are prudent men *(tous phronimous)*" (1140a25).[19] "Now it seems to belong to the prudent man to be able to deliberate well concerning the things good and advantageous for himself, not in part, such as what sort of things [are good and advantageous] in relation to health [or] in relation to strength, but what sort of things [are good and advantageous] in relation to living well as a whole" (1140a25–28). Aristotle's mention of health and strength points to the arts of medicine and gymnastic; he thus suggests that prudential deliberations belong to a different order than the deliberations of the ordinary arts, even the arts most directly concerned with particular human goods. Equally clearly, his use of the phrases "not in part" *(ou kata meros)* and "as a whole" *(holōs)*, phrases that also appear in his description of *sophia*, suggests that the prudent man's deliberations are somehow universal in character. Aristotle's later extension of the objects of the prudent man's concern from "the things good and advantageous for himself" to "the things good and bad for man" or "the human goods" underscores this suggestion and makes the conclusion seem inescapable: *Phronēsis*, like *sophia* and in contrast to the *technai*, is in some sense knowledge of what is universal *(to katholou)*; the wholeness or generality of its objects distinguish it from other forms of deliberation (1140b4–6; 1140b20–22).

The moment we draw this conclusion, however, we find ourselves forced to retreat from it. I proposed earlier that Aristotle makes *phronēsis* the object of inquiry in part because of the inadequacy of law: The man who possesses complete virtue must be able to reason out for himself what is good and bad because the law fails to give an adequate account of such things. Yet according to Aristotle, the law fails precisely *because* of its universality: Its pronouncements are too general to "do justice" to the variety of circumstances and situations that arise in the course of political life. How, then, can *phronēsis* be a solution to the problem posed by the law if it is also characterized by universality? If anything, insofar as *phronēsis* is an alternative to law, we should expect it to be characterized by the particularity of its focus—and indeed, Aristotle describes it in just these terms later in the same chapter. Toward the end of chapter seven, he insists that *phronēsis* is not knowledge "of universals alone" (*tōn katholou monon*), but requires familiarity with "the particulars" (*ta kath' hekasta*) as well, "for it is practical, and action is concerned with particulars" (1141b14-16). Within the same context, he observes that "those with experience" (*hoi empeiroi*), that is, those who possess a thorough knowledge of particulars, are "more able to act" (*praktikoteroi*) (1141b16-18). Finally, he ends chapter seven with the claim that "it is necessary to have both [forms of knowledge], or this one [namely, knowledge of particulars] more" (1141b21-22).

Where do these remarks leave us? Is *phronēsis* not, after all, characterized by universality? Is the prudent man prudent primarily because he has what Aristotle calls in Book I experience of "the actions in accord with life" (1095a3)? The answer to this question will clearly bear on our understanding of the relation between *phronēsis* and *nous* as well, for, at least as Aristotle presents it in chapter six of Book VI, *nous* is the power of soul that provides immediate access to universals (1140b31-36; 1141a3-8). If *phronēsis* is not, or not in any decisive sense, universal knowledge, then it cannot be closely allied to *nous*. In fact, Aristotle says just this in chapter eight: "[*Phronēsis*] is clearly in opposition to *nous*; for *nous* is of the definitions, of which there is no *logos*, while [*phronēsis*] is of the ultimate [particular] . . ." (1142a25-26).[20] Taken together, what Aristotle says in chapter six about *nous*, in chapter seven about *phronēsis*, and in chapter eight about the relation between them suggest that *phronēsis* is anything but universal knowledge. We are forced to conclude that *sophia* and *phronēsis*, rightly understood, lie at opposite extremes from one another: the roots of the one lie in the apprehension of unchanging universals, the roots of the other in apprehension of changing particulars.

YET, EVEN IN CHAPTER SEVEN, where he emphasizes most strongly its "empirical" character, Aristotle admits that *phronēsis* somehow involves knowledge "of universals." Nor can we forget what he says in chapter five about the "impartiality" and "wholeness" of *phronēsis*. Can we make sense of these claims in light of Aristotle's emphasis elsewhere on the particularity of its focus? Could *phronēsis* be, not incidentally but in its very nature, both universal and particular in character?

Let us take a closer look at the object of the prudent man's concern. In chapter two of Book VI, Aristotle tells us that "practical" thought, the best disposition of which is *phronēsis*, is concerned with ends that are "ends simply." In chapter five he notes that the prudent man is the man able to deliberate well "concerning the things good and advantageous for himself, not in part . . . but in relation to living well as a whole." These are clearly two ways of saying the same thing, for "living well" is one of Aristotle's synonyms for happiness or the human good, and the good is precisely the end we seek and choose simply for its own sake. *Phronēsis*, in other words, is that disposition of soul which allows us to think well about things that contribute to or make possible human happiness; it is deliberative thought that has as its end not just any "work" or activity, but precisely that being at work of the soul in which human life reaches its completion.

How does knowing this aid us in understanding why Aristotle sometimes characterizes *phronēsis* in terms of universality? Consider again the relation between its end—the human good—and the ends pursued by the various *technai*. The man who fashions bridles, the cavalryman who puts bridle, stirrup, and steed to work in battle, the general who makes "strategic" use of his cavalry and infantry—all do what they do and make what they make, as we observed earlier and as Aristotle observes on the opening page of the *Ethics*, for the sake of some "larger" end (1094a9–16). But to say this is to say that there is something "partial" about the ends that each of the arts pursue. The maker of bridles, and, still more, the horseman who spends his days with friends exercising his horses may forget from time to time that their "works" make sense only within a larger context. Perhaps it is even good or at least necessary that they do forget. But the point remains: Victory and the thrill of victory, to take the case of the general, are not ends in themselves; they presuppose something like the common good, the well-being, the happiness of the political community. But this means that happiness or the good bears to the ends of even the "highest" arts something resembling the relation of whole to part. In short, we can see now why Aristotle is inclined in chapter five to contrast deliberating about "living well as a whole" (*holōs*) with the "partiality" of deliberations about strength and health. Living well, understood as a synonym for human happiness, is the being whole, the being at an end (*entelecheia*), in which all other human pursuits find their completion; accordingly, the form of reasoning that has living well as its end can be appropriately regarded as reasoning "about the whole" (*kath-holou*).[21]

This does not mean that *phronēsis* must be regarded as a type of reasoning about and from universals in the ordinary sense of the term. The ends at which the arts aim may be *partial* in comparison to the end of prudence, but the end at which prudence aims may be no less *particular* than the ends of the arts. Aristotle hints at this when he tells us in chapter two that the end of practical reason is faring or acting well (*eu-praxia*) and then says in chapter seven and elsewhere that "*praxis* is concerned with particulars (*peri ta kath' hekasta*)." If the end of right reason is right action, and if not only actions but all the things that concern right action are particulars, then the capacity for right thinking about right action—*phronēsis*—would seem to be wholly concerned with, wholly "about" (*peri*), particulars.

WE ARE NOT ACCUSTOMED to thinking about thinking in this way. In this, as in other respects, our model for reason tends to be "epistemic"—the kind of reasoning found, for instance, in mathematics. Here thought is wholly bound up with universals. The object of thought in any given demonstration may be, as in the case of ancient as opposed to modern mathematics, *this* triangle ABC.[22] Nevertheless, universal claims form the end as well as the beginning of a demonstration. What is sought is not what belongs to this triangle "in particular," but what belongs to every such triangle. Similarly, what is taken for granted in the course of a demonstration is not what belongs to this triangle and no other, but what has been demonstrated before to belong to triangles *as* triangles or figures *as* figures or even quantities *as* quantities. Indeed, as anyone who has attempted to teach mathematics knows, an inability to grasp the full universality of a demonstration's conclusion, to see that what holds for *this* mathematical object holds for *any such* object, constitutes the most common failing of the mathematical tyro.

What does the alternative to this kind of thinking—what does thinking in which the most common failure lies in an inadequate appreciation of the uniqueness, the ultimate particularity, of the situation at hand—look like? To ask this question is to ask what part reason plays in the day to day workings of the ethical life, where as a matter of course particular human beings must make particular decisions about particular situations. Accordingly Aristotle's answer is to be found in just those sections of the *Ethics* where the relation of reason to the ethical virtues is at issue, for example, in Book III, where he further refines and clarifies the meaning of ethical virtue by discussing deliberation and choice, and in the final chapter of Book VI, where he explicitly discusses the relation of prudence to the ethical virtues (1111b4–1113b1; 1144a11–1144b17).

The picture of practical reason and *praxis* in general that emerges in these passages serves to qualify something that Aristotle says in the final chapter of Book I. In that chapter he calls the appetitive part of the soul the "listening" part, and thus implies that the ethical virtues, which are dispositions of it, are intended merely to dispose or attune the various human desires to follow the dictates of reason (1103a1–3). What Aristotle says in Book III and at the end of Book VI, on the other hand, makes it clear that reason can equally well be said to listen to the ethical virtues. For it is the ethical virtues that supply the good man with what Aristotle calls the wish or the appetite for the end; the work of practical reason lies in discovering whether the wished for end can be realized and, if it can be, in finding out how best to realize it.[23] In other words, being at work in accordance with virtue—right action—is the result of a kind of conversation between *phronēsis* and the ethical virtues. *Phronēsis* listens to the ethical virtues, which disclose to it some possible end to be achieved, while the ethical virtues, in turn, hearken to the plan for achieving that end at which *phronēsis* arrives. "Choice" (*proairesis*) is Aristotle's name for this conjunction of right reason and right desire. Thus Aristotle can say, in chapter two of Book VI, that "choice is either appetitive thought (*orektikos nous*) or thoughtful appetite (*dianoētikē orexis*)" (1139b4–5). Because choice is the point of intersection of appetite and reason, it makes no difference, in its description, which of the two is treated as a noun and which as an adjective: both are equally co-conditions or co-efficient causes of any given right action.

This picture of *phronēsis* and the ethical virtues "at work" tells us, among other things, that the prudent man need never depart from the realm of the "ultimate particular" in the course of his day to day thinking. The process of practical reasoning may *resemble* the process of reasoning from universals. Indeed, in Book III Aristotle likens it to the process of mathematical analysis, in which a universal assumption is tested by following out its consequences to see whether or not a contradiction with something known to be true universally can be reached. Nevertheless, deliberation is only *akin* to this type of universal reasoning. As Aristotle points out in the same passage, "not every process of inquiry (*zētēsis*), for example, mathematical inquiries, appears to be deliberation, though every deliberation appears to be a process of inquiry" (1112b20–24). What occupies the place of the universal assumption to be tested in the case of practical reason is the "vision" of the end supplied by the ethical virtues. But this "vision" is not a universal vision. For instance, the good man *qua* generous does not wish to help all men (or for that matter wish for world peace); his wish, his appetite for the end, is directed toward *this* man in *this* context who stands before him in need. Nor, when he reasons, is he required to think in or by means of universal terms. On the contrary, what the generous man must do is look closely at the particulars of *this* situation—no doubt drawing as well on his experience of other particular situations—in order to decide what, if anything, he can do for *this* man in *this* quandary, right here and now (1112b15–20; 1112b24–31). In short, at no point in the process of practical reasoning is it necessary for the prudent man to have recourse to universal reasoning: he need never "abstract" himself, pull himself away, from the situation at hand.[24]

AT LAST WE APPEAR to have achieved some clarity about the relation of *sophia* and *phronēsis* to one another. Both are distinguished from other intellectual dispositions by the excellence of their objects. Both are characterized by a kind of universality. And both are marked by the directness with which they apprehend their objects, that is, both meet the criterion of truthfulness that Aristotle lays down in chapter two. This is clearly so in the case of *sophia*, which is distinguished from the remaining *epistēmai* by its inseparability from *nous*, from the immediate apprehension of its objects. But seeing things as they are, truth in this sense, also seems to characterize *phronēsis*. Like the wise man, and unlike the artisan, whose success depends on his ability to see trees and stones, not as they are, but as "material" for ships and statues, the prudent man is successful in proportion to his ability to see what stands before him as it truly is.

Yet these points of resemblance between *sophia* and *phronēsis* must not be allowed to conceal the still greater differences that exist between them. In contrast to the objects of *sophia*, which must, as objects of an *epistēmē*, be universal in the strict sense of the term, the objects of *phronēsis* merely possess a kind of quasi-universality. The human good may bear to the ends pursued by the various *technai* something like the relation of whole to part, but "in practice" happiness is as particular an end as any of the ends of the arts: it must be discovered and brought forth within the realm of the "ultimate particular." This means that the kind of truth and the kind of reasoning that characterize *sophia* and *phronēsis* differ radically from one another: the perceptions and deliberations of the prudent man are as particular as the insights and syllogisms of the wise man are universal. In short, the very things that make *sophia* and *phronēsis* virtues—the excellence of their objects and the directness with which they apprehend them—also serve to divide them irrevocably from one another.

C. The Kinds of *Phronēsis*

Certain passages in Book VI appear to call into question, or at least to qualify, this rather tidy account of the differences between *phronēsis* and *sophia*. For instance, in chapter eleven Aristotle claims that "*Nous* is of the ultimate things in both directions; for there is *nous* and not *logos* of both the first definitions and the ultimate things, the one according to demonstrations is of the unchanging and first definitions, while the one in practical matters is of the ultimate [particular] and that which admits [of being otherwise] and of the other premise" (1143a35–b2). Now it might seem as if Aristotle merely means to affirm here what he has already implied elsewhere: *Phronēsis* as well as *sophia* is characterized by directness of apprehension; practical as well as theoretical reasoning rests on trans-logical insight into its objects, even though its objects differ in kind from the objects of *sophia*. And yet, especially in light of his earlier claim that *phronēsis* "is in opposition to *nous*," Aristotle's use of *the same name* here to denote the capacity for direct apprehension comes as a surprise. Does he mean to concede that, after all, *phronēsis* and *sophia* are rooted in, and are perhaps even modes of, *the same* intellectual activity?

Aristotle proceeds to add fuel to this particular fire: "for these [namely, the changeable particulars] are the starting points [or sources] of the for the sake of which; for out of the particulars [arise] the universals" (1143b3–4). Here Aristotle obviously identifies "the for the sake of which" with "the universals." Does he not suggest thereby that the end about which the prudent man reasons has for him, in the moment when he reasons about it, the status of a universal? Is this passage not of a piece with the passage, which we mentioned but did not discuss earlier, where Aristotle claims that prudent men "are able to contemplate [*theōrein*] the things good for themselves and the things good for men" (1140b7–10)?

Elsewhere in Book VI Aristotle uses language that further undercuts the distinction between theoretical and practical thought. In chapter two, for example, he calls the two parts of the reasoning part of the soul "*noetic* parts," as if to suggest again that the work of both parts is grounded in *noēsis*, that is, in the same activity of elementary apprehension. Even in chapter one, where Aristotle first asserts that there are two parts of the soul which possess reason, he uses language that suggests there is something "theoretical" about practical (and poetic) reason. If we substitute "contemplate" for the somewhat misleading "observe" as a translation for the verb "*theōrein*," Aristotle's initial hypothesis runs as follows: "Let two parts having reason be assumed, one by which we contemplate those sorts of beings the principles of which do not admit of being otherwise [than they are], and one by which [we contemplate] those beings which admit of being otherwise [than they are]" (1139a6–8).

WHY DOES ARISTOTLE BLUR the distinction between theoretical and practical thought in this way? Given what he says in Book III and elsewhere about deliberation, there seems to be no need for the prudent man to engage in reasoning from universals, and certainly no reason for Aristotle to link his activity with the activity of *theōria*. As we have just seen, according to that account, the ethical virtues supply the good man with the "equivalent" of universal premises, that is, right desires or wishes that are always already particular. The work of right reason lies simply in determining whether and how best he can bring about what he desires, and this the prudent man can do by sorting through the particulars of his past and present experience, by weighing one particular possibility against another. What matters, according to this account, is awareness of particulars, what Aristotle calls at one point an "eye from experience": sound judgment in practical matters requires no appeal to the universal, no "epistemic" knowledge (1143b11–15). But suppose the work of practical reason were not exhausted by this sort of activity. Suppose there were times when the ends disclosed by the ethical virtues were not sufficient guides for reason; when appeals to something beyond experience and the ethical virtues were unavoidable; when the *particular* situation in which the prudent man found himself compelled him to think in *universal* terms, to call on something like theoretical knowledge. Suppose, in other words, that there were not one but two types of practical reason, one grounded more or less exclusively in particular experience, the other grounded in this, and in some sort of universal knowledge as well. Aristotle's waffling would in this case make good sense: the complexity of his account would simply mimic or reflect the complexity of *phronēsis*, which would in turn reflect the complexity of our human condition.

What might these situations might be? On what occasions might a trans-particular, somehow theoretical *phronēsis* be called for? Aristotle hints at one possible answer to this question in the first part of chapter eight, where he discusses politics or political *phronēsis* (1141b23–33).[25] Here he draws a distinction between two types of political *phronēsis*. One type he calls "architectonic" or "legislative" *phronēsis*. The other type, which he observes has taken on "the common name" politics, he characterizes as "practical" or "deliberative;" this second type he further divides into "deliberative" and "judicial" *phronēsis*. The latter type of *phronēsis*, which Aristotle likens to the manual arts (*cheirotechnai*), he explicitly associates with knowledge of particulars. Architectonic *phronēsis*, the *phronēsis* of the legislator, Aristotle implies, somehow involves knowledge of universals.[26]

Can we make sense of this claim about architectonic or legislative *phronēsis*? In the ordinary course of political life, there is little need for men to think in terms of universals. What members of the assembly must do when they deliberate, what jurymen in the courts must do when they pass sentence, is focus on the particulars of the situation at hand. "Did Alcibiades in fact deface the

Hermai?" "Can we manage to finish the Long Walls by spring?" are the kinds of questions that must be dealt with as a rule in political life.[27]

The situation changes when we take into account the legislator's view of the city, and the more so, the more deeply we think about his work. We ordinarily call the men who make what Aristotle would call decrees, legislators, and the decrees they make, laws.[28] But if we think, as Aristotle does, of the legislator or lawgiver (*nomo-thetēs*) as the man who lays down or sets forth (*tithenai*) those fundamental beliefs or customs (*nomoi*) that shape and inform the life of a city and its citizens, the universality of his activity comes into view. Every founder of a political order must take into account—along with many other things—the particular character of the people whose way of life he intends to shape. But if he is to be more than a mirror of his people, if he is to do more in his capacity as lawgiver than just confirm what is already given to him, he must also be able to look beyond that character to other possibilities that lie dormant within them. If, for instance, his people lack the courage they need to defend themselves against hostile neighbors, the lawgiver must be able to see this and also see how to persuade them that courage is a virtue worth having; he must know that courage is a virtue, must understand the conditions for its realization, and must see how to bring it forth within the souls of his citizens. But courage without moderation is a disaster in the making; the lawgiver must also see this, must see that moderation is a virtue, and must understand how to weave courage and moderation together in just the proportion and in just the measure that best suits his people. In short, the genuine legislator must possess a knowledge of the range of enduring human possibilities and a knowledge as well of the end that those possibilities are intended to serve. He must understand the human soul and the human good; and the more unsettled and unsettling the situation in which he finds himself, the deeper, more comprehensive, and more articulated his understanding must be.[29]

Here, then, we see one reason why Aristotle might speak at times as if *phronēsis* could have a universal, quasi-theoretical character. Founders or lawgivers must be able to see political situations with different eyes than ordinary citizens; they must be able to see the political present as a situation ripe with possibilities, as an instance, a particular "realization," of human nature and the human good "in general." Founders must, in other words, "be able to *contemplate* the things good for themselves and the things good for human beings." But the situation of the legislator or founder points to another situation that might demand something resembling a theoretical *phronēsis*. Earlier in this chapter, when we first noted that Aristotle sometimes characterizes *phronēsis* in terms of its universality, we wondered how this could be so. Previously I had suggested that Aristotle takes up the investigation of *phronēsis* in Book VI because it was now important to explore the way of thinking of the equitable man, who first comes into view at the end of Book V. But equity shows itself precisely in the *correction* of the universality of the law: How, then, could *phronēsis* be marked by universality when its work lies, in part, in the setting right of what is universal?

We can see now just how misguided this way of putting the question was. The legislator, no less than the equitable man, possesses a particular knowledge of the particular situation of the community he founds at the moment when he founds it, but the reverse is true as well. If the equitable man is to speak and act, as Aristotle says he must, as the legislator would have had he been present, then he, no less than the legislator, must possess a comprehensive knowledge of human things. Put otherwise: if the equitable man is to correct the law as the legislator would have, he must be able to see the law as the legislator saw it, as a particular set of universal claims or directives intended to bring forth, to set into work, the best possible form of the human good available in the circumstances. In effect, every act of genuine equity is an act of re-founding, and it presupposes a mind and knowledge at least equal to that of the founder.

Let us remind ourselves why equity becomes an issue in the *Ethics* in the first place. The man of complete virtue simply cannot be honored by his political community as he deserves, and the more clearly he recognizes his own goodness—the more magnanimous he is—the more clearly he must see its failure to do him justice (1124a7–9). The man who possesses complete virtue thus stands outside the law, and if he is not to become an outlaw or, at any rate, if he is not to withdraw his allegiance from his city altogether, he must find some way to accommodate himself to this state of affairs. But this can happen only if he does not identify the "universe" of the law with the "universe" as such. Only if he can appeal beyond the law to an order of things that makes sense of his position in the world, only if he possesses an understanding of the good different from that of his city, in short, only if he can see the law as a set of conventions that of necessity leave him out of the picture, and see as well that *according to nature* he still has a place in his city, will there be any chance that he can reconcile himself to his lack of external recognition. In other words, equity (*epi-eikeia*), that "seemliness" of soul which disposes a man to receive less than his due with grace, appears to require, as one of its necessary conditions, a *phronēsis* grounded in an understanding of the nature of things, at least human things.

Perhaps this explains why Aristotle links equity to *syngnōmē*, *gnōmē*, and *orthē krisis* toward the end of Book VI (1143a19–24). *Syngnōmē* means, in the first instance, something like pardon or forgiveness—Aristotle uses it in Book III to signify what we show those who do wrong out of ignorance or of necessity—and this seems to be just what the equitable man must grant his fellow citizens, and perhaps the legislator as well (1109b30–35). *Gnōmē*, in turn, can mean understanding or the faculty of understanding; this is what the equitable man must possess if he is to grant *syngnōmē* to his fellow citizens. Finally, the understanding of the equitable man shows itself, above all, in his ability to separate (*krinein*) himself from the self-understanding of the city, to distinguish between the intention of the legislator and the laws he has made; this capacity for critical thinking, for right discernment, is captured perfectly in the phrase *orthē krisis*.

IN ANY CASE, it has become clear that *phronēsis*—like magnanimity and justice—is a word with at least two distinct, but related, meanings. Above and beyond the workman-like *phronēsis* of the ordinary citizen or decent man, there is architectonic *phronēsis*, the *phronēsis* of the legislator and the equitable man. This latter form of *phronēsis* makes sense of Aristotle's occasional blurring of the distinction between theoretical and practical reason, for unlike the ordinary man, who need only deliberate about particular means for particular ends and who sees the good, as it were, only through the noble ends disclosed by the ethical virtues, the man with architectonic *phronēsis* must possess something like universal or theoretical knowledge. The architect of the good must know the human things, know the full range of human possibilities, and be able to see all such things—including the ethical virtues—in light of the good.[30]

IV. *SOPHIA* AND *PHRONĒSIS*

Even this "higher" form of *phronēsis*, however, differs decisively from *sophia*. To say that it involves theoretical or universal knowledge is a far cry from saying that it is one with the virtue of the epistemic part of the soul. In the first place, the *activity* of every form of prudence differs from the activity of wisdom. The being at work of wisdom has its end in itself: the wise man thinks what he thinks for its own sake. This is not the case with prudence, even architectonic prudence. The *phronēsis* of the legislator may rest on or include *theōria*, and he may not himself "do" anything in the ordinary sense of the term, but insofar as he deliberates, he thinks for the sake of some further end. *Phronēsis* may be a word with multiple meanings, but its meanings are related to one another in just this respect: It is, as Aristotle says, "epi-tactical" rather than theoretical; its activity lies in ordering and giving orders, not seeing for its own sake (1143a8; 1145a10–11).

Moreover, the *objects* of *sophia* differ from the objects of *phronēsis*. In Book VI, Aristotle says next to nothing about the objects of *sophia*, but what little he says is enough to make us see that the human things and the human good are distinct from those "most honorable things" with which the wise man concerns himself. Indeed, Aristotle spends the greater part of the chapter on *sophia* making just this point. Insofar as *phronēsis* is concerned with the *human* good and *human* things, he argues, it lacks the comprehensiveness that marks *sophia*. And even if *sophia* were not so much knowledge of all things as knowledge of the highest things, *sophia* and *phronēsis* would still not have the same objects. Man may be the best of all living things, the human good may be of a higher order than, say, the good of fish, but man is not "the best thing of the things in the *kosmos*" (1141a21–22). Just look up, Aristotle says, and you will see "other things much more divine in their nature than man" (1141a34–b2).

The importance of this last claim cannot be underestimated. Were man the highest being in the *kosmos*, and hence the chief object of interest for "epistemic" as well as "calculative" reason, there would exist a kind of ultimate unity in the reasoning part of the soul. In spite of the differences in their activities and the differences in their foci, *phronēsis* and *sophia* would be "about" the same thing; their unity would be displayed, above all, in the workings of architectonic *phronēsis*. Like the master gardener, who somehow knows what the botanist knows—the unchanging natures and forms of plant life—and who knows as well what his experienced workmen know—the particular soil and climate and seeds with which they must work—the man with architectonic *phronēsis* would unite within himself the universal knowledge of the wise man and the particular knowledge of those who possess "ordinary" *phronēsis*.

The aim of the man with architectonic *phronēsis* would naturally differ from the aim of the wise man. The task of the former would be the cultivation and fostering of the highest available human possibilities, while the work of the wise man would lie in the contemplation of the range of human possibilities and the possible peaks of human life, but this difference would in no way compromise the unity of the reasoning part of the soul. Indeed, if man were the highest of all beings, it's easy to imagine that *phronēsis* and *sophia* could naturally arise and co-exist within the same man, to imagine, that is, that the same man could be at once the cause and the contemplator of the highest human possibilities. In at least some men, we could imagine, "ordinary" *phronēsis*, grounded in the experience of particulars, could gradually yield a universal knowledge of human things, which knowledge would result in the capacity to contemplate as well as order the human good.

But man is *not* "the best thing of the things in the *kosmos*." There are "other things much more divine in their nature than man," and this seems to mean that there is no "natural" harmony or unity within the reasoning part of the soul (1141a20–22; 1141a34–b2). The excellence of "epistemic" reason has its end in the contemplation of things far higher than man, the excellence of "calculative" reason has its end in the cultivation of the human good, and there seems to be no reason to suppose that the twain would ever meet, that the same man would be or should be both wise and prudent. Certainly there is no reason to think that the union of wisdom and prudence within one soul could be "fruitful." In fact, in the closing line of Book VI, Aristotle acknowledges the absolute separation of *phronēsis* and *sophia*. He responds to the question "Does *phronēsis* govern and give orders to *sophia*?" by saying this would be like saying "politics rules the gods because it gives orders concerning all things in the city" (1145a10–11). *Phronēsis* and *sophia* belong to separate realms: *phronēsis* to the realm of politics and *praxis*, *sophia* to the realm of *theōria* and the divine, which not only lies outside, but also above, the realm of the human-all-too-human good.

Need we draw this conclusion? Does this separation necessarily follow from the fact that *phronēsis* and *sophia* are distinct virtues with distinct objects? Or in spite of the differences between them, might there be grounds for saying that *phronēsis* and *sophia* belong together within the soul? Could it be the case, for instance, that human happiness—which is the larger issue that leads Aristotle to examine *phronēsis* and *sophia* in the first place—*requires* the presence within the soul of both virtues?

Let us consider what can be said in favor of this possibility. In the first place, it seems clear that the activity of *sophia* must constitute at least some part of the human good. In the final chapter of Book VI, Aristotle calls it a "part . . . of whole virtue," and for good reason: If the goodness of dispositions depends on the goodness of their objects, then *sophia*, with its divine and most honorable objects, must be the best possible disposition in man, and its activity must be the best activity of the distinctively human part of man (1144a5). Thus happiness in the full sense of the term, activity in accordance with *complete* virtue, certainly presupposes *sophia*. Does it also depend on the presence of *phronēsis*? Do *phronēsis* and *sophia* perhaps together constitute whole or complete virtue? "In itself" *sophia* seems able to exist apart from a knowledge of human things and the human good. But can the wise *man*? It seems not: the wise man must presumably live and act among other men. At the very least, then, he must know how to live and act so that others will "let him be." Moreover, his way of life surely depends on *his* having a clear sense of the relative importance of the virtues: If he does not see that being wise is ultimately a better and more choiceworthy activity than, say, being courageous, he will be liable to expend his "energies" in the wrong way and for the wrong objects. Doesn't this suggest that the wise man must possess something like practical reason, that is, a capacity to see the human good clearly and an ability to reason well and in detail about what to "do" in light of that vision? In fact, doesn't it suggest that the wise man must possess precisely that type of *phronēsis* that Aristotle calls "architectonic," that is, a *phronēsis* that transcends the ethical virtues, which disclose the good now as being courageous, now as being generous, but never as being wise?[31]

I do not mean to suggest that all wise men must be legislators or all legislators wise men. Presumably—given his understanding of the good—the wise man could be a legislator if circumstances so dictated. One can even imagine the wise man engaging regularly in a sort of "legislation": in addition to using his prudence to secure his own good, he might find ways of securing the possibility that others might know and practice the highest human good, perhaps by educating potential legislators to see the ultimate superiority of *sophia* to the other virtues. All in all, however, the wise and prudent man seems to bear a closer resemblance to the other type of man who must possess architectonic *phronēsis*—the equitable man. Indeed, the more closely we examine our account of the equitable man, the clearer it becomes that ultimately "equitable" and "wise" (and "prudent," "magnanimous," and "just" as well) are different modifiers that express different "modes" of the same man.³² The virtue of the equitable man simply cannot be seen or recognized adequately by his fellow citizens and the law. Of whom can this be said with greater truth than the wise man? What virtue is more likely than wisdom to escape the notice and recognition of action-oriented men? As a consequence, the equitable man stands outside the law and must therefore possess a trans-legal understanding of the good. Again, of whom can this be said more than the wise man? Finally, if the equitable man is to take part willingly in the life of his city, if he is to exercise "complete virtue" in the form of justice, he must be able to see the law as a set of conventions that of necessity leave him out of the picture, and also see that according to nature he still has a place in the city. Once again, what man would be more likely to have to face and overcome this "para-dox" than the wise man?

I mean to suggest that Aristotle's various attempts to "think" complete virtue are of a piece. In different ways and from different angles, he gradually uncovers the conditions and the problematic character of the conditions for human happiness. What Aristotle says about *sophia* makes it clear that it forms the core, or rather core condition, of the human good: happiness lies above all in the being at work of wisdom, in the *noēsis*, the immediate apprehension, of the most divine objects. His accounts of magnanimity and justice, in turn, point to the tension the wise man must face between his own good and the good of the city. The more aware the good man is of his own goodness—the more magnanimous he is—the more clearly he will see the gap between his own virtue and the virtues his city recognizes, and the less likely he will be to make its affairs his concern. The more eagerly he strives to practice the virtues as they are understood by the city—the more he exercises whole justice toward and for (*pros*) others—the more unjust he must be toward himself, that is, the more likely he is to violate, or at least compromise, the best things in himself. Finally, Aristotle's hints about equity and his discussion of *phronēsis* suggest a solution to the problem faced by the good man or, at any rate, suggest the necessary condition for a solution. Only if the wise man can look beyond the self-understanding of his city to an understanding of the human good that makes sense of his predicament, only if he possesses a knowledge of his own good and the city's good that shows him the connection between them, and only if he can reason well about that connection and thus correct the city's understanding of the good by way of his own, will there be any chance for him to find a true place for himself within his city—or any city.

WHY SHOULD THE MAN with complete virtue practice equity? *Is* there an understanding of the good that connects the political good and the good of the man who possesses complete virtue? These are questions we had to raise at the close of our inquiry into the ethical virtues, and, if anything, our examination of the intellectual virtues has brought them into sharper focus. As long as our inquiry remained bounded by the understanding of the cultivated and active, it seemed plausible to suppose that happiness would turn out to involve the practice of the ethical virtues; sooner or later a position would emerge wherein the everyday and the true understanding of happiness would be reconciled. But once Aristotle raises the specter of wisdom in Book VI, the gap between the everyday and the true understanding of happiness widens, and we must ask ourselves whether that gap has not become a chasm that simply cannot be bridged.

Put otherwise: Even in the course of our inquiry into the intellectual virtues, we have supposed for the most part that Aristotle's account of the virtues is additive—that in addition to the "ordinary" ethical virtues, the simply good man must possess magnanimity, whole justice, equity, prudence, and wisdom. Perhaps we may be excused for temporarily making this assumption. At no point in the first six books of the *Ethics* does Aristotle wonder out loud whether happiness might ultimately be an "impractical" activity. Even in the final chapters of Book VI, where he considers the relation between prudence, wisdom, and the ethical virtues, Aristotle exercises remarkable restraint: he calls wisdom a "part of whole virtue" and leaves unanswered, indeed unarticulated, the question of whether whole or complete virtue might be a whole in which the ethical virtues have no part. Yet it would be inexcusable—given the results of Aristotle's investigation of the distinctively human part of the soul in Book VI—not to face this question squarely at some point in our inquiry. This we must now do, as we attempt to understand the full implications of Aristotle's "new beginning" in Books VII through X.

4

||||||||||||||||||||||||||||||||||||||||||||

FRIENDSHIP
AND HAPPINESS

THE BEGINNING OF ARISTOTLE'S new beginning is anything but loud. Given the results of his inquiry in Book VI—
the discovery that the everyday understanding of virtue is far
from complete, that above and beyond the ethical virtues there
lies a virtue, *sophia*, that is a strong contender for the title of "best
and most complete" virtue—we might expect him to make the
relation among those virtues the leading theme of Book VII. At
the very least, we expect him to include wisdom and its claims as
an integral part of that discussion.[1]

This Aristotle does not do. To be sure, he makes it clear in
the opening lines of Book VII that the sphere of virtues and
vices—or rather the sphere of conditions of soul to be pursued
and avoided—is larger than the sphere of *ethical* virtues and vices,
that is, he quietly acknowledges the limitations of the scope of
his inquiries in Books II through V (1145a15–17). Moreover, he
alludes in the lines that follow to his discovery in Book VI of wisdom, the knowledge of the "divine" and "most honorable" things:
he mentions the existence of a "divine" virtue, indeed, a condition
of soul "more honorable than virtue" (1145a17–27). Yet Aristotle
effectively conceals the import of this discovery by assimilating it to the "heroic" view of virtue: He likens the possessor of
divine virtue to Hector, who dies a noble death in defense of his

city (1145a15–22). He leaves us with the impression that the virtue "over us" is simply a type of supra-courage, an extension or magnification of the everyday understanding of courage.[2]

Aristotle displays a similar reticence (and restraint) in the account of self-restraint and unrestraint that forms the body of Book VII.[3] Once again, the discerning reader of the *Ethics* might see in Aristotle's discussion of self-restraint a hint that the ethical virtues are not all they appear to be. Any claim they might have against wisdom to be the properly human virtues would surely rest in part on the further claim that most men *could* acquire them with proper habituation, but Aristotle observes in Book VII that most human beings drift between restraint and unrestraint— and lean in the direction of unrestraint (1150a9–16; 1152a25–27).[4] Most of us spend most of our lives plagued by desire and pinched by regret. Even moderation, which we suggested earlier is a sort of prerequisite for the other ethical virtues and which Aristotle says is a prerequisite for prudence, is unavailable in its full form to most human beings (1140b11–20).

The discerning reader might also see in Aristotle's discussion of the self-restrained man an image of the man who takes his bearings by another standard than that of the ethical virtues. As the very word "self-restraint" (*en-krateia*) suggests, the self-restrained man is the one within (*en*) whom thought holds sway (*kratein*), not in partnership with the ethical virtues, but by itself (1150a33–1150b1; 1151b23–1152a2). Aristotle suggests that within the soul of the self-restrained man there is something approaching the legislative function or architectonic reason, a power of reason unmediated by the law-ordained ethical virtues (1152a19–24).[5] Still, these hints about the possible inadequacy of the ethical virtues and possible adequacy of reason remain only hints. As in the case of his allusion to a divine virtue, Aristotle's discussion of self-restraint and unrestraint leaves the general impression that he has added nothing fundamentally new to his account of practical matters. He has merely supplemented his examination of moderation and immoderation in Book III by describing the somewhat shadowy middle ground between them.

Yet at least at one point in the course of his inquiries in Books
VII through X, Aristotle seems to drop his guard. As we saw at
the very outset of this inquiry, in chapters six through eight of
Book X, Aristotle not only lays to rest once and for all the claim
that happiness lies in bodily pleasure, that is, in a life of play and
amusement; he also takes up what has surely become, by the end
of Book VI, the ruling form of the ruling question of the *Ethics*:
What part do *theōria* and *praxis* play in the happy life? It is now
time to examine in more detail Aristotle's answer.

I. HAPPINESS

In at least one respect, Aristotle's answer is clear. He says, in effect:
"Take any measure for happiness you wish—indeed, take each of
the possible criteria for happiness that came to sight in the course
of my inquiries in Book I—and you will find, in each case, that
theōria meets the criterion to a greater degree than *praxis*."[6] That
is, *theōria* is at once the "most continuous" or enduring, "most
pleasant," "most self-sufficient," and most intrinsically choiceworthy of activities (1177a21–1177b4). What is more, and what is perhaps most important, given Aristotle's derivation of his definition
of happiness in Book I, wisdom rather than any of the action-
oriented virtues is the best disposition of the distinctively human
part of the soul. For the ethical virtues and even prudence belong
to man insofar as he is a composite being, a "synthesis" of body
and soul, and Aristotle goes out of his way to stress how bound up
they are with the body (1178a9–22). But *theōria* is, as Aristotle says
in Book X and as we have already gathered from his discussion of
wisdom in Book VI, the best activity of the best thing in man and
is best because, by virtue of being wise, men are able to contemplate the best of all possible objects of knowledge (1177a12–21).
   This is not to say that actions play no part in the good life. The
wise man, the man with *sophia*, may be god-like, and it may be
ludicrous to suggest that the gods perform acts of courage or moderation or justice, but in truth the wise man is no more a god than
he is a beast (1178b7–22).[7] Like other men, he must dwell in some

political community: He may be most at home with the objects of wisdom, but he must make his home day by day with other men. The wise man must act in relation to others (*pros heterous*), and Aristotle is quite clear about how he will act: ". . . insofar as he is a human being and lives together with many he chooses to do (*prattein*) the things in accordance with virtue" (1178b5–6).

Chapters seven and eight of Book X thus provide us with a reasonably clear picture of the relation between *theōria* and *praxis*. Contemplation and action are equally parts of the good life, but the parts they play are by no means equal: activity in accordance with wisdom has a far greater weight or dignity than does activity in accordance with the ethical virtues and prudence. Yet even this way of formulating their relation may give too much weight or dignity to practical activity. Aristotle does say at one point in chapter eight that a life lived in accordance with the practical virtues is happy "in a secondary way" (*deuterōs*) (1178a7–10). This might lead us to think that noble actions, like contemplation, are activities worthy of being chosen for their own sake but are simply less worthy ends than contemplation. Yet Aristotle emphasizes in chapter seven that *all* actions, *all praxeis*, are chosen for the sake of some further end: even "political and military" actions, which "stand out" before other virtuous actions "in beauty and greatness," are "unleisurely and aim at some [further] end and are not chosen for themselves" (1177b16–18). Only *theōria*, it seems, meets in full the requirements of Aristotle's definition of happiness.

Why, then, does the wise man choose to perform such actions, or choose "to do (*prattein*) the things in accordance with virtue" at all? For surely, given the results of our earlier inquiries, it is not enough to say that he chooses to do them simply because they are the actions most often praised or honored by others. If virtuous actions are not worthy of being chosen for their own sake, if happiness in the strict sense lies simply and exclusively in the activity of contemplation, then the wise man would presumably choose such actions because they somehow make possible his engagement in *theōria*. His choice would be grounded in some deliberation about the best means of achieving what is good—in this case a deliberation that treated ethical actions, not as ends in themselves, but as means to the end of contemplation.[8] On what grounds might the man who knows what it is to contemplate think it good to do those things that others—at least "the cultivated and active"—regard as worth doing for their own sake?

Aristotle hints at several possible answers in the course of Book X. "[Human] nature," he observes at one point in chapter eight, "is not self-sufficient with respect to contemplation." "For someone who is human there will also be need of external prosperity," that is, "nourishment" and other "service" as well as a healthy body (1178b33–35). But such prosperity is found, or found in sufficient abundance, only in the company of other men. Thus "insofar as he is a man," insofar as he is a composite being, the wise man will need to "live together with many," that is, will need to dwell in some sort of political community. But not every such community would be likely to afford the wise man equal opportunities for the employment of his particular gift. A city of cowards, constantly besieged by stronger neighbors, would not. Nor would a city rent by faction and filled with lawless men. If he is to have the leisure that Aristotle tells us is a condition for contemplation, the wise man needs a reasonably prosperous and reasonably well-ordered city (1177b4–6). To say this, however, is to say that he needs a city in which most men, whether freely or from compulsion, do those very things that it would be ridiculous to ascribe to the gods: make and keep contracts, confront dangers and run risks, give money to those in need, etc. (1178b7–22). Would it not make sense, then, for the wise man to do such things as well—since to do them would be to promote the very conditions that make possible the activity he seeks to enjoy?

This argument has to do with the external conditions for contemplation. There may also be an internal reason—a reason bound up with the very activity of contemplation—for the wise man to exercise at least one of the ethical virtues. In the course of his discussion of pleasure in Book X, Aristotle observes that activities and their accompanying pleasures are intimately bound up with one another, so much so that it is often difficult to distinguish them (1175a10–21; 1175b30–35). Thus a given activity is "intensified" by the presence of its proper pleasure and "hindered" or "destroyed" by the presence of an alien pleasure: the man who enjoys geometry will do well at it, and the man who enjoys music more than argument will be seduced by the first passing melody (1175a30–1175b13). Clearly one consequence of this phenomenon is that our ability to take part in higher-order activities—and it is striking how often Aristotle mentions thinking and contemplation in his second discussion of pleasure—will be limited by any undue attachment to lower pleasures (1173b16–19; 1174b20–23; 1174b33–1175a2; 1175a10–16; 1175a21–1175b1; 1175b34–1176a2).[9] There is, of course, a place in human life for the measured enjoyment of such pleasures. Aristotle says as much in his treatment of moderation back in Book III and, if anything, his attitude toward bodily pleasure in the second half of the *Ethics* is more tempered than it is in the first (1119a16–20).[10] In Book VII he emphasizes the *naturalness* of basic bodily pleasures, and while remaining critical of a life dedicated to amusement, he admits in Book X that "amusement is like rest, and, being unable to toil continuously, men have need of rest" (1176b34–35).[11] Bodily pleasures and amusements are, then, a natural and necessary feature of every human life. Nevertheless—to apply Aristotle's observation about pleasure and activity to the case at hand—the exercise of wisdom and the immoderate pursuit of bodily pleasures are clearly incompatible; the man who habitually desires his dinner (and dinner parties) more than the exercise of wisdom cannot be wise.

Still, it does not follow—and Aristotle does not imply—that the wise man, the man capable of contemplation, must possess moderation in the strict sense of the term, according to which a man delights in the measured pursuit of bodily pleasure for its own sake. Indeed, his observation implies that the wise man will have no need for a *separate* virtue of moderation; the very delight he takes in the activity of wisdom will serve to hinder or limit his desire for bodily pleasures (1175b6–11). I am suggesting, however, that the lowly virtue of moderation may be the only ethical virtue that has an analogue tightly bound up with the wisdom of the wise man. That is, there seems to be no reason in principle why the wise man *qua* wise should be "disposed" to risk his life in battle or be generous with his wealth or even keep his hand out of the city's till.[12] He will do all these things, but for prudential reasons, that is, because a well-ordered city is essential or at least conducive to his own well-being. But if a man's soul is not disposed to prefer intellectual activity to bodily pleasure, wisdom will be beyond his reach.

Aristotle's peculiar way of treating self-restraint and unrestraint in Book VII may be connected to this point. He could have chosen—and in the interest of completeness, one might think, *should* have chosen—to make the territory covered by self-restraint and unrestraint co-extensive with that of the ethical virtues and vices. At any rate, one can easily imagine equivalents for self-restraint and unrestraint in the case of each of the ethical virtues and vices, for example, the man who is not a habitual coward but finds himself fleeing in the face of impending danger or the man who behaves generously in spite of a tendency toward stinginess. Yet Aristotle does not proceed in this way. Instead he limits his discussion of self-restraint and unrestraint to the much narrower territory marked out earlier in his discussion of moderation and immoderation.[13]

What we have just seen may help to explain why he does this. If giving a full account of the possible conditions for right and wrong action is no longer Aristotle's primary concern after Book VI, and if giving an account of the conditions for contemplation *is* one of his primary concerns, then his decision to focus his inquiry as he does makes sense, for if our current line of reasoning is correct, the wise man *qua* wise need not be courageous or generous or just. But the possibility of contemplation (at least for human beings) stands or falls by the possibility that desire can somehow be brought into line with reason. Seen in this light, Aristotle's discussion of self-restraint would be a first attempt to solve the problem posed by "the pleasure principle"—the self-restrained man has strong desires but controls them by means of reason—while his discussion of pleasure in Book X would hint at its final solution (1151b32–38). Here reason or thought would act, not as an efficient cause, mastering the desires, as it were, in spite of themselves, but as the final cause or end of human desire. The wise man loves or delights in the activity of wisdom for its own sake, and precisely because he does, he is "naturally" disposed to love bodily pleasures in due proportion.

ARISTOTLE'S ACCOUNTS OF SELF-RESTRAINT, pleasure, and the relation between contemplation and action all point us in the same direction—toward the view that there *is* an unbridgeable chasm between the true understanding and the everyday understanding of happiness. Those who seek a life of bodily pleasure and amusement are not the only ones mistaken about the meaning of happiness; the very best among the unwise—those who do what is courageous or generous or just, because they regard such actions as intrinsically choiceworthy—are, too. To those who might claim that bodily pleasures are the highest good, Aristotle says, in effect, that the pleasures of *theōria* far surpass their bodily counterparts in "purity" and "steadfastness" (1177a22–27). To those who might claim that right actions are worthy of being chosen for their own sake and who might argue that, in any case, rigorous training or habituation is needed to combat the temptations posed by bodily pleasures, Aristotle says, albeit more discreetly, that from the point of view of *theōria* noble actions are not much more choiceworthy than bodily pleasures. Indeed, he suggests, the truly happy man will choose to dwell among others, not because the city provides him with a place and opportunity to perform noble actions, but because it supplies him with the very things that tempt most men to behave immoderately. From the point of view of the truly happy man, the city exists not for the sake of the good life, that is, the life of actions in accordance with virtue, but for the sake of mere life.[14] What he seeks from the city, the only good that connects his life to that of the city, is the bodily good; not honor, but goods such as food and shelter form the true basis of his relation to it.

Does this view of the wise man and his relation to political life square with what we see in the final chapter of the *Ethics*? Having brought his inquiry into the nature of happiness to completion in the course of chapters six through eight—the last line of chapter eight is ". . . and so in this way, too, the wise man would be happy above all"—Aristotle turns to the consideration of its genesis in chapter nine (1179a31–32). Within this context he asks how the young might best be led to virtue. Given what Aristotle has just said in the two preceding chapters, we naturally expect him to make suggestions about how the young might be induced to care for wisdom: if happiness lies in *theōria*, then surely wisdom must be the goal of education. But he does not. Neither wisdom nor *theōria* are mentioned in chapter nine. Instead the question is how best to lead the young to love what is noble and hate what is base (1179b23–31). Education in virtue is a matter of habituating the young, or those who are of good birth among the young, in the ethical virtues, that is, those very virtues that seem, in chapters seven and eight, to have little to do with genuine happiness (1179b31–1180a1; 1180a14–18). In short, *theōria* makes a brief appearance in the final book of the *Ethics* only to be bundled off stage in its closing moments.[15]

After a long journey we have returned to another of the questions that first set our inquiry into motion: How are we to reconcile Aristotle's claims about the superiority of *theōria* to *praxis* in chapters seven and eight with his apparent abandonment of this position in chapter nine? It may make sense for Aristotle to assume in the early books of the *Ethics* that happiness lies in action—this, we recall, was one aspect of our initial question. If Aristotle is to bring his intended audience, that is, the cultivated and active, to see that his understanding of happiness is the true one, he must make their understanding the starting point of his inquiry. But to return to this assumption in the final chapter of his inquiry seems to make no sense at all. Once he has demonstrated that contemplation forms the true content of happiness, it can do nothing but confuse the issue to bring the ethical virtues back into the picture.

How are we to "save the appearances" in Book X? Why does Aristotle take back in chapter nine what he has given us in chapters seven and eight, that is, a reasonably coherent account of the relation between *theōria* and *praxis*? Two alternatives come to mind. In the first place, it might be the case that Aristotle *means* to confuse the issue in chapter nine. That is, we might suppose that what he says in chapters seven and eight *is* at odds with what he implies in chapter nine, but that he must speak out of both sides of his mouth in order to preserve and promote the conditions for true happiness. For true happiness, that is, contemplation—which in any case is available only to a very few—depends upon leisure, good order, and in general, a community in which most men, whether freely or from compulsion, do what is right. Thus, although right actions do not themselves constitute true happiness, to encourage men to cultivate and practice the ethical virtues would be to secure the possibility of genuine happiness for some.[16] Seen in this light, Aristotle's sudden shift away from *theōria* in chapter nine would be a sort of "gracious ruse," a relatively harmless deception for the sake of the good: those who can understand what he says about the superiority of contemplation will not be fooled by it, and those who cannot, but are persuaded by chapter nine, will at least be of service to the wise.[17]

The second alternative proceeds differently. Perhaps Aristotle does *not* contradict himself in the closing chapters of the *Ethics*, and any appearance of contradiction results from too literal a reading of Aristotle's account of the relation between contemplation and action. In other words, perhaps Aristotle is exaggerating for the sake of clarity in chapters seven and eight; perhaps he is simply telling us that wisdom *would* be the only true virtue and that the ethical virtues *would* pale in comparison with it *if* human beings could be wise. But in truth—so this argument runs—contemplation and wisdom are the peculiar province of the gods: what human beings or at least some human beings *can* do is love and pursue wisdom, on the one hand, and acquire and practice the ethical virtues, on the other. Seen in this light, chapter nine would serve, and would be intended to serve, as a corrective to possible misreadings of the chapters that precede it; chapter nine brings Aristotle's inquiry into the good to a fitting conclusion by reminding us that *human* happiness requires the possession of the ethical as well as intellectual virtues.

Both of these alternatives have an air of plausibility about them. Aristotle does argue in chapter seven that even the greatest virtuous actions exist for the sake of some further end, and given what he says there about contemplation, it seems reasonable to suppose that he thinks contemplation is that end. It is not too much of a stretch to suggest that the city and the ethical virtues ultimately exist for the sake of contemplation. Similarly, it is not difficult to find evidence, in chapters seven and eight and elsewhere, to support the contention that wisdom in the fullest sense is beyond the reach of mortals. For instance, after arguing that the only activity befitting the gods is contemplation, Aristotle says that "of human activities the one most *akin* to this is happiest" and that "happiness extends *just so far* as contemplation does, and being happy belongs *more* to those who contemplate *more*" (1178b24; 28–31). In the *Metaphysics*, too, Aristotle seems to conclude in the end that there is no science of wisdom in the strict sense of the term: our knowledge of the divine is more a matter of momentary insight than steady vision (*Meta.* 1072b25–28). Perhaps, then, wisdom and contemplation for human beings are a matter of more and less: one can speak of wiser, but not wise men, *philosophoi*, but not *sophoi*.

Still, it is unclear what conclusion we are to draw from this last point. More generally, it is unclear whether either of the alternatives we have just spelled out account for the discrepancy between what Aristotle says in chapters seven and eight and what he says in chapter nine. Suppose Aristotle means to say that men can at best be lovers of wisdom. Does it follow that he also means to say that happy men must possess the ethical virtues and exercise them for their own sake? It seems not. On the contrary, the passages just cited in support of the view that men cannot be wholly wise suggest that happiness is directly proportional to the degree of contemplation; Aristotle says nothing in them about the ethical life. Again, does it follow that because men cannot be wise they need to have the *ethical* virtue of moderation? In arguing for the pleasantness of activity in accordance with wisdom, Aristotle speaks of the "purity" and "steadfastness" of the pleasures of *philosophy* (1177a25–27). Does he not thereby suggest that the longing for wisdom will itself suffice to limit the desire for bodily pleasures? In short, we must apparently draw the same conclusions, whether we regard wisdom as an achievable end or as an object of immortal longing for mortal beings. The ethical life and ethical virtues pale in comparison to the life and virtue of the best man, whether he be *sophos* or *philosophos*.

Does it follow from this that our first alternative—that Aristotle promotes the ethical virtues because others must practice them if the truly happy man is to fare well—provides an adequate explanation for Aristotle's turn in chapter nine from contemplation to action? It might if Aristotle did nothing more in chapter nine than suddenly speak as if happiness lay in the exercise of the ethical virtues, but he does do more. He asks his readers to take it *upon themselves* to see that others acquire the ethical virtues. Indeed, he suggests that the task of educating others in the love of what is noble and the hatred of what is base is bound up with the highest human activity.

In the opening lines of chapter nine, Aristotle brings the issue to the fore. He begins by saying that we must now put into "practice" what we have learned about the human good: "or, just as is said, the end in practical matters is not to contemplate (*theōrēsai*) each thing and to know it, but rather to do (*prattein*) them" (1179a35–1179b1). Now, by stretching the meaning of *prattein* a bit, we *might* take this sentence to mean that, in accordance with Aristotle's recommendation in chapter seven, we must begin striving "to make ourselves immortal" and "to do all things according to the best of the things in us;" that is, we *might* take it to mean that we must leave off "minding" (*phronein*) human and mortal things and begin striving, as best we can, to acquire the virtue of wisdom (1177b31–34). Taken in context, however, the sentence surely means something different. Aristotle quickly identifies the attempt "to possess and employ" virtue with the task of nurturing the ethical virtues in others, and it becomes clear, as the chapter unfolds, that this task is virtually identical to the task of legislation (1179b1–4; 1179b32–34; 1180a15–24; 1180b24–28). The conclusion seems inescapable: happiness, being at work in accordance with virtue, is connected to the work of educating others in the ethical virtues; being "wise" and being a lawgiver, *theōria* and a certain form of *praxis*, are both features of the best life.[18]

OUR QUESTIONS ABOUT THE LINK between the parts of Book X therefore stand. We must admit, on the one hand, that the man who delights in wisdom has, as such, no need of the ethical virtues and that the life of pursuing or exercising wisdom is far superior to the ethical life. And we must admit, on the other, that the man who loves wisdom, who knows what it is to contemplate, will at the same time take an active interest in the well being of his city, that is, will actively nurture and promote activities and virtues that have no apparent connection to his own activities and virtues. How are we to resolve—how does Aristotle resolve—this paradox? If our labors thus far are any indication, it is unlikely that Book X can itself provide answers to the questions it raises. It makes sense, then, to look elsewhere for answers; the most promising place is Books VIII and IX, if only because they immediately precede Book X. Is Aristotle's account of friendship intended to prepare us to see as one what our reasonings thus far have kept asunder? Can it be said that the simply good man, who possesses complete virtue, concerns himself with the well-being of his community out of a kind of friendship with it? Does *friendship* provide the as yet missing link between *theōria* and *praxis*, between care for wisdom and care for the city, between the true and the everyday understanding of happiness?[19]

II. FRIENDSHIP

A. The Problem of Honor Revisited

Some evidence appears to point in this direction. For instance, in the opening lines of Book VIII, Aristotle links friendship to virtue, saying that it is "either a virtue or [goes] with virtue" (1155a3–5). Somewhat later in the first chapter, he tells us that "friendship seems to hold cities together" (1155a22–24). Moreover, he suggests that friendship transcends justice: "those who are friends have no need of justice, while those who are just have an additional need of friendship" (1155a26–27). Because Aristotle's accounts of magnanimity and justice first led us to wonder why the simply good man should take an active interest in the well-being of his community—the city cannot honor him adequately and hence cannot give him his just due—it is tempting to suppose that Aristotle is here indicating that friendship supplies what justice cannot, and that his account of friendship is intended to supplement or even supersede his account of justice.[20] That is, it is tempting to conclude that friendship is the unifying principle, the virtue or concommitant to virtue, that holds the city and its very best men together in spite of their apparent "incommensurability." Yet for a variety of reasons, we must beware of embracing this conclusion too readily.

In the first place, Aristotle's very definition of friendship seems to preclude, in advance, the possibility that one might speak of friendship between the very best men and ordinary men. At the outset of chapter two, he observes that there are three "objects of love" (*philēta*)—the good, the pleasant, and the useful—and this leads him to conclude, in chapter three, that there are three kinds or forms of friendship (*philia*), each based on a different form of "affection" (*philēsis*) (1155b18–19; 1156a6–8). But friendship (*philia*), Aristotle argues, depends on more than affection.[21] We may love or like a certain kind of wine, but only a man very deep in his cups would speak of friendship with his favorite bottle (1155b27–31). Friendship requires, above and beyond mere affection, affection in return (*anti-philēsis*), mutual good will (*eu-noia*), and mutual recognition (1155b28–1156a5). On all three counts, and perhaps especially the last, the relation between the best man and others seems to fail to meet the test of friendship. It is difficult enough to imagine most men genuinely caring for the best man and wishing him well—as Aristotle later observes, men do not wish to see others become gods (1159a5–12). But recognition by such men of the best man, in fact any but the most superficial understanding of who he is and what he lives for, seems impossible in principle. The virtue of the best man in fact must of necessity escape notice or remain concealed (*lanthanein*) (1155b34–1156a5). This is simply another way of saying that there can be no honor adequate to complete virtue. Hence, it seems, there can be no friendship between the simply good man and ordinary men.

Aristotle's discussion of friendship between unequals in chapter seven of Book VIII adds more force to this point. As in the case of distributive justice, friendship between unequals depends on "equalization" or proportionate equality. That is, friendship between unequals obtains when the better man receives affection from the lesser in proportion to his superiority (1158b23–28). But friendship differs from distributive justice in what might be called the limiting conditions for equalization. Justice obtains whenever a distribution according to merit is made, a condition that we have already seen cannot be met in the case of the best man and his community. But the conditions for friendship are even more stringent, for "in friendship the equal according to quantity is primary, that according to merit is secondary" (1158b31–33). That is, even in cases where a distribution according to merit *can* be made, friendship may be impossible; if the distance (*diastema*) between one person and another is too great, they simply cannot be friends (1158b33–1159a3).[22] This, however, is precisely the situation in which the best man finds himself. If any man can be said to be beyond friendship with ordinary men, it is surely the wise man or philosopher. To put the same point in a different way, if justice cannot obtain between the best man and ordinary men because the distance between them is too great to be bridged by even the greatest of honors, then the same must be true—*a fortiori*—of friendship.

Further evidence for the view that Aristotle's account of friendship is not intended to explain the simply good man's relation to ordinary men can be found in those places in Books VIII and IX where Aristotle discusses the type of friendship that *does* befit the good man. Two passages clearly speak to this issue. In chapters three and four of Book VIII, Aristotle discusses complete or perfect friendship (*teleia philia*), that form of friendship in which the primary object of affection on both sides is not the usefulness or pleasantness, but the goodness or virtue of the other person. In chapter nine of Book IX, he raises, and answers in the affirmative, the question of whether the good or happy man needs friends. Aristotle's precise reasons for this answer need not concern us just now. What is important is that in both discussions friendship with unequals is not at issue. This is obvious in the case of Aristotle's account of complete friendship. At this point in the argument of Book VIII, he is still talking about friendship between equals: perfect friends are those who are "alike," that is, equal, in virtue (1156b7–9). But it is no less clear in the case of Aristotle's account of the good man's need for friends. The kind of men the happy man wishes to have as friends are those who mirror his own virtue; what he seeks is "another self," someone with whom he can "share in conversations and thought" (1170b6–7; 10–12) In other words, what the best man seeks in a friend is a fellow lover of wisdom, someone with whom he might share the philosophical life. "For living together would seem to mean this in the case of human beings, and not, as in the case of cattle, grazing together in the same place" (1170b12–14).[23]

To sum up: Only if there were a kind of friendship between unequals that did not depend on the three qualities of mutual affection, good will, and mutual recognition would friendship between the best man and ordinary men be possible, and only if this friendship could somehow provide the best man with the equivalent of "another self," a reflection of his own goodness, would it be choiceworthy. But the first of these conditions is inconsistent with Aristotle's own definition of friendship, while the second seems to be inconsistent with everything we have learned about the differences between *theōria* and *praxis*. Would it not be safer to assume that Aristotle means to say that genuine friendship, the kind that is "a virtue or with virtue," can only exist among friends of wisdom and that, as a consequence, friendship between the best man and other human beings—even the best among "the cultivated and active"—is out of the question?

B. Mothers and Benefactors

It might be. Yet even in the passage from chapter seven discussed above, where Aristotle pushes to the limit the argument for the impossibility of friendship between certain unequals, he hesitates to draw this conclusion. He does insist—here—that there can be no friendship between gods and men (1159a4–5). Moreover, he brings forward as evidence for his claim that distance makes all the difference in friendship the observation that ". . . those who are worthy (*axioi*) of nothing . . . do not think themselves worthy (*axiousin*) to be friends . . . with *the best and wisest men*" (1159a1–3). But he also says that a "precise determination in such matters, that is, up to what point men [can remain] friends, is not possible" (1159a3–4). Again, in the final chapter of Book VIII, Aristotle appears to reverse his position on the relation of friendship to justice. Rather than arguing that the conditions for justice are more easily met than the conditions for friendship, he says that in certain cases friendship can exist even in the absence of a just distribution of honors. That is, he claims that "friendship seeks or demands what is possible, not the thing according to merit (*to kat'axian*)" (1163b15–18).

What are we to make of these passages? It is hard to say. But I think it is possible to take them to mean that under certain conditions, for example, where those who are inferior are not altogether unworthy, something like friendship between such men and "the best and wisest men" *is* possible, even in the absence of adequately returned affection, good will, and recognition. This would mean, in turn, that Aristotle's definition of friendship in chapter two of Book VIII does not exhaust the meaning of friendship. We may find this somewhat difficult to accept. After all, Aristotle's definition—as well as his discussion of friendship between unequals—seems to articulate what all of us think about friends and friendship. Don't we insist that our friends wish us well and return our affection? And when one of us "brings more" to a friendship—more money, more power, more beauty—don't we expect (secretly) to be liked, or rather loved, the more for it? Breaking up may be hard to do, but when these conditions are not met, don't our friendships tend to do just that?

With dramatic aptness, a first answer to these questions comes to light in chapter eight of Book VIII just after Aristotle has made his argument for the importance of "proportion" and "quantity" in friendship. Everyone else may quarrel endlessly about unsettled debts and loyalties betrayed, and accordingly Aristotle records and does his best to adjudicate such squabbling in Books VIII and IX.[24] But there is at least one class of human beings that stands, or tends to stand, above the fray: mothers. Mothers lead Aristotle to conclude that friendship must lie in loving rather than being loved, for they love without demanding that they be loved in return (1159a27–28). Given the choice between being loved in return (*antiphileisthai*) and seeing those whom they love fare well (*eu prattontas*), mothers choose the latter (1159a28–31). What is more, mothers do this even when it means that their children "on account of ignorance distribute (*apo-nemōsi*) nothing [to them] of the things which befit a mother" (1159a32–33). In other words, the principle of distributive friendship or distributive justice breaks down in the case of mothers and thus breaks down in precisely the sort of case in which one would least expect that it could. That friendship or love could survive the separation of mother and child is strange enough; only a few chapters earlier Aristotle observed that (too much) absence makes the heart less fond (1157b11–13). But, as Aristotle notes later, children also owe their parents a debt that no quantity of honor or returned affection could ever repay; they owe their very being (*to einai*) to those who brought them into being (*hoi gennēsantes*) (1162a4–7; 1163b15–18).[25]

We don't yet know, however, what light the case of motherly love will shed on the question we are attempting to answer. One might admit—who could deny it?—that mothers as a rule behave as Aristotle says they do. One might also admit Aristotle's initial definition of friendship does not therefore cover every conceivable case of friendship. One might even admit that Aristotle's observations about motherly love *would*, if they could be extended to cover the case of the best man, provide us with just the sort of answer we have been looking for. For if friendship between the truly happy man and those who find their happiness in acting well (*eu prattein*) is to be possible, he must be willing, motherlike, to let himself and his virtue remain concealed from them. In order that his city might fare well, in order that its honors and customs might retain their meaning, he must keep a certain distance, be willing to forgo the honor and affection that is his due, and pardon his fellow citizens for their ignorance of his virtue.

Can the kind of friendship that mothers exhibit toward their children be extended to cover the case of the simply good man? After all, mothers have every reason to behave as they do. As Aristotle later argues, parents, and mothers in particular, love their children and tend to love them more than they are loved by them, because their children are their own; they are, quite literally, "other selves in separation" (1161b8–33). Can the same be said of any other relation between unequals? And if it can be, can it be said of the relation between the best man and those of lesser virtue? If the distance between them is great enough to warrant the best man's concealment of his virtue, how can it be small enough to permit him to see his fellow citizens as other selves, that is, as friends worthy of the care and effort that Aristotle suggests, in Book X, he should expend on them? Put otherwise, is motherly love more than an interesting exception to the rules that otherwise apply to friends—an exception surely worth thinking about, but in no way serviceable as a model or paradigm for the kind of relation we are attempting to understand?

We find the beginnings of an answer in Aristotle's discussion of beneficence in chapter seven of Book IX. Here Aristotle observes that there *are* cases of friendship between unequals that are not based on proportional or even mutual affection. Indeed, it is precisely this phenomenon that he attempts to account for in his discussion. Why, he asks, do benefactors care more for those whom they have benefited than those whom they have benefited care for them (1167b17–19)?

Most people explain the relation between benefactors and benefited by assimilating it to the relation between lenders and debtors—most think that just as lenders care for the safety of those to whom they have lent money because they hope to get a good return on their investments, so, too, benefactors "wish [those whom they have benefited] to be (*einai*), . . . intending to recover favors (*charitas*) for themselves" (1167b19–25). But this explanation, Aristotle argues, is simply not adequate to the phenomenon of beneficence. One can see why people tend to think this way. Most prefer to receive rather than bestow benefits; they therefore make benefactors over in their own image by making them out to be people who postpone, for a time, the return of the benefits they bestow (1167b25–28). But in fact, the case of lenders is "not even similar" to the case of benefactors. Lenders do not care for their debtors—there is no love lost on either side of the lender-debtor relation—while benefactors *do* care for those whom they benefit, and care for them "even if they should neither be useful nor might become useful at a later time" (1167b28–33). The case of benefactors forms a precise parallel to that of mothers; it is no accident that Aristotle concludes his discussion of beneficence by likening the two (1168a24–27). For benefactors, like mothers and unlike lenders, prefer seeing those they have benefited fare well to any benefit or honor or affection they might receive from them.[26]

Why is this? How does Aristotle answer the question he raises at the outset of his account of beneficence? "The cause," he says, is "more natural (*physikoteron*)," by which he means, in the first instance, that it can be traced back once again to the natural relation between mothers and their children. Just as artisans (*technitai*) and, above all, poets love the things they make "as if they were children (*tekna*)," so, too, benefactors love those whom they have benefited because they are their own; "for that which has suffered well is their own work" (1167b33–1168a5).[27] But nature is at work in the phenomenon of beneficence in another sense as well, or rather, "makers" of all kinds, mothers and poets as well as benefactors, exhibit the same fundamental principle of nature in their activities. "Being (*to einai*) is choiceworthy and loveable for all [men]." But "we are" only insofar as we are "at work (*energeia*)," and "the work (*to ergon*) is in some sense the maker at work (*en-ergeia*)" (1168a5–7). In other words, benefactors can dispense with honor and recognition, can care for those whom they help even in the absence of returned affection, because they *are*, in the most fundamental sense of the term, those whom they help. They *see themselves* alive and at work in their deeds or works (*erga*), and for precisely this reason find lovable the objects of their activity. "For that which is in potency (*dunamei*), *this* the work discloses in its being at work (*energeia*)" (1168a8–9).

AT LONG LAST we have hit upon the principle we have been searching for. Aristotle's account of beneficence not only tells us *that* there can be cases of friendship between unequals that do not depend on returned affection and recognition; it also explains *why* this should be the case. Motherly love is not an isolated exception to the rules that otherwise apply to friends; it is rather the clearest or most familiar instance of what we might call the cunning of nature. For nature itself has provided the connection between one's own good and the good of others: That connection is built into the very being of things. To be sure, most men miss the point. They help others only because they expect to receive in return (external) goods at least equal to those they have given. But as the word beneficence (*eu-ergesia*) suggests, the benefactor (*eu-ergetēs*) finds the good or happiness *in* the activity (*en-ergeia*) of beneficence itself. The benefactor's happiness, his being at work well (*eu en-ergein*), is manifested in his doing well by others (*eu-ergetein*), which doing well is in turn manifest in the faring well or acting well (*eu prattein*) of those others.

C. Beneficence and Complete Virtue

As yet we do not know who Aristotle's "benefactors" are. We have been trying to understand why the best man, the man who possesses complete virtue, should work at cultivating the ethical virtues in others. Aristotle's account of beneficence seems to provide an answer. It explains why certain men might be willing to benefit others even in the absence of returned affection and recognition. Does the simply good man fall into this category? Is Aristotle's discussion of beneficence meant to apply to the best man?

Certain features of Aristotle's account of beneficence suggest that it is. For instance, his rejection of the everyday explanation of beneficence makes it clear that most men are incapable of it: whatever else one can say about the benefactor, he is no ordinary man. Aristotle's initial discussion of motherly love points to the same conclusion. Here he observes that most men—and now "the many" must include "the cultivated and active"—prefer being loved to loving because being loved is like being honored (1159a12–24).[28] Only those who are beyond honor, only men who can dispense with the admiration of others because they know themselves to be good, are able to take a mother's-eye view of the situation in which they find themselves.

Moreover, if we consider what Aristotle says in the final chapter of Book X in light of his account of beneficence, we can see that the activity he describes and proposes there is the very model of beneficence. The benefactor takes delight in the well-being of others because he sees those others and their well-being as his own work. But apart from parents, who are responsible for the very existence of their children, no one is more responsible for the being and well-being of others than the man who shapes the character of his fellow citizens. The man who is "free" with his wealth may provide others with the necessary external conditions for their well-being, but the man who forms character makes others *who* they are, and in the measure that he makes them good he provides them with the core condition for their well-being. If any man can be said to "make" others happy, if any man deserves to be called the "architect of the good," it is surely the legislator of virtue.

We find the best evidence for the claim that "benefactor" is yet another name for the man who possesses complete virtue in the discussion of the good man's need for friends in chapter nine of Book IX. There Aristotle couches his argument in the same terms and, indeed, in the same language as his discussion of beneficence. He reasons roughly as follows. In the case of each of our activities, there is an accompanying perception (*aesthēsis*) or awareness (*noēsis*) of that activity, a perception that we *are* in this or that respect (1170a29–33). But this perception, especially in the case of the good man, is intrinsically pleasant, for being or being alive is in itself pleasant or good, and the more so, the better we are (1170a25–29; 1170b1–5). In other words, blessedness—that is, happiness in the fullest sense—involves not only being good but being aware of one's goodness. But friends are other selves. Hence the perception of *their* happiness, *their* being at work well, is as desirable, or nearly as desirable, as the perception of one's own well-being (1170b5–8). Indeed, since, as Aristotle suggests at another point in the argument, it is easier to see (*theōrein*) our neighbors than ourselves, a good friend may be not only desirable but necessary for the good man. A friend is "the greatest of external goods" because the full self-awareness or self-consciousness that brings happiness to completion is only possible in the presence of a friend (1169b30–1170a4).[29]

The connection between this argument and Aristotle's discussion of beneficence is clear. His account of the good man's need for friends depends, as did his account of beneficence, on an appeal to nature: "For those who look at [the matter] more naturally (*phusikoteron*) the serious friend seems to be choiceworthy by nature (*phusei*) to the serious man" (1170a13–14). And his argument turns, as did his account of beneficence, on the claim that happiness is to be found, at least in part, in the perception or awareness or contemplation of one's goodness at work in another. Although there are significant differences between what Aristotle says in chapter nine and what he says in chapter seven—he says nothing about need in chapter seven and his discussion in chapter nine has to do with friendship between equals—the continuity of language between the two chapters indicates that the issue in both is in a decisive respect the same: the simply good man's relation to others. Perhaps complete (*teleia*) friendship exists only between men who possess complete (*teleia*) virtue, for it is only in this friendship, in the sharing of words and thought that marks a life of common inquiry and insight, that human life reaches its end (*telos*) or completion (*entelecheia*). Still, a kind of friendship can exist between the man who possesses complete virtue and those who do not. From such men the best man may not receive honor and affection, but he has no need for honor, and in any case his beneficence provides him with the very good that lesser men seek in their pursuit of honor. He receives confirmation of his goodness, not through the recognition of others, but through his own recognition of his goodness at work in the *eupraxia*, the faring well, of those others.

Perhaps for this reason the word "beneficence" first appears in Aristotle's discussion of the great-souled man—in fact, appears only in that discussion and in his discussion of friendship. Perhaps for this reason, too, Aristotle says of the magnanimous man that he is "incapable of living for (*pros*) another except for a friend" (1124b31–1125a1). For it is Aristotle's account of magnanimity that first forces the reader of the *Ethics* to ask why the man who is self-sufficient with respect to honor, the man who possesses all virtue in completion (*pan-telēs aretē*), should take an active interest in the affairs of ordinary men, and it is Aristotle's account of friendship in the form of beneficence that provides a final answer to this question. It explains why the great-souled man, who otherwise prefers "to speak and act openly," should be willing to speak and act "ironically toward most men (*pros tous pollous*)," that is, in such a way that he conceals the greatness of his virtue (1124b26–31). Put in terms of Book V, Aristotle's discussion of beneficence explains why the simply good man should be willing to practice equity in relation to others (*pros heterous*), that is, should be willing to take a legislator's-eye view of the community in which he finds himself and so demand less honor from it than he deserves.

IT DOES SO IN PRINCIPLE, at any rate. Aristotle's account of beneficence fails to address a question of critical importance. Beneficence can serve as a paradigm for the best man's relation to those of lesser virtue if he can see *himself* at work in them, that is, only if those whom he benefits in some sense mirror his own virtue. We have been assuming for the last several pages that this is possible, that friendship between the simply good man and men of lesser virtue differs in degree rather than in kind from the friendship of the good. But in the case of complete friendship it is clear that a shared delight in *theōria* forms the basis for friendship. As good men think and converse together, they *see* in one another what they *are* in themselves. They think thinking, understand understanding; as such, they seem to participate in, or at least reflect, what Aristotle claims in the *Metaphysics* is the highest or the divine activity, *noēsis noēseōs* (*Meta.* 1074b15–35). There is at least one case in which something resembling this kind of completeness can be found in a relation between the good man and his inferiors. One can easily imagine the philosopher taking delight in seeing and causing the burgeoning of *philosophia* in another, for in this case he sees and brings forth an image of himself: a young man taking his first stumbling steps along the path to wisdom "is" a philosopher in the same sense as a puppy or child "is" its mother.[30] But that is not, it seems, the case we are attempting to understand. In the final chapter of Book X, Aristotle is saying or seems to be saying that the lover of wisdom should see to it that the young acquire the *ethical*, not the intellectual, virtues.

The question we must now face is clear. Mutual affection and recognition are marks of what we ordinarily call friendship; they are also found in the highest degree in the friendship of good men. Nevertheless, as Aristotle's observations about motherly love and his account of beneficence make clear, friendship does not in every case depend on the return of affection and recognition. To this extent, Aristotle provides a solution to what is in some sense the central problem of the *Ethics* and what is certainly a problem raised by its conclusion: why the philosopher might be willing to take an active interest in the well-being of those who cannot, in principle, see him for what he is. Yet the very manner in which Aristotle resolves the problem also makes clear that beneficence depends on *some* kind of kinship between benefactor and benefited. Honor is not needed to bridge the gap between them, but if their virtues and the lives lived in accordance with them are *simply* incommensurable with one another, there can be no community, no friendship, between the good man and men who possess what are commonly called virtues.[31] We must therefore ask: Do *theōria* and *praxis* bear at least a "familial" resemblance to one another? Is it conceivable that the man who loves wisdom, in his capacity as legislator of ethical virtue, cultivates in others what is after all a reflection of his own virtue? Does faring well (*eu prattein*) in the ordinary sense of the term perhaps "disclose in its being at work . . . [what the simply good man] is in potency"?

III. THE KINSHIP BETWEEN *THEŌRIA*
   AND *PRAXIS*

Aristotle's answer seems to be "no." Were the ethical virtues among the necessary conditions for true happiness, we might be justified in regarding the ethical life and the ethical virtues as a partial reflection of the highest life and complete virtue, but, as we have seen, prudence is the only "practical" virtue needed by the good man. Of the ethical virtues, only a non-habit-formed moderation is a condition for the pursuit or exercise of wisdom. Indeed, even if nothing that Aristotle says or suggests in Book X convinced us of the truth of this last point, his depiction of the state of soul of the good man in Book IX would. In chapter four of Book

IX—a chapter I have not yet considered—Aristotle argues that the characteristic marks of friendship are all rooted in the good man's relation to himself (1166a1–3; 10–14). Unlike most men, whose souls are rent by conflicting desires, who are constantly in a state of faction (*stasis*) with themselves, the good man "shares the same opinions with himself and desires the same things with his whole soul" (1166a13–14; 1166b18–22).[32] He "wishes good things for himself . . . for the sake of himself" (1166a14–16). But the "self" for whose sake he wishes good things, the part of himself that he always strives to gratify, is "the *dianoetic* [part];" for this or rather the "activity of thinking" (*to nooun*) is what "each man is or is most of all" (1166a16–23).[33] In other words, the picture of the good man's soul that emerges in the course of chapter four is precisely the one we inferred on the basis of Aristotle's discussion of pleasure in Book X. For most men, the ethical virtue of moderation, a balanced disposition toward bodily pleasures, is the best that can be hoped for; it is the only cure possible for the state of "paralysis" or civil war that exists within their souls (1102b16–21). But for the man who enjoys true happiness—the man in whom the *hexis* of self-friendship or friendship with wisdom occupies the place of ethical virtue—moderation is the natural consequence of his love for himself. He is at peace with himself because he loves, honors, and obeys at every turn the distinctively human part of himself.[34]

A. The Potential Philosopher

Still, it may be one thing to say this, and another to say that there is simply no connection between the virtue of moderation and the virtue of the simply good man. After all, in chapter four of Book IX, Aristotle is describing the state of soul of the man who is *already* good, *already* in love with wisdom. In the final chapter of Book X, he is talking about the education of the young. This distinction may make a difference. Could what is dispensable from the point of view of the man who *is* a philosopher be indispensable to his *becoming* one? If so, the situation Aristotle describes in the final chapter of the *Ethics* would meet the requirements of his account of beneficence. In cultivating the ethical virtues—or at least moderation—in the young, the philosopher would be establishing the pre-condition in others of his own activity. There is some evidence that this is Aristotle's point. At the outset of that final chapter he emphasizes the inefficacy of reason or argument as a guide to virtue and the good (1179b4–7). It is less clear whether he means to say that reason is ineffective in all cases; he notes initially that arguments "appear to have the power to encourage and stimulate" the best among the young (1179b7–10). Some young men, he suggests, are naturally open to reason, that is, are by nature given to moderation in the sense described above. Yet, as the chapter unfolds, Aristotle backs away from this position. All men when they are young, he seems to conclude, are in need of external constraints on their appetites (1179b31–34). Perhaps the point is that appearances are deceptive in the case of the best among the young: what appears as natural moderation in them is instead a readiness to become open to reason, a natural readiness to be led toward reason. While nature makes some souls more open to reason than others, *all* souls— even the soul of the potential philosopher—may need initial cultivation with respect to moderation.

Can one say the same thing about the remaining ethical virtues? Do the ethical virtues and the ethical life taken as a whole in some sense prepare a person for the philosophical life? Once again, Aristotle's closing arguments provide some evidence for this view. Aristotle does not limit the discussion to moderation, but tells us that "it is necessary to cultivate the soul of the listener beforehand by habits (*ethesi*) with respect to loving and hating well (*kalōs*)" (1179b23–26). Again, a few lines later, he says that "it is necessary for the character (*ēthos*) somehow to be there beforehand, akin to virtue, loving what is noble (*to kalon*) and disliking what is base" (1179b29–31). These passages hint at a kind of kinship between the ethical virtues, that is, the virtues acquired through habituation, and virtue in the strict sense. Beautiful actions may not themselves constitute true happiness. The ethical virtues may not in *this* sense be necessary conditions for the good life. Nevertheless, the theoretical life rests on a love of the beautiful, presupposes a cultivated awareness of the distinction between the noble and the base.[35]

What Aristotle says elsewhere in the *Ethics* about the character of his audience lends support to this conclusion. In chapter three of Book I, he tells us that his inquiry will be of use only to those who "fashion their appetites and act in accordance with *logos*" (1095a10–11). And in chapter four of the same book, he says that his audience must have been "led well by habits (*ethesi*)" (1095b4–6). True, these remarks are originally intended to set forth the conditions for understanding an inquiry "concerning beautiful, just and, in general, political things" (1094b5). But it is also true that Aristotle's inquiry into the good gradually becomes an inquiry into the theoretical life, indeed, a defense of the superiority of that way of life to any other. The inference we are to draw here seems obvious. Only those who possess the right habits will be able to understand the full force of Aristotle's *logos* in the *Ethics*, and only those who understand it will be able and willing to put that *logos* into "practice." Put otherwise, only those who, as younger men, have already tasted the excellence of a life of beautiful action can appreciate the excellence and beauty of *theōria*.

B. The Ethical Man

Here, then, we have one explanation for the turn Aristotle's argument takes in the final chapter of the *Ethics*. The ethical life, quite literally, "discloses in its being at work" what the philosopher is "in potency." It is the seedbed in which love of wisdom first takes root, and for just this reason it is worthy of the care and attention of the philosopher. But this explanation prompts another question. In *some* men, right desire might gradually give way to the desire for wisdom; prudence might gradually turn from enabling noble deeds to "see[ing] how [wisdom] is to arise;" the ethical virtues might gradually take up their properly subordinate and instrumental places within a larger whole, a new "*kosmos* of the virtues" (1134a1–3; 1145a8–9).[36] In *some* men—those large-souled enough to harbor a desire for contact with the ultimate sources of all things—there might arise that constellation of virtues properly called *philosophia*, friendship with wisdom. But surely not in *all*. Aristotle nowhere suggests that all men who practice the ethical virtues can also practice the highest virtue. On the contrary, in chapters six through eight of Book X he suggests that full access to the pleasures of *theōria* is reserved for the very few. What about the others, those who can be courageous, moderate, generous, and just, but not wise or lovers of wisdom? Does Aristotle say anything to lead us to think that the philosopher's beneficence might extend to such men as well? Is the ethical life "in itself" a reflection of the theoretical life and hence worthy, in its own right, of the best man's care?

There is some evidence for this possibility. I begin with the most obvious point of resemblance: In contrast to the "life of enjoyment" sought after by most men, the ethical life and the theoretical life are both marked by restraint toward the pleasures that human beings share with other living things. Moderation is an ethical as well as a philosophic virtue. Of course, "natural" moderation and ethical moderation differ from one another with respect to their source. In this sense they are different virtues. But whatever their causes, the effect in each case is the same: a taking of bodily pleasures in stride.

Moreover, in the case of each form of moderation, *reason* plays a decisive part in bringing about the desired effect. The parts of the habitually moderate man's soul, no less than those of the philosopher's soul, speak and must speak with the same voice (*homophōnei tō logō*) (1102b25–28). Indeed, in this sense reason is an essential feature of the ethical life as a whole. As Aristotle argues in the final chapter of Book VI, the ethical virtues can no more exist in the absence of prudence than prudence—or at least "ordinary" prudence—can exist in the absence of the ethical virtues (1144b30–32). The ethical life, like the theoretical life, is a life informed by the presence of reason; it is a life in which the distinctively human part of the soul somehow holds sway. Of course, *logos* does not occupy a position of unqualified supremacy within the ethical life; it does not serve as or even dictate the end. But this is just another way of saying that the ethical life is *incomplete*, that it contains an only *partial* realization of what is fully realized or fully at work within the theoretical life.

How much should this partiality or incompleteness concern us? What is at stake here can be framed more fully in terms of two difficulties that haunt Aristotle's whole inquiry but that come closest to surfacing during his second discussion of pleasure—and hence just before he re-opens the question of happiness in Book X. As with all major issues in the *Ethics*, these difficulties have to do with being complete (*teleios*) or being at an end (*entelecheia*). Here in Book X, for the first time in the *Ethics*, Aristotle makes a clear-cut distinction between those quasi-activities he calls motions (*kinēseis*) or becomings (*geneseis*) and activities (*energeiai*) in the strict sense.[37] Temple-building is an example of the first type: building temples takes time and at no time before the installation of the last statue is the process complete (1174a19–29). Seeing is a low-level but significant example of the second: it may take time for the eye to take in a whole landscape, but the act of seeing (and in fact every act of sensing) is complete *as seeing* at every moment (1174a14–16). Clearly, contemplation is the paradigmatic instance of sheer activity: Seeing with the mind's eye is the timeless taking in of timeless objects. But it seems equally clear that actions (*praxeis*) are processes of the first type.[38] Not only does the deliberation that is integral to every genuine action take time, but so do acts of generosity and courage. Withdrawing funds, handing them over, reining in one's fear, avoiding a spear-thrust—all are time-bound parts of time-bound wholes.

Here the difficulties begin. If all contemplation is a form of sheer, timeless activity and every action is a form of time-bound motion—if *theōria* and *praxis* are fundamentally different modes of being—it is difficult to see how one can be truly akin to the other. For that matter, it is difficult to see how the life of action, a life composed of discrete motions, could even count as a lower-order form of happiness; happiness is, after all, a form of *energeia*. The second difficulty follows closely upon the first. According to

Aristotle's account, *pleasures* not only accompany and complete activities—so much so that he initially identifies pleasure with unimpeded activity—they also share all the qualities that distinguish genuine activities from mere motions.[39] Pleasures, too, are timeless wholes—this claim is in fact the starting point of Aristotle's own account of pleasure in Book X (1174a13–19; 1174b5–9). But since pleasure and contemplation share features that separate them both from actions—and link them both to happiness—it is difficult to avoid drawing the further conclusion that pleasure is more akin to contemplation—and a better candidate for true happiness—than virtuous action.

Though a full resolution of these difficulties lies beyond the scope of this inquiry, I will try to make some progress toward one. Let us begin with pleasure. It is surely true that pleasures, *all* pleasures, bear a certain resemblance to sheer activity. Nor can it be denied that pleasure completes even the most complete activity— even the best activity of the best thing in the best condition in relation to the best object (1174b14–33). But this only proves that people who dedicate themselves to the pursuit of bodily pleasure are on to something. In Book I Aristotle had likened such people to cattle; now he lets us see that, while they may behave like beasts, they want to be gods. "And perhaps [people who pursue bodily pleasure] do not pursue what they imagine nor what they would say they do, but the same pleasure; for all things by nature possess something divine" (1153b30–32). The pursuit of bodily pleasure is a misguided attempt to achieve a completeness only truly available in the activity of contemplation. It is to mistake the *form* of activity for its proper content, and thus to pursue a content that cannot sustain itself. In pursuing the rush of pleasure, in seeking to lose themselves in the now, men seek to participate in what is eternal and divine. In living for the moment, they attempt to dwell, if only for a moment, in the timeless present.

The situation of the man who lives in accordance with ethical virtue is very different. For such a man, time is of the essence. He must heed the past, look to the future, and above all take into account the ever-changing circumstances before him. Moreover,

he is pressed by time and pressed for time. Once his deliberations are done, he must act with decision and dispatch. He must
make his move—move forward into the world—without rush-
ing and without delay (1142b2–5; 26–28). Still, this involvement
of the man of action with motion and time does not prove that he
and his way of life have no kinship with sheer activity and therefore no connection with happiness. On the contrary, precisely
by taking time into account and precisely *by* putting himself "in
motion," he brings something akin to "the activity of motionless-
ness" into the world of motion (1154b26–28). To act in accordance
with reason and ethical virtue is to bring the measuredness and
integrity, the stillness and harmony, of a well-balanced soul into
the world at large. It is to bring some semblance of order into the
rough and tumble of human life. To put it another way: To act
for the sake of the beautiful, to do something generous or just or
courageous simply for its own sake is to bring a temporary halt
to the one-step-after-another, one step-*for*-another movement of
human life. A beautiful deed, like a beautiful melody, crystallizes
time; it gives time a syntax and meaning it could not otherwise
have. What Aristotle says about the magnificent man—he is "like
someone who knows (*epistēmoni*), for he is able to contemplate
(*theōrēsai*) what is fitting and spend great things harmoniously"
for a beautiful object—holds true of everything the man of action
does (1122a34–35). He contemplates what is fitting and spends
his greatness accordingly. He is a maker of time-bound, insight-
infused wholes—beautiful temples dedicated to the unchanging
god. Motion and therefore *praxis* may be an incomplete activity,
the being-complete of what is in potency *as* something in potency
(*Physics* 201a10–12; 201b28–34). Nevertheless, it is an activity, and
in shaping his motions in accordance with reason, in allowing
his thought to be at work in the world, the man of action comes
as close as humanly possible to mirroring the sheer activity of
contemplative thought in the medium of becoming. We could
even say the ethical life is in potency what the theoretical life is
in activity; *as* motion, *as* incomplete activity, it is always tend-
ing, always stretching, toward the sheer activity of contemplation.

Seen from the point of view of *theōria*, *praxis* is always already on the way to it.[40]

Let us try to take this line of reasoning a step further. The differences between the ethical and theoretical life are most apparent in the case of such commonly recognized virtues as courage and justice. Because actions or deeds form the ends of these virtues, the part played by right reason in their realization is liable to escape notice: their "look" or actuality bears little resemblance to the activity of philosophizing. But Aristotle's account of the ethical virtues is not limited to such virtues. Near the end of Book IV, he describes certain unnamed, that is, generally unrecognized, virtues that have less to do with right action than right speaking (1108a9–20). At issue is the question of the proper use of leisure. Once the city is at peace, once the daily business of distributing goods and righting wrongs is done, what will the ethical man do with himself? Once he is done moving, how will he rest? How will he spend the time that most men devote to the pursuit of bodily pleasures and that the philosopher devotes to the pursuit of wisdom?

Aristotle's answer is illuminating. Like most men, the ethical man will "play" (*paizein*). But unlike most men, and like the philosopher, he will spend his time in conversation. His play takes the form of witty conversation, a kind of verbal gymnastic, which reveals the character of the soul in much the same way that gymnastic proper reveals the character of the body, the "shape" it is in (1128a9–12). Among other things, the ethical man will not make—or put up with—certain jests. Being a "law unto himself," he will exhibit a kind of moderation in speech (1128a28–33). He will also tell the truth. Being a man who keeps his word in matters of justice, a "lover of truth," he will make his words correspond to things even when nothing further is at stake; he will exhibit a kind of justice or fairness in speech (1127a32–b7). Or rather, he will tell the truth except when speaking about himself. In this case, he will be inclined to understate the truth, to be "ironic" about his own virtue, thus exhibiting a kind of equity in speech (1127b7–9; 29–31).

Do we not see in this picture of ethical men at leisure a kind of image—playful, to be sure—of the philosopher and philosophic friendship? Can it be an accident that truth-telling is the central unnamed virtue and that Socrates' name is mentioned in the course of Aristotle's description of it (1127b22–26)? It is, of course, one thing to be truthful about everyday matters, another to seek the truth about the highest matters; one thing to use reason to uncover ambiguities in language and foibles in men, another to use reason to uncover and explore the natures of things. Above all, it is one thing to regard conversation as a break from the serious business of political life—as the ethical man appears to do—and another to regard it as the best justification for political life. Still, the *resemblance* is unmistakable. Indeed, it is not too far-fetched to suppose that—moderation aside—it is the unnamed ethical virtues rather than the commonly recognized ones that most of all prepare the potential philosopher for entrance into the philosophical life. Aren't tact and a certain suppleness of wit, love of truth and a certain willingness to understate one's goodness precisely the qualities of soul that must be developed in the budding philosopher?

C. The Philosopher as Benefactor

The ethical life and the theoretical life come closest to crossing paths at those moments when the principle they share—right speech or reason—comes to the fore, but they only come *close* to crossing paths. The ethical life is at best a partial realization of the highest life, a playful, that is to say, incomplete image of it. Recognizing this, recognizing the kinship and the limits of the kinship between his own life and the life of the ethical man, the philosopher as benefactor would have to seek to keep both ways of life intact. Mother-like, he would have to content himself with seeing others fare well as best they can. That is, he would see to it that those who can acquire only the ethical virtues do so. Although he might hint at the kinship between the life of action and his own, and even at the superiority of his way of life to theirs, he would not make too much of his own virtue or too little of theirs. His own *praxis*, in other words, would be informed by equity.

But his work could not stop here. He would also have to provide for the very best natures, those for whom the ethical life is a preparation for the philosophical life. He would have to name, that is, to recognize as virtues in their own right, the ethical virtues that matter most to potential philosophers but are taken for granted by the man of action. He would have to make it clear, at least to such men, that for the best natures the ethical virtues are a means to a further end. Above all, he would have to make visible the end that those virtues serve; he would have to make apparent the character and the superiority of understanding for its own sake. In short, the task faced by the philosopher would be exceedingly complex. Doing well by others, making it possible for each man to attain the good proper to him, would require the philosopher to strike a balance at each point between affirming the intrinsic worthiness of the ethical life and pointing beyond it.

In the final chapter of the *Ethics*, Aristotle points to this difficulty. Legislation, he argues, has its advantages as a means of leading men to virtue. In contrast to the commands of one man, which are liable to be resented by some men and which in any case lack force, laws possess authority. Combining the impersonality of reason with compulsive force, they offend no one and, if well made, can be a means of bringing men to live in accordance with right reason and right order (1180a14–24). But legislation has its disadvantages as well—the very disadvantages that Aristotle first points out at the end of his account of justice in Book V. Precisely because laws are impersonal, they fail to take into account differences between men. They lack what might be called the personal touch (1180b7–13). In the case we are considering—and this must be the issue for Aristotle in chapter nine as well—laws that promoted the ethical virtues, that is, laws that enjoined or impelled men to act well, would fail or would at least tend to fail to represent those virtues in the way most appropriate to the potential philosopher. Perhaps in the best of all possible circumstances the philosopher might find a way to deal with the problem. Given an opportunity to found or radically refound a regime, he might devise some way to enact a set of laws that promoted the good at every level, that compelled some and habituated others to practice the ethical virtues while somehow making room for the pursuit of wisdom.[41] But in all other circumstances it is difficult to see how active participation in public life, legislation in the usual sense of the term, could make a difference worthy of the effort—especially when we remember that the philosopher is more interested in thinking than doing and is interested in doing only insofar as it and its products are in some sense effluences of his thought. How is the man who loves wisdom to benefit others—and to preserve the integrity of his own life while doing so?

D. *Theōria* and *Praxis* in the *Ethics*

The *Ethics* itself may point to—or rather *be*—the answer to this question. It may itself represent the final answer to the questions it raises concerning the relation of *theōria* to *praxis*. I suggested earlier, near the end of our inquiry into Book VI, that the philosopher might regularly engage in a sort of legislation. In addition to using his prudence to secure his own good, he might seek out ways of enabling others to know and pursue the highest human good, perhaps by educating potential legislators to see the ultimate superiority of *sophia* to the other virtues. Don't we see Aristotle himself engaged in just this sort of education in the *Ethics*?[42] Don't we see him present potential legislators with an account of human things that makes right action the principal aim of legislation, and then see him correct that account by gently suggesting that happiness may not lie simply in the performance of noble deeds? It is difficult to judge in these matters, but it seems reasonable to assume that the impression left in the minds of most readers of the *Ethics*—especially those suited by temperament to be legislators—would be a somewhat distant respect for wisdom coupled with a firm conviction that the ethical virtues must be cultivated in the young. Isn't this just what is needed? Isn't it the best a philosopher exercising his beneficence at a distance could hope to achieve?

It may be. Yet there is another sense in which the *Ethics* represents or rather *enacts* a final resolution of the tension between *theōria* and *praxis*. Aristotle not only educates potential legislators—a risky business at best for the reasons given above—he also provides the private education, the "education for the particular man" (*paideia kath' hekaston*) that he proposes as an alternative to ordinary legislation (1180b6–7). Consider what I have just said about the impression left by the *Ethics* on its "average" reader. Aristotle spends the greater part of the *Ethics* discussing the ethical life, and while doing so he acts as if that life were the locus of human happiness. He does just what I suggested the beneficent philosopher must do when faced with men to whom *theōria* must remain a somewhat mysterious alternative to their own way of life: Aristotle practices equity. He conceals his own virtue, contenting himself for the most part with articulating and refining their understanding of the good. In short, he does not make much of his own virtue, and refuses to make little of theirs.

Aristotle's beneficence does not stop there. The *Ethics* is also written with the potential philosopher in mind: Aristotle the inquirer writes for inquiring minds. He engages in a philosophic deliberation and invites anyone who can be engaged by his questions to participate.[43] He himself names, and thus acknowledges, the unnamed virtues of tact and truthfulness; he makes visible, in some fashion, the character and superiority of *sophia*; and he provides an account, however indirect, of the tension and ultimate resolution of the tension between *theōria* and *praxis*. In other words, Aristotle shows at least some of those who "act and fashion their appetites in accordance with reason" what it might mean to live a life that is truly *kata logon* (1095a10–11). That he presents these matters in an oblique manner and, for the most part, focuses his attention on the pre-philosophic understanding of the good need not trouble us: The ability to follow a tactful argument is as much a mark of the potential philosopher as the ability to make one is a mark of the actual philosopher. Like the doctor who uses his simultaneously universal and particular knowledge to care for bodies, Aristotle prescribes different "regimes" for different souls (1180b7–23). In this case, the regime prescribed—vigorous exercise for the mind—is also a test of its applicability. Those who cannot grasp the full force of Aristotle's *logos* need not, and those who can, will.

TO WHAT EXTENT DOES Aristotle himself benefit from his peculiar mode of beneficence? Is "legislating" as Aristotle does in the *Ethics* the best means for the philosopher to secure his own good? Is it the best way to preserve the integrity of his own life, while being of use to others? There is an obvious sense in which the answer is "yes." Writing rather than legislating in the ordinary sense of the term spares the philosopher from the distractions of political life and leaves him free to pursue a life of inquiry. This is especially true of the kind of writing and thinking we find in the *Ethics*, for Aristotle's "action" is itself an inquiry; his *praxis* is also a form of *theōria*. As he teaches potential legislators, and as he culls out and cultivates the best among his readers, he comes to see, or see again, what it is to be human. By "leaving actions" in the ordinary sense to his "friends," by "being a cause of acting" rather than an actor himself, he "distributes the greater share of the beautiful" to himself (1169a31–35). He provides himself with an occasion to contemplate the full range of possible forms that human being can take on; he "brings to mind" the order and the conditions for order within human things.

Let us keep in mind, however, that in Aristotle's view human things are not "the things most honored by nature" (1141b2–3). The human order is one thing; the order of the whole is another. And it is the order of the whole or rather the source, the *archē*, of order within the whole that is the true target of the philosopher's inquiries. Still, we need not take this to mean that Aristotle's inquiry in the *Ethics*, and by implication every inquiry into human things, is not so much an instance of genuine *theōria* as a distraction from it. Something Aristotle says in one of his biological works sheds light on the matter. He argues that the study of living things in some sense completes the study of what is divine and imperishable (*De Part. Anim.* 644b23–645a7). The "look" of the lower animals may hold few charms for the senses. But seen with the mind's eye, even the meanest animal shows some trace of the divine (*De Part. Anim.* 645a7–11):

> For within all natural things there is present something wondrous (*thaumaston*); and as Heracleitus is said to have responded to strangers who wished to meet with him and who hesitated when they approached and saw him warming himself at the stove—for he bid them enter and take heart, saying, 'For here, too, there are gods'—so, too, we must approach the inquiry concerning each of the animals without grimacing, since there is something natural and beautiful in all of them (*De Part. Anim.* 645a17–23).

What holds true of the study of even the meanest animals holds true *a fortiori* of the study of man. To engage, as Aristotle does in the *Ethics*, in "the love of wisdom concerning human things"— to hold up a mirror to human nature—is to see reflected in the tangle and flow of human things a moving image of the unmoving mover of all things (1181b12–15).[44] For what "moves" human beings, especially those who live their lives *kata logon*, is in some sense what moves the whole. Thus to study human things as Aristotle studies them is not to study a part of the whole in abstraction from the whole. Nor is it to study one of many wondrous parts of a still more wondrous whole. To study human things as Aristotle does—taking seriously the everyday understanding of them, then ascending from that understanding, through that understanding, to the delightful recognition of "himself" at work in those things—is to study that part of the whole which reveals most about the source of the whole. For here, too, as it turns out, there are gods.

A BRIEF BIBLIOGRAPHY

T HE SECONDARY LITERATURE ON the *Nicomachean Ethics* is large and ever growing. The following bibliography is restricted to works by Aristotle in English translation, the secondary texts I refer to directly, and the Greek texts of Aristotle that formed the principal basis of my inquiries. More extensive bibliographies relevant to the topics treated here can be found in Richard Kraut's *Aristotle on the Human Good*, in Sarah Broadie's *Ethics with Aristotle*, and in Aristide Tessitore's *Reading Aristotle's Ethics: Virtue, Rhetoric, and Political Philosophy.*

Works by Aristotle in English Translation

Basic Works of Aristotle. Ed. Richard Mckeon. New York: Random House, 1941.

The Complete Works of Aristotle, Revised Oxford Translation. Ed. Jonathan Barnes. Princeton: Princeton Univ. Press, 1984.

Aristotle's Eudemian Ethics, Books I, II, and VIII. Trans. Michael Woods. Oxford: Clarendon Press, 1982.

Aristotle's Metaphysics. Trans. Joe Sachs. Santa Fe, N.M.: Green Lion Press, 1999.

Aristotle's On the Soul and On Memory and Recollection. Trans. Joe Sachs. Santa Fe, N.M.: Green Lion Press, 2001.

Aristotle's Physics: A Guided Study. Trans. Joe Sachs. New Brunswick, N.J.: Rutger's Univ. Press, 1995.

Metaphysics. Trans. Hugh Tredennick. Loeb Classical Library 271–272. Cambridge: Harvard Univ. Press, 1935.

Nicomachean Ethics. Trans. Martin Ostwald. Indianapolis: Bobbs-Merrill, 1962.

The Nicomachean Ethics. Trans. H. Rackham. Loeb Classical Library 73. Cambridge: Harvard Univ. Press, 1926.

The Nicomachean Ethics. Trans. David Ross. Oxford: Oxford Univ. Press, 1980.

Nicomachean Ethics. Trans. Joe Sachs. Newburyport, Mass.: Focus Publishing, 2002.

On the Soul, Parva Naturalia, On Breath. Trans. W. S. Hett. Loeb Classical Library 288. Cambridge: Harvard Univ. Press, 1936.

Parts of Animals, Movement of Animals, Progression of Animals. Trans. A. L. Peck and E. S. Forster. Loeb Classical Library 323. Cambridge: Harvard Univ. Press, 1961.

Physics. Trans. Robin Waterfield. Oxford: Oxford Univ. Press, 2008.

The Politics. Trans. Carnes Lord. Chicago: Univ. of Chicago Press, 1984.

Politics. Trans. H. Rackham. Loeb Classical Library 264. Cambridge: Harvard Univ. Press, 1932.

Posterior Analytics, Topica. Trans. Hugh Tredennick and E. S. Forster. Loeb Classical Library 391. Cambridge: Harvard Univ. Press, 1960.

Works Cited

Ackrill, J. L. "Aristotle on *Eudaimonia.*" In *Essays on Aristotle's Ethics,* ed. A. Rorty, 15–33. Berkeley: Univ. of California Press, 1980.

Aquinas, Thomas. *Commentary on Aristotle's Nicomachean Ethics.* Trans. C. I. Litzinger. Notre Dame, Ind.: Dumb Ox Books, 1993.

Aubenque, Pierre. *La Prudence chez Aristote.* Paris: Presses Universitaires de France, 1963.

Benardete, Seth. *Herodotean Inquiries.* The Hague: Martinus Nijhoff, 1969.

Berns, Laurence. "Plato's *Meno* and Aristotle's *Nicomachean Ethics.*" In *The Envisioned Life: Essays in Honor of Eva Brann,* ed. Peter Kalkavage and Eric Salem, 1–26. Philadelphia: Paul Dry Books, 2007.

Berti, Enrico. *Aristotle nel Novecento.* Roma-Bari: Editori Laterza, 1992.

Broadie, Sarah. *Ethics with Aristotle.* New York: Oxford Univ. Press, 1991.

Burger, Ronna. *Aristotle's Dialogue with Socrates: On the Nicomachean Ethics.* Chicago: Univ. of Chicago Press, 2008.

Burnet, John, ed. *The Ethics of Aristotle.* London: Methuen, 1900.

Gauthier, R. A., and J. Y. Jolif. *L'Éthique à Nicomaque: Introduction, Traduction et Commentaire.* 3 vols. Louvain: Publications Universitaires de Louvain, 1958–59.

Heidegger, Martin. "The Question Concerning Technology." In *The Question Concerning Technology,* trans. William Lovitt, 3–35. New York: Harper & Row, 1977.

———. *What is a Thing?* Trans. W. B. Barton, Jr., and Vera Deutsch. Chicago: Regnery, 1967.

Irwin, T. H. "The Metaphysical and Psychological Basis of Aristotle's Ethics." In *Essays on Aristotle's Ethics,* ed. A. Rorty, 35–54. Berkeley: Univ. of California Press, 1980.

Jaffa, Harry V. *Thomism and Aristotelianism: A Study of the Commentary by Thomas Aquinas on the Nicomachean Ethics.* Westport, Ct.: Greenwood Press, 1979.

Joachim, H. H. *Aristotle: The Nicomachean Ethics.* Ed. D. A. Rees. Oxford: Clarendon Press, 1951.

Klein, Jacob. *A Commentary on Plato's Meno.* Chapel Hill: Univ. of North Carolina Press, 1965.

———. *Greek Mathematical Thought and the Origin of Algebra.* Trans. Eva Brann. Cambridge, Mass.: MIT Press, 1968.

———. "The World of Physics and the Natural World." Trans. David R. Lachterman. In *Lectures and Essays,* ed. Robert B. Williamson and Elliott Zuckerman, 1–34. Annapolis: St. John's College Press, 1985.

———. "Aristotle, an Introduction." In *Lectures and Essays,* ed. Robert B. Williamson and Elliott Zuckerman, 171–95. Annapolis: St. John's College Press, 1985.

Kraut, Richard. *Aristotle on the Human Good.* Princeton: Princeton Univ. Press, 1989.

Nagel, Thomas. "Aristotle on *Eudaimonia.*" In *Essays on Aristotle's Ethics,* ed. A. Rorty, 7–14. Berkeley: Univ. of California Press, 1980.

Rorty, Amélie, ed. *Essays on Aristotle's Ethics.* Berkeley: Univ. of California Press, 1980.

———. "The Place of Contemplation in Aristotle's *Nicomachean Ethics.*" In *Essays on Aristotle's Ethics,* 377–94. Berkeley: Univ. of California Press, 1980.

Sachs, Joe. "Aristotle's Definition of Motion." *The College* 27.4 (1976): 12–18.

———. "An Outline of the Argument of Aristotle's *Metaphysics.*" *St. John's Review* 32.3 (1981): 38–46.

Sorabji, Richard. "Aristotle on the Role of Intellect in Virtue." In *Essays on Aristotle's Ethics,* ed. A. Rorty, 201–19. Berkeley: Univ. of California Press, 1980.

Stewart, J. A. *Notes on the Nicomachean Ethics of Aristotle.* 2 vols. Oxford: Clarendon Press, 1892.

Strauss, Leo. *The City and Man.* Chicago: Univ. of Chicago Press, 1977.

———. *Natural Right and History.* Chicago: Univ. of Chicago Press, 1950.

———. *Thoughts on Machiavelli.* Chicago: Univ. of Chicago Press, 1958.

Tessitore, Aristide. *Reading Aristotle's Ethics: Virtue, Rhetoric, and Political Philosophy.* Albany: State Univ. of New York Press, 1996.

Wilkes, Kathleen. "The Good Man and the Good for Man in Aristotle's Ethics." In *Essays on Aristotle's Ethics,* ed. A. Rorty, 341–57. Berkeley: Univ. of California Press, 1980.

Greek Texts

Aristotle. *Analytica Priora et Posteriora.* Ed. W. D. Ross. Oxford: Clarendon Press, 1964.

———. *De Anima.* Ed. W. D. Ross. Oxford: Clarendon Press, 1956.

———. *Ethica Nicomachea.* Ed. I. Bywater. Oxford: Clarendon Press, 1894.

———. *Metaphysica.* Ed. W. Jaeger. Oxford: Clarendon Press, 1957.

———. *Physica.* Ed. W. D. Ross. Oxford: Clarendon Press, 1950.

———. *Politica.* Ed. W. D. Ross. Oxford: Clarendon Press, 1957.

NOTES

Introduction

1. Page references to Aristotle's works here and elsewhere are those of the Bekker edition. Chapter references correspond to the Roman numeral divisions in I. Bywater, ed., *Ethica Nicomachea* (Oxford: Oxford Univ. Press, 1894). All references not otherwise noted are to the *Nicomachean Ethics*. Translations from the *Ethics* and elsewhere are my own. Italicized words and phrases within translations represent my emphasis.

2. The tension between what Aristotle says in the body of the *Ethics* about the good life and what he says in Book X remains an issue for his interpreters. For a sample of "mainstream" essays that discuss Aristotle's understanding of the relation between *theōria* and *praxis*, see Amelie Rorty, ed., *Essays on Aristotle's Ethics* (Berkeley: Univ. of Calif. Press, 1980). Thomas Nagel's "Aristotle on *Eudaimonia*," J. L. Ackrill's "Aristotle on *Eudaimonia*," Kathleen Wilkes' "The Good Man and the Good for Man in Aristotle's Ethics," and Amelie Rorty's "The Place of Contemplation in Aristotle's *Nicomachean Ethics*" bear most directly on the problem. Ackrill, p. 15, puts it nicely: "Most of the *Ethics* implies that good action is—or is at least a major element in—man's best life, but eventually in Book 10 purely contemplative activity is said to be perfect *eudaimonia*; and Aristotle does not tell us how to combine or relate these two ideas." Two books that belong to roughly the same milieu as *Essays* and that treat the *theōria/praxis* issue at some length are Sarah Broadie's *Ethics with Aristotle* (Oxford: Oxford Univ. Press, 1991) and Richard Kraut's *Aristotle on the Human Good* (Princeton: Princeton Univ. Press, 1989). My own approach to the *Ethics* is closer to that of Aristide Tessitore in *Reading Aristotle's Ethics: Virtue, Rhetoric and Political Philosophy* (Albany: State Univ. of New York Press, 1996) and of Ronna Burger in her wonderful new book *Aristotle's Dialogue with Socrates: On the Nicomachean Ethics* (Chicago: Univ. of Chicago Press, 2008). For a helpful account of the ways that different approaches to Aristotle have shaped and been shaped by different schools of thought in Europe, England, and the United States, see Enrico Berti, *Aristotele nel Novecento* (Roma-Bari: Editori Laterza, 1992).

3. For revealing accounts of the difference between ancient and modern science and the relation of modern science to modern technology, see Martin Heidegger, *What is a Thing?*, trans. W. B. Barton, Jr., and Vera Deutsch (Chicago: Regnery, 1967), 66–96, and "The Question Concerning Technology," in *The Question Concerning Technology*, trans. William Lovett (New York: Harper Colophon, 1977), 3–35. Missing from Heidegger's accounts, however, is a clear sense of the extent to which modern science is a project, an enterprise, deliberately intended to overturn ancient science (and Christianity) and deliberately wed, from the outset, to the task of relieving man's estate. In other words, Heidegger neglects the political aspect of the modern enterprise. Cf. Leo Strauss, *The City and Man* (Chicago: Univ. of Chi-

cago Press, 1977), 1–12, and *Thoughts on Machiavelli* (Chicago: Univ. of Chicago Press, 1958).

4. Thus Descartes writes in one of his "Cogitationes Privatae": "So far I have been a spectator in this theater which is the world, but I am now about to mount the stage, and I come forward masked" (*The Philosophical Writings of Descartes*, 2 vols., trans. John Cottingham, Robert Stoothoff, and Dugald Murdoch [Cambridge: Cambridge Univ. Press, 1985], 1:2). Cf. also his remark to the Abbé Mersenne: "I hope that readers will gradually get used to my principles, and recognize their truth, before observing that they destroy Aristotle's" (Descartes: *Philosophical Letters*, trans. and ed. Anthony Kenny [Minneapolis: Univ. of Minnesota Press, 1970], 94). Presumably the principle that Descartes above all seeks to destroy or overturn is the notion of final cause.

5. John Burnet, *The Ethics of Aristotle* (London: Methuen, 1900). For obvious reasons, Burnet is especially good at picking up allusions to the Platonic dialogues and "Academic" positions. Moreover, his immersion in the study of Plato also seems to have made him particularly sensitive to the "dialogic" character of the *Ethics*. Perhaps for this reason I have often found his to be the most useful of the standard commentaries on the *Ethics*.

6. For an account of the difference between the ancient and post-ancient (including scholastic) attitudes toward the world of common sense, see Jacob Klein's *Greek Mathematical Thought and the Origin of Algebra*, trans. Eva Brann (Cambridge, Mass.: MIT Press, 1968), 117–125, and "The World of Physics and the Natural World," trans. David R. Lachterman, in *Lectures and Essays*, ed. Robert B. Williamson and Elliott Zuckerman (Annapolis: St. John's College Press, 1985), 1–34.

7. For Aristotle's use of *dokein* (seems, is thought) and related words, see Burnet's introduction, xxxvii–xliii, and (for instance) pages 1–2, 11, 16, 18, 48–49, and 56 of his commentary. Other features of Aristotle's "style" of writing—which some would claim is no style at all—include frequent use of impersonal (and passive) constructions and ubiquitous use of the first person plural. (How many times does Aristotle say "I" in the entire corpus? Probably fewer than ten.) All of these grammatical features point in the same direction, *away* from the self-assertive "I" of the lecturer or author who lays out his views before a largely passive audience and *toward* a community of active learning that keeps the object of thought (and the everyday opinions that oscillate and flicker around it) at the center of the inquiry. The Heraclitean dictum, "Listen not to me but to the *Logos*" could easily function as Aristotle's motto. Likewise, it is no accident that the "I" first moves to the center of philosophic discourse, as topic of discussion and stylistic feature, in that great battle cry of anti-Aristotelianism (and rejection of everydayness), Descartes' *Discourse on Method*.

1 ‖ Happiness

1. For a discussion and history of this view, see R. A. Gauthier and J. A. Jolif, *L'Éthique à Nicomaque, Introduction, Traduction et Commentaire*, 2nd. ed., 3 vols. (Louvain: Publications Universitaires de Louvain, 1958–59), 1:1–60. Its hold on a certain type of reader is evidenced by the willingness of Gauthier and Jolif, the authors of the standard edition of the *Nicomachean Ethics*, to accept it without question. Although Burnet, too, believes that the *Nicomachean Ethics* was not put into its final form by Aristotle himself, his reading of the text suggests an alternative explanation—the explanation that I have adopted—for the repetitions and apparent inconsistencies

that we find in it, namely, that Aristotle is reasoning dialectically (and rhetorically) in much of the *Ethics*. See Burnet, xi–xix, xxxi–xlvi. Gauthier and Jolif reject Burnet's reading on the grounds that it suggests that the *Nicomachean Ethics* is not a scientific work (1:35–36, 87–88). Just what they mean by "scientific" in this context is not clear. In the *Topics*, Aristotle suggests that dialectic is useful, among other things, for establishing the first principles of the sciences (101a25–b4).

2. See Broadie, 39, and Kraut, 241–44 and 313.

3. That is, he could have said "and of the virtues, the best and most complete" or simply (along the lines of his second qualification) "and further, in accordance with the best and most complete virtue."

4. Whether and in what sense virtue is one or many is, of course, a Socratic question. It turns up, in various forms, in the *Meno*, the *Laches*, the *Charmides*, and to some extent, the *Republic*. Aristotle is clearly aware of its Socratic origin (1144b28–30). For an extended discussion of the question, see Jacob Klein, *A Commentary on Plato's Meno* (Chapel Hill, N.C.: Univ. of North Carolina Press, 1965). It should become clear as I proceed that Aristotle's answer is no less difficult to ferret out than that of Socrates.

5. Cf. Plato *Meno* 70a1–4. For a helpful account of the many connections between this dialogue and the *Ethics*, see Laurence Berns, "Plato's *Meno* and Aristotle's *Nicomachean Ethics*" in *The Envisioned Life: Essays in Honor of Eva Brann*, ed. Peter Kalkavage and Eric Salem (Philadelphia: Paul Dry Books, 2007), 1–26.

6. Cf. Herodotus *Histories* 1.29–45; Sophocles *Oedipus Rex* 1523–1530, and *The Trachiniae* 1–8. Burnet, 42–45, notes Aristotle's frequent use of poetic or tragic language in chapters nine through eleven. Given this, and given that Priam's name and story turn up repeatedly in the discussion, one wonders whether Aristotle is representing and subtly countering the "tragic sense of life" in the concluding chapters of Book I. Does the view that happiness either is or is radically dependent on good fortune, that is, "divine lot," perhaps stem ultimately from the poets? Cf. also Seth Benardete, *Herodotean Inquiries* (The Hague: Martinus Nijhoff, 1969), 19–21, for a discussion of the "tragic" tone of the Solon/Croesus episode.

7. This latter claim may seem strange, but it is a commonplace in Greek tragedy, where the happiness or misery of a whole "house," often identified with its founder, e.g., Atreus, is a frequent theme. Within this context the sins and sufferings of sons can be visited on their fathers no less than those of fathers can be visited on sons. Cf. Aeschylus *The Oresteia*. Once again, then, the view that happiness is largely dependent on good fortune seems to have its roots in the "poetic" understanding of things.

8. In fact the various "equipment" words used here and elsewhere in the *Ethics* all come from *chorēgos*, chorus-leader or play-producer: *chorēgia* include everything that's needed for the show to go on.

9. George Eliot's *Middlemarch* is an extended meditation on precisely these questions. For Eliot, as for Aristotle, the real issue is not whether excellent human beings need to eat (of course they do) but whether the activity of excellence, the full shining-forth of virtue, presupposes a certain kind of world—for instance, a world that acknowledges and welcomes human greatness.

10. See Tessitore, 21.

11. Liddell and Scott list as meanings of *eudaimonia* (in this order): "prosperity," "good fortune," "wealth," "weal," "happiness." (Our own word "happiness," derived from "happen," and the German "*Glücklichkeit*," derived from "*Glück*" {"luck"}, point

in the same direction.) Embedded in this everyday understanding of happiness is surely some sense of the original meaning of *eudaimonia*: an *eu-daimōn* is a man with a good or kindly spirit on his side.

12. Sardanapollos, an Assyrian king notorious for immoderation verging on effeminacy, apparently served in antiquity as a kind of image of excess in high places. See the comments of Burnet, 20; Gauthier and Jolif, 2:31; and J. A. Stewart, *Notes on the Nicomachean Ethics of Aristotle*, 2 vols. (Oxford: Clarendon, 1892), 1:63-64. In the *Eudemian Ethics* Aristotle again mentions Sardanapollos in connection with "the life of enjoyment" (1216a16). Henceforth I shall often use the word "Sardanapollist" to denote those who "sympathize with Sardanapollos."

13. For a fuller and more precise account of the relation between pleasure and virtuous activity, see Aristotle's discussion of pleasure in Books VII and X.

14. *Ergon*, related to the English "work" and German "*Werk*," can mean everything from job or task to deed or accomplishment—it cuts across the distinction between craft and action. In the present context, it is worth emphasizing that not every *ergon* has to serve a larger or further purpose. For instance, seeing is a work or activity that we sometimes engage in (and take delight in!) for its own sake. Sometimes we just like to take in the world around us. See *Metaphysics* 980a22-28.

15. Socrates enunciates the principle "at work" here in *Republic* 352d8-353b1; he later uses a peculiar version of it to found his city in speech—"one being, one work" becomes "one man, one *ergon*" (here in the sense of job) and thus "one man, one art" (370a7-c5). Later still, other versions are used to define justice, sort out the structure of the soul and distinguish the philosopher from the non-philosopher. See also *Sophist* 246d-e. Is it possible to reject this principle? Certainly. Is it possible to carry on a serious, coherent inquiry into the human good without accepting some version of it? Probably not.

16. His discussion of courage in Book III is a case in point. For that matter, so is the *Ethics* as a whole. Aristotle begins with an outline or sketch and then gradually fills in the details. He describes this approach and argues for its naturalness in Book I, chapter one of the *Physics*.

17. The argument as well as the language of this passage closely parallels Aristotle's discussion of the soul in *De Anima*. For a list of relevant passages, see Stewart, 1:98-99. In "The Metaphysical and Psychological Basis of Aristotle's *Ethics*" in *Essays*, 35-53, T. H. Irwin takes this to mean that Aristotle's "ethical theory" depends, not only on "ordinary language and ordinary beliefs," but on the view of the soul that he works out in *De Anima*. Cf. also Wilkes, 343, in *Essays*: "Hence a reading of the account of human psychology in the *De Anima* is essential to a proper understanding of this argument." I think one need not go this far. A reading of *De Anima* would surely help one to appreciate the force and reasonableness of Aristotle's derivation in chapter seven, but I believe its argument is intelligible on its own terms. It presupposes nothing more than a willingness on the part of the reader to reflect on his everyday experience of living things.

18. See 1118a23-32 where Aristotle claims that the pleasures with which moderation and immoderation are concerned, that is, the pleasures associated with eating, drinking and sexual intercourse, are common to other animals and ultimately based on touch. Cf. also *De Anima* 413b5: "Of sensation, touch belongs first to all [animals]."

19. See *De Anima* 415a24-415b2.

20. For "the life of cattle" as an image of the life devoted to the pursuit of bodily pleasures, see Plato *Republic* 586a and Heraclitus fr.4.
21. See Broadie, 26.
22. The word I have translated as "active" here (and earlier in the phrase "active life" in chapter seven) is related to the noun *praxis*, action—to be *praktikos* is to be up to and ready for *praxis*—but not related to the noun *energeia*, activity or being at work. Every genuine *praxis* is a form of *energeia*, but not every *energeia* is a form of *praxis*—a distinction that will prove to be crucial later on.
23. Not to mention that—as so many of those who seek the elixir of immortal fame in political life have discovered to their chagrin—the public giveth and the public taketh away.
24. I am assuming here that the understanding of human life that belongs to those who engage in politics is a species of the natural understanding. Aristotle provides reasons for this assumption in the *Politics* (1252b28–1253a20).
25. Cf. *Politics* 1253a11–18.
26. In what follows I will generally translate *logos* as reason. The reader should beware, however, of construing the meaning of this all-important term too narrowly, as, say, a power of inference. *Logos* can mean thought, sentence, judgment, definition, account, argument, and even ratio. All of these meaning are related more or less directly to its most basic, everyday meaning, speech or the power of speech, and its root-meaning, gathering or collection.
27. Note that the analogy through which Aristotle arrives at his definition suggests that virtue is, or is at least akin to, an art: here in chapter seven virtue looks like the art (*technē*) of being human.
28. This meaning of virtue accords well with its most likely etymology. *Aretē* is related to the verb *arariskō*, to join or fasten together, to fit up or be fitted up for a certain task. *Harmonia*, a fitting together of tones in a certain way to form a scale, is another word related to *arariskō*. To have virtue is simply to be fit, to be well-equipped, to be in the right shape, for the work at hand. It is to be attuned to a certain situation and ready to respond to it.
29. Cf. Plato *Republic* 353b2–e5. The question I am raising here is presumably the same question that leaves Thrasymachus—and perhaps Socrates as well—dissatisfied at the conclusion of Book I. Why should he believe that justice, that is, justice as most men understand it, is the virtue that allows men to be at work well?
30. Cf. Broadie, 39.
31. For the three ways of life, see Plato *Republic* 581. Gauthier and Jolif, 2:30, note one important difference between the two passages. In Socrates' account the three ways or "three tribes of human beings" are, as it were, deduced from the tripartite division of the soul; in Aristotle's account they are the primary "fact of experience" *from* which he reasons. Another important difference is that in the Socratic account different pleasures are associated with each tribe or each part of the soul; hence the lowest type of human being is not called a lover of pleasure, but a lover of gain (*philokerdēs*). Given that Aristotle is clearly aware of the Socratic account, it seems reasonable to wonder whether his transformation of it is deliberate. Is he intentionally giving short shrift to pleasure, shunting it aside in Book I in much the same way as he does reason? If so, his way of proceeding would be fully in keeping with Socrates' own. In the *Republic*, too, pleasure (and *erōs*) only comes into its own in the final books.

32. Put otherwise: The careful reader begins wondering, as early as Book I, whether political life or the ethical life is a mean between the "bestial" life of the Sardana-pollist and the somehow divine life of the lover of wisdom.

33. Even his defense of virtue in chapter eight turns into a defense of activity, presumably because of his opposition to the "Academic" or Platonic identification of virtue with happiness (1098b30–1099a7). See Burnet's comment on the passage (p. 42).

34. See, for instance, I.1, II.1–4, VII.11–14, and X.1–5.

35. See Aristotle's account of pleasure in Books VII and X, where, as I noted earlier, he comes close to identifying pleasure with activity. That Aristotle ultimately refuses to do so does not detract from the point. Those who identify happiness with pleasure may simply mistake what lies at the fringe of their desire, that is, the pleasures that accompany eating, drinking, and sex, for the true object of their desire, that is, those activities themselves.

36. The possible exceptions are not, I think, books like the *Metaphysics* and *Physics*, "abstract" as they may seem at first reading, but the zoological works, which clearly presuppose a more detailed knowledge of living things than most of us possess. Yet even there, in works like the *History of Animals* or the *Parts of Animals*, Aristotle's primary intent seems to be to describe, order, and account for what *we would see* if we paid closer attention to things that for the most part occupy the background of our ordinary experience.

37. Once again, then, I must disagree with Irwin, who argues in "'The Metaphysical and Psychological Basis" that the *Ethics* ultimately depends on principles not found in it but in the *Metaphysics*: "the starting point of ethics is a feature of human agents which is part of their soul and essence, as understood in Aristotle's general theory of substance" (p. 50). Irwin is certainly right to suggest that the *Metaphysics* can shed light on the *Ethics*. But it can, only because the understanding that forms the starting point of the *Ethics* itself contains a kind of "metaphysics" of human things, that is, because the commonsense understanding of human things and human happiness is of a piece with the commonsense understanding of the world "at large" that Aristotle articulates in the *Metaphysics*.

38. Also *Metaphysics* 1025b7–10.

39. *De Anima* 412a1–6; 28–29.

40. See *Metaphysics* 998b 22–27.

41. Cf. Joe Sachs, "An Outline of the Argument of Aristotle's *Metaphysics*," *St. John's Review* 32.3 (1981): 41. The following discussion owes much to this and another essay by Sachs, "Aristotle's Definition of Motion," *The College* 27.4 (1976). I am also deeply indebted—here and elsewhere—to Klein's very fine essay "Aristotle, an Introduction" in *Lectures and Essays*, 171–195.

42. For an account of the difference between equivocal (or "homonymous") and uni-vocal (or "synonymous") predication, see chapter one of the *Categories*. For an account of the defining characteristics of the most important categories, see chapters five through nine of the same work. A question I will ask later is whether the many virtues are one in just this (limited) sense. Are some conditions of soul virtues only insofar as they tend to produce or preserve or otherwise make possible other conditions more properly called virtues?

43. *Metaphysics* 1028b8–13; 1029a33–b12. By "primary" here I mean first, in the sense of "first for us." For one of the questions Aristotle raises in the opening chapters of Book VII is whether there are *ousiai* that are not bodies, and his answer, given in Book XII, suggests that natural bodies are ultimately to be regarded as second-

ary *ousiai*. Works of art are at best tertiary *ousiai*; their identities depend wholly on those who use them. An empty Coke can becomes an ashtray in the twinkling of an eye; one man's book is another man's doorstop.

44. See, e.g., 1029a27–30.
45. Cf. Sachs, "Aristotle's Definition of Motion," 13–14.
46. For the meaning of *hexis*, see Aristotle's "lexicon" of fundamental terms in Book V of the *Metaphysics*. A *hexis* is a peculiar kind of *diathesis* or arrangement, one that disposes something well or badly; *diathesis* is in turn defined as an "ordering of that which has parts either according to place or potentiality or form" (1022bl–14). This suggests that virtue is to be understood as that order or ordering (*taxis*) of the parts of the soul which makes possible its good or being at work well and which, for this very reason, cannot be *identified* with that good. Cf. also Aristotle's first attempt at a definition of (ethical) virtue in Book II (1105b25–28).

2 ‖ Magnanimity and Justice

1. 109410–1095a3; 1095a31–b13; 1098a20–b8. I say "at least" not only because in the *Ethics* it is often difficult to disentangle inquiry and reflection on inquiry but also because it's difficult to know whether to include Aristotle's critique of the Good in I.6 with these "pauses." In other cases, Aristotle is working out details, thinking through how best to carry out the inquiry. I.6 serves a different, quasi-transcendental purpose. It clears the way for Aristotle's pursuit of the good: Through an ordered series of abbreviated dialectical arguments, Aristotle establishes the very possibility of an *a posteriori* inquiry such as the *Ethics*. By arguing that there is no univocal, cross-categorical meaning of good, that there is no single meaning even if the good is taken narrowly to mean what is good "in itself," and that even if there were a universal good, knowledge of it wouldn't be useful, Aristotle moves his readers away from the opinion that the good is "something great and beyond us" and prepares them for the focused inquiry that begins immediately afterwards in chapter seven (1096a23–34; 1096b8–26; 1096b32–1097a14; 1095a25–26). I.6 also serves other purposes. It introduces us to the thought that there might be a connection between being and the good (1096a19–28)—a connection I explore in my discussion of activity in chapter one. And it provides us with an important first glimpse of philosophic friendship and the principles that govern it (1096a11–17)—an issue I'll take up later in chapter four.
2. See also 1098a33–b2.
3. For a useful discussion of these and other passages in Aristotle's works where Aristotle emphasizes the peculiar character of his intended audience, see Burnet, xxxi–xxxiv. For a useful discussion of the intended audience of the *Ethics* in particular, see Tessitore, 15–20.
4. A *meth-odos* is literally a way-after. It is a going after something, a pursuit, an inquiry—a particular path, leading in a particular direction, toward a particular object.
5. See also Aristotle's prefatory remarks in the *Physics* 184a10–b5 and *De Anima* 402a12–23. There are, to be sure, certain features common to every sort of inquiry, and Aristotle discusses them at length in the *Topics*. But it is one thing to say this and another to say that there can be a universal method, separable from and applicable to any subject matter. Descartes' conviction that such a method exists, that the paradigm for it is to be found in mathematical analysis, and that, as a conse-

quence, merely "probable" reasoning from opinion, from what seems to be the case, is to be rejected is expressed with great clarity in the opening chapters of the *Rules for the Direction of the Mind*. What this conviction amounts to in practice is that only those features of things, human as well as natural, which can be formulated in mathematical terms are treated as legitimate objects of inquiry. The study of natural things becomes mathematical physics, while students of human affairs lead lives of quiet desperation, hoping yet always failing to account for the variable richness of human life in terms of the latest mathematical or physical theories, e.g., statistical mechanics, game theory, catastrophe theory, and so on.

6. He does not, however, stop altogether. For instance, we find brief observations at the beginning of II.2, where Aristotle emphasizes the "practical" character of his inquiry, and at the beginning of II.7, where he reminds us that in the case of ethical (as opposed to mathematical, e.g.) inquiries, the more particular the *logos*, the truer, that is, the more precise, it is.

7. Put in a slightly different way: Aristotle's discussion of magnanimity allows us to see a meaning of the word *hexis* that is not so apparent elsewhere. *Hexis* is an action word built on the future root of the verb *echō* (have, hold) in its intransitive meaning (hold on, remain, be in a certain condition). A *hexis* is a particular readiness for a particular activity; it is, as it were, that activity "on hold." But a *hexis* is also a way of carrying oneself, an attitude toward the world, an inner posture that shows itself in the smallest details—and this is the meaning that comes through here. Aristotle can present the man rather than the *hexis* in his account of magnanimity because the man—in the way he walks, talks, treats wealth and poverty, rich and poor, honor and dishonor—*is* the *hexis*.

8. What about the rest of us? Many of us have been brought up to believe that honor is certainly not the good ("Don't worry about what other people think!") and that virtues are obviously to be exercised for their own sake ("Virtue is its own reward!"). Our horizon is not that of Aristotle's intended audience, and accordingly we may find it difficult to take seriously the issue that Aristotle is thinking through here. But the case is not entirely hopeless. Literature (beginning with the *Iliad*) and political biography (beginning with Plutarch) can help us to feel our way into the situation of the cultivated and active. Or we can look around and inside ourselves. Almost all of us live to some degree in the eyes of others. We are pleased when our opinions (or books) are well received, especially when the people who receive them are in a position to understand them. We are hurt or offended when our views are ignored or willfully misunderstood. We admire people who carry on in spite of everything, and are not surprised to see people in show business collapse in the face of either great success or bad reviews. We may not chime in with the recently-crowned Prince Hal when he says, "If it be a sin to covet honor, I am the most offending soul alive"—but all the elements we need to understand what's at stake in Aristotle's treatment of honor and the great-souled man are there in our everyday experience, if in a slightly altered form.

9. See Aristotle's discussion of courage and *thumos* in III.8, especially 1116b30–1117a5.

10. A passage at the beginning of Book II about moral virtue and habituation makes this point beautifully: "The virtues come to be within us neither by nature nor against nature, but instead [come to be] within us who are of a nature to receive them and who are completed by habit" (1103a23–26).

11. See Aristotle's characterization of the genus that includes virtue and vice: "Dispositions (*hexeis*) are those things in accordance with which we hold well (*echomen eu*)

or badly with respect to passions . . ." (1105b24–26). Courage is neither fearlessness nor a feeling of confidence in the face of extreme danger. It is fearing (and being confident) in its proper shape. To be more precise, it is the shape or ordering of soul that puts (or rather *is*) the well in fearing well.

12. Thus Aristotle claims at the outset of his account of moderation that courage and moderation are the virtues of "the irrational (*a-logon*) parts" of the soul, that is, *epithumia* and *thumos* (1117b23–24). See also his account of the virtues and passions associated with different stages of life in the *Rhetoric* II.12–14. There Aristotle suggests that courage and moderation are, for different reasons, "youthful" virtues. The young are naturally courageous and naturally inclined to immoderation; hence both their *thumos* and *epithumia* are in need of being checked and balanced.

13. Consider, for instance, the definitions of *agathos* and *aretē* in Richard Cunliffe, *A Lexicon of the Homeric Dialect* (Norman: Univ. of Oklahoma Press, 1963).

14. Perhaps it would be more precise to say that courage is *the* virtue in the *Iliad* and moderation *the* virtue in the *Odyssey*. At any rate, courage seems to be the distinguishing feature of Achilles' character, while *sōphrosynē*, in the broad as well as narrow sense of the term, is Odysseus' defining trait.

15. See his encounters with the Laistrygones as well as the Cyclopes and Skylla (Homer *Odyssey* IX 231–374; X 80–132; XII 222–59).

16. I am thinking here, not only of his companions' immoderate devouring of the cattle of Helios, but also of their initial encounter with Circe as well as the "Lotus-eaters" episode (IX 82–104; X 229–243; XII 260–402). Such details, taken together with the descriptions of the suitors, strongly suggest that if the *Odyssey* is "about" anything, it is about the importance of what might be called "right eating."

17. It is worth noting that Socrates, too, seems to think courage and moderation are "first for us" as human beings and citizens. See, for instance, his discussion of the education of the guardians in Plato *Republic* II–III, especially 374e–376c and 389d–e. In this respect, then, there seems to be no quarrel between philosophy and poetry.

18. If the relation of virtue to honor is *the* issue for his readers, why doesn't Aristotle put his discussion of magnanimity immediately after his accounts of courage and moderation? Why discuss generosity and magnificence before magnanimity? I can think of two answers to this question: First, Aristotle is ascending, in his presentation of the virtues, from the lowest to the highest forms of external goods, that is, from wealth used to help those in need (generosity) to wealth used to beautify or adorn life (magnificence) to honor, "the greatest of external goods" (magnanimity). Second, by placing magnanimity where he does, Aristotle underscores its importance and points to the passion that forms its natural basis. Thus if we regard the three unnamed virtues discussed at the end of Book IV as a unit—and Aristotle gives us every reason to—magnanimity turns out to be the central moral virtue. If, on the other hand, we take the moral virtues one by one, magnanimity, "right" love of honor, and "right" anger become the central virtues: a link between *orgē* or *thumos* and *philotimia* is suggested.

19. See Burnet, 178–87 and H. H. Joachim, *Aristotle: The Nicomachean Ethics*, ed. D. A. Rees (Oxford: Clarendon, 1951), 124–25. For a very helpful discussion of this issue and the whole account of magnanimity, see Tessitore, pp. 28–35.

20. Perhaps this is the appropriate place to mention a time-honored controversy concerning the meaning of magnanimity, exponents of which include Gauthier and Jolif, and Harry V. Jaffa, *Thomism and Aristotelianism: A Study of the Commentary by Thomas Aquinas on the Nicomachean Ethics* (Westport, Ct.: Greenwood

Press, 1979). Jaffa argues—as does Burnet (179)—that magnanimity does not represent Aristotle's last word on the subject of complete virtue: together with justice, it represents the peak of the active life. Thus, although one can perhaps speak of the magnanimity of the philosopher, Aristotle's portrait of the magnanimous man is in the first instance a picture of the complete "man of action" (121–23; 141). (See also Tessitore, 34.) Gauthier and Jolif disagree. Rejecting Jaffa's view explicitly, and following Stewart and others, they treat Aristotle's portrait as a description of the contemplative life. In the *Nicomachean* as opposed to the *Eudemian Ethics*, they claim, Socrates is *the* prototype of the magnanimous man. See Gauthier and Jolif, 2:272–73 and Stewart, 1:335–37. It should be clear by now, and should become still clearer in the sequel, that my sympathies lie with Jaffa on this point. The same objections that Jaffa levels with devastating clarity against Thomas—he neglects the "developmental" or "dynamic" features of Aristotle's writings—can, I think, be leveled against Gauthier and Jolif (48–52; 67–69). In their desire to make Aristotle a "scientific" or "systematic" author, they systematically overlook the dramatic or dialectical character of the *Ethics*. Hence their attempt to conflate Aristotle's accounts of the contemplative and active ways of life.

21. Although *megalopsychos* never appears in the *Iliad* or *Odyssey*, it has clear Homeric antecedents. *Megalētor* (great-hearted) and *megathumos* (great-spirited) are everywhere used to describe the combination of touchiness and endurance that distinguishes Homer's heroes. See Cunliffe, 257–58, for their full range of meanings. That *megalopsychos* is Aristotle's "translation" of *megathumos* provides further support for the claim that *thumos* is *the* passion of the soul at issue in magnanimity. Cf. also the *Politics* 1327b36–1328a16, where Aristotle makes the connection perfectly clear. The passage should be compared with Socrates' discussion of the nature of the guardians in the *Republic* (especially 375c) on which it is a commentary.

22. Homer *Iliad* XI 595–614.

23. Homer *Iliad* XXIII (especially 532–62) and XXIV 471–676. That both the "higher" and "lower" forms of magnanimity are aspects of the everyday understanding of it is further suggested by *Posterior Analytics* 27b17–26. The "apathy" of Lysander and Socrates with respect to fortune and the unwillingness of Alcibiades, Achilles, and Aias to put up with dishonor are equally elements of its ordinary meaning. Cf. the remarks of Gauthier and Jolif, 2:273.

24. Burnet, p. 180, tells us that "[t]he literal sense of this word is 'gaping.' It is then applied to anything porous, spongy or loose (Liddell and Scott) as for instance snow." Porous and spongy are just right. The vain man, like snow, presents the appearance of solidity, but caves in at the slightest pressure; his "look" belies the hollowness of his character (1125a27–32). The magnanimous man, by contrast, is solid, three dimensional, as it were. His greatness consists, at least in part, in the *depth* of soul that allows him to endure, to remain himself, in the face of changing circumstances.

25. "Pan" can also be taken adverbially. In this case the adjective would mean "altogether complete."

26. Thus *periaptos* (translated by Ross as "adventitious charm") is used in Book I to describe the relation of sensual pleasures to happiness, in contrast to those "natural" pleasures that the life of virtuous activity possesses "in itself" (1099a11–16).

27. I must disagree, then, with Burnet (182) who insists that *kosmos tōn aretōn* means "[s]imply 'an adornment of goodness.'" It surely means this, but the meaning points

beyond itself. Magnanimity adorns or makes beautiful the remaining moral virtues by making them and their possessor whole—at any rate, this is the thought experiment Aristotle is playing out in Book IV.3.

28. Jaffa takes this passage seriously and contrasts it with Aristotle's accounts of the gods and the friendship of the good in Books IX and X (139–41). Gauthier and Jolif admit that it poses difficulties for their interpretation of magnanimity, and then refer us to Book IX for Aristotle's true view (2:287). In effect, they concede that there are, in fact, discrepancies between Aristotle's account of magnanimity and his account of friendship—a scant eight pages after they criticize Jaffa for making just this point (2:278–79).

29. Hence our admiration for Achilles. His noble anger at Agammemnon is rooted in his desire to have *to kalon*, his inner nobility, be *kalon*, be beautiful in the eyes of the world. The terrible price that must be paid for the satisfaction of this desire is disclosed to us in Book XVIII of the *Iliad*. Achilles becomes fully—and literally—luminous only in his moment of greatest agony, when, having at once lost and destroyed his dearest friend, he stands naked before both armies and thus gains the day for the Greeks (202–38). The alternative to this demand for full disclosure is represented by Homer in the person of Odysseus. Odysseus succeeds because he is willing to appear other—and often less—than he is. He calls himself "no one" to escape from the Cyclopes (*Odyssey* IX 360–408). And in contrast to the youthful Telemachos, who longs to see his father arrive in a blaze of glory, he knows that if he is to be a king once again he must first play the beggar (I 113–17).

30. It seems to be, at any rate. Burnet (206) and Stewart (382–84) both point out that Aristotle later calls the various meanings of justice "synonyms" (1130a33). Burnet takes this to mean that Aristotle is here using "homonym" in a loose sense, to mean simply "sharing the same name." I think it more likely that Aristotle is imitating the natural path of understanding. We begin in confusion, then see only the different meanings of justice, and then, in turn, see the connections between those meanings. But ultimately, I suspect, justice is neither a synonym nor homonym. Instead, like "being," it is a word with several irreducible but related meanings. And as is the case with so many of Aristotle's key terms in the *Ethics*, it is a word the full and central meaning of which becomes apparent only in the latter part of Aristotle's inquiry—in this case, in his discussion of friendship in Books VIII and IX. Cf. Stewart, 385.

31. The most persuasive accounts of Aristotle's discussion that I know of are those of Jaffa (167–88) and Leo Strauss, *Natural Right and History* (Chicago: Univ. of Chicago Press, 1950), 156–63.

32. For definitions of ratio (*logos*), sameness of ratios, and proportional (*analogon*), see Euclid, *Elements* Book V, Defs. 3, 5, and 6. For definitions and mathematical justifications of the "operations" employed by Aristotle in the argument—*alternando* and *componendo*—see Book V, Defs. 12 and 14; Props. 16 and 18. It is perhaps worth noting that Aristotle violates strict mathematical procedure in drawing his conclusions. He compares and then compounds persons and goods (1131a27–b17). But, according to Euclid, only homogeneous magnitudes can be said to "have a ratio" to one another (V, Defs. 3–4). Could Aristotle be suggesting that, even at the most basic level, there is something problematic about the attempt to "mathematicize" justice? Cf. Berns, op. cit., 10–13.

33. Cf. Burnet, 218.

34. Thus Burnet remarks that, in speaking about whole justice, Aristotle "is only clearing the ground as usual by narrowing the application of the word" (206). According to Burnet, then, the connection between whole and partial justice is "a mere accident of the Greek language, and we should not erect the distinction between 'universal and particular injustice' into a part of Aristotle's system" (206).

35. See Hobbes, *Leviathan*, chapter 30: "For the use of laws, which are but rules authorized, is not to bind the people from all voluntary actions; but to direct and keep them in such a motion, as not to hurt themselves by their own impetuous desires, rashness or indiscretion; as hedges are set, not to stop travellers, but to keep them in their way." Locke picks up on Hobbes' image in *The Second Treatise of Government*, para. 222: "The Reason why Men enter into Society, is the preservation of their Property; and the end why they chuse and authorize a Legislative, is, that there may be Laws made, and Rules set as Guards and Fences to the Properties of all the Members of the Society, to limit the Power, and moderate the Dominion of every Part and Member of the Society." In the case of Hobbes, at any rate, this view of the law seems to be part and parcel of his outright denial of Aristotle's initial hypothesis: "To which end we are to consider, that the Felicity of this life, consisteth not in the repose of a mind satisfied. For there is no such *Finis ultimus* (utmost ayme) nor *Summum Bonum* (greatest Good) as is spoken of in the Books of the old Morall Philosophers" (*Leviathan*, chap. 11).

36. On this point and the contrast between "our" understanding of law and Aristotle's, see Tessitore, 35–36.

37. In fact we get an instance of this in Book XXIII of the *Iliad*. The same touchiness about honor that erupts in Book I and sets the whole drama in motion still simmers just below the surface at the funeral games for Patroklos in Book XXIII. In quick succession we see quarrels begin to break out between Idomeneus and lesser Aias, and Menelaos and Antilochos. It is Achilles who saves the day through a combination of skillful speech and even more skillful apportioning of prizes and honors: Achilles accomplishes in Book XXIII what poor Nestor could not in Book I. Achilles' accomplishment rests on two things: 1) He at long last occupies the position of authority that should always have been his "by nature"; and 2) His own honor is no longer at stake; the man of complete virtue has, as it were, taken himself out of the equation. Achilles can be generous and just because he no longer cares.

38. But see Berns, 13.

39. For the mathematical meaning of "incommensurable," which Aristotle is clearly playing on in these passages, see Euclid X, Def. 1. Another name for incommensurable magnitudes, that is, magnitudes that have no common part or share (*meros*), is "irrational" (*a-loga*). The perplexing discovery that there are irrational or incommensurable magnitudes was one of the great achievements of Greek mathematics. The discovery that a *logos* of such magnitudes could nevertheless be given, that the ratios or relations between them could be understood, was another. I think the argument of the *Ethics* parallels these two discoveries. In its first half, the incommensurability of complete virtue and the everyday understanding of virtue is quietly disclosed. In the second, we are shown—again quietly—how they can nevertheless be said to belong together, to, as it were, "have a *logos*" to one another.

40. See Tessitore, 40–41. Aristotle's account of equity survives, albeit in a somewhat altered form, in Locke's teaching on "prerogative" (*The Second Treatise*, chap. 14).

3 || **Prudence and Wisdom**

1. Thus Aristotle notes that "[happiness] seems to be virtue to some men, prudence to others, a sort of wisdom to others, while to others [it is] these things or some one of these things with pleasure or not without pleasure; and others bring in external prosperity" (1098b23–26). He then discusses all the items on this list *except* prudence and wisdom. As in the case of his definition of happiness in chapter seven, reason is conspicuously absent in chapter eight.

2. See Plato *Phaedo* 99e, where Socrates speaks of his decision to "take refuge in *logoi*." Gauthier and Jolif also see in the passage an ironic allusion to the *Charmides* 157a (2:131). Of course Aristotle is doing in the *Ethics* precisely what Socrates is advocating in the *Phaedo*—thinking about the good by thinking through what people say about it. Here he is objecting to those who take Socrates' turn to *logoi* as an excuse for idle talk. Not those who philosophize, but those who don't take philosophy and the consequences of philosophy seriously enough are his real target. Hence the word "imagine."

3. For instance, Aristotle discusses deliberation in the course of an attempt to define choice, while choice in turn is discussed only because it forms part of the definition of ethical virtue. That the rationality of the ethical life is an ongoing issue for commentators on the *Ethics*, that, for instance, Richard Sorabji must go to such lengths to argue that "the role given to practical wisdom in Book 6 represents no change of direction and should come as no surprise," is itself evidence that a surprising change of direction takes place in Book VI ("Aristotle on the Role of Intellect in Virtue" in *Essays*, 218).

4. I am not suggesting that the argument sketched out in the preceding paragraph—which corresponds roughly to the account given by Sorabji and others—is false, but rather incomplete. To use Jaffa's terms, it emphasizes the architecture of the *Ethics* at the expense of its developmental or dynamical features. See Sorabji in *Essays*, especially 218.

5. The phrase "law unto himself" in fact turns up in Aristotle's account of the witty man who knows better than to make fun of everything (1128a30–33).

6. Aristotle touches on these issues a number of times in the *Politics*. In the lead-up to his discussion of the *pambasileus* in Book III, Aristotle entertains seriously the possibility of men so "outstanding in virtue" that they cannot be regarded as "part" of the city; such men "are themselves a law" and like god[s] among men—here the emphasis is on the incomparability or incommensurability of the greatest virtue and ordinary virtue (*Politics* 1284a3–17). In Book V the accent falls instead on equity: In the course of spelling out the root causes of political faction and revolt, Aristotle observes that men "outstanding in virtue" have the greatest right to stir up trouble but are least likely to do so (*Politics* 1301a39–b2). As befits the *Politics*, both the problem and its solutions—handing the city over to such men in the first case; such men not pressing their just claims in the second—are pitched at a somewhat lower level than in the *Ethics*: The possibility of a virtue and way of life that completely transcends political life, office, and honor is not broached—at least not in these passages. In his discussion of the best regime, Aristotle quietly points to this possibility in a variety of ways (*Politics* 1325b17–22; 1331a24–b1; 1331b12–13).

7. In what follows, I have chosen to translate "*epistēmē*" as "science." I do this not only because the alternative translation, "knowledge," seems somewhat too broad,

but because part of my point is that there is a fractured continuity between ancient *epistēmē* and modern *scientia*. The differences between them are very great, and I try to detail some of these in my notes, but the truth is that modern science was meant to develop, transform, and supplant ancient science all at once. Modern science, one might say, is the *Aufhebung* of ancient *epistēmē*, and depending on one's orientation, it will be seen as the preservation and elevation or destruction and suppression of the truth of its ancient counterpart.

8. My descriptions of scientists and mathematicians here apply primarily but not exclusively to ancient science. Some modern biologists still make it their business to identify and order new species of living things, others search for the at least semi-permanent molecular structures that underlie the manifold of pheno-types; even evolutionary biologists must grant in their thinking a kind of permanence to the properties and forms they try to account for. The final formulation of the fundamental (and in themselves unchanging) laws of nature—which Leibniz, for one, saw clearly were the modern replacement for substantial forms—remains the holy grail of modern physics. And mathematicians today are no less concerned with the changeless features of their objects of study than was Euclid. The real difference between ancient and modern science has to do, I suspect, with the character of those objects and the character of our thinking about them—not their permanence.

9. Burnet (253) traces this argument from kinds of beings to kinds of "faculties" or "powers" of the soul back to Socrates' distinction between knowledge (*epistēmē*) and opinion (*doxa*) in Plato *Republic* 476d–480a. Stewart traces its still more ancient roots in Empedocles and others, and summarizes Aristotle's own critique of the vulgar formulations of the principle in *De Anima*, Book I (2:11–15). In Book III of *De Anima*, Aristotle himself provides the starkest formulation imaginable of the kinship between knower and known: Knowing (*noein*) is a matter of becoming, or rather *being*, the object of knowledge, and the possibility of its occurrence rests on the intellect's being nothing but the pure potency to be, the pure receptivity for, the form of what it knows (429a10–24). To say that the man who knows geometry *is* geometry may sound ridiculous to our ears—and yet we say, without thinking about it much, that a person who really knows something knows it "from the inside out."

10. As Burnet (253) points out, there is something curious about this way of naming the parts of the "rational" soul. Given that Aristotle's division is based on Socrates' distinction between opinion and knowledge, one might expect Aristotle to call the "lower" half *to doxastikon*—as he does at 1140b26. Instead he gives it the name—*to logistikon*—that Socrates gives to the highest part of the soul in the *Republic*. Could Aristotle be reminding us, even as he begins to make the argument for a trans-practical virtue, that practical reason and the cognitive power it completes are not to be treated lightly?

11. That these five dispositions are being presented by Aristotle as *candidates* for intellectual virtue and not as intellectual virtues is made clear at 1143b14–17. I have difficulty, then, understanding what—apart from a desire to have Aristotle contradict himself—could ever have led some commentators to think otherwise. See the apt comments of Stewart (2:32–33), Burnet (257), and Gauthier and Jolif (3:450–52). Because the usual translations of these terms are among the most "loaded" of all Aristotelian translations, I shall for the most part transliterate them in the remainder of the chapter.

NOTES TO PAGES 96–98   **183**

12. Or at any rate this is Aristotle's claim here, in the *Posterior Analytics* (71b9–17), and elsewhere. The pre-philosophic meaning of *epistasthai* is not quite so clear-cut. In Homer, for instance, it seems to mean—as does the conditional form of the French *"savoir"*—"to know how to do something" or simply "to be able": *epistēmē* and *technē* are virtually indistinguishable. Yet even here a link with Aristotle's claim is perhaps discernable. The Homeric artisan or warrior or statesman *is* able because he knows "what counts," because he possesses an enduring knowledge of the enduring features of the "stuff" he works with. In other words, one can argue that Aristotle—like Plato or Socrates before him—is simply making visible what is already present in the everyday understanding of *epistasthai*.

13. One way to get at Aristotle's notion of induction is to read the final chapter of the *Posterior Analytics*, especially 99b33–100b4. Another way is to reflect on what is going on in most of Aristotle's works when he thinks through a problem by reflecting on experience and opinion. A third way is to read the opening chapter of the *Physics* and ask oneself how it is that small children learn to recognize (quickly and unerringly) cats as cats and dogs as dogs.

14. *Apodeixis* is the word commonly used for mathematical demonstration (and demonstration is a literal translation of it). But we should beware, I think, of picturing Aristotle's knower as someone who commands an ordered body of propositions (à la Euclid's *Elements*) that he can both parade at will and hand on to others if necessary. For one thing, there are apparently non-mathematical *epistēmai*. For another, an *epistēmē* is a *hexis*, a condition of soul, and conditions of soul can neither be paraded nor handed over to others. Perhaps it would be more helpful to picture the knower as someone who has taken up residence within a territory the boundaries of which he knows very well and parts of which he has explored thoroughly—thoroughly enough so that he can get from place to place without too much difficulty. Teaching, according to this image, would involve helping others to take up residence within the same territory—showing them the lay of the land (always with reference ultimately to the boundaries of the territory), showing them where the really interesting or really beautiful or really dangerous places are, and perhaps in the end exploring with them some as yet unexplored sub-regions.

15. In Homer, for instance, *noein* often simply means "to see" or "to perceive" with the eyes. Cf. Cunliffe, 280–81. Its philosophic meaning—seeing purely with the "mind's eye" what can be laid hold of in no other way—can be gathered from Plato *Republic* 510b–511c, where Socrates assigns *noēsis* to the highest part of the divided line. Between these two extremes lies a whole range of meanings, present in Homer and elsewhere, all of which, however, are concerned in one way or another with directness of apprehension. Is the relative importance given to seeing perhaps what chiefly distinguishes ancient *theōria* from modern theory? Aristotle's insistence that anything worthy of the name of science be grounded in the apprehension of elementary noetic structures and the contrary emphasis in modern mathematics (and the mathematical sciences) on formalization and formal reasoning (not to mention the sheer difficulty of following and making sense of so much of the latter) might lead us to think so. And yet we cannot forget that modern science-and-mathematics (more or less) begins with Descartes' demand that knowledge be founded on clear and distinct ideas and that its progress is marked by periodic attempts to return to beginnings and clarify basic principles and insights. (Maxwell, Dedekind, Mach, Einstein, and Bohr are a few of the names that come to mind.) Once again, I sus-

pect, the issue is not "seeing" as such, but the way seeing and the object of sight are conceived.

16. See Stewart's helpful note on the everyday meanings of *sophos* (2:54). See also the opening chapters of the *Metaphysics*, where Aristotle derives the "proper" meaning of *sophia* from ordinary usage (980a21–983a23).

17. *Ta mathematika* are literally "things that can be learned or understood." That Aristotle regards them as such is evidenced by the *Posterior Analytics*: the chief examples of rigorous demonstration (*apodeixis*) in that book are taken from mathematics and the physical sciences most closely allied with mathematics, that is, optics and astronomy.

18. It seems reasonable to ask at this point how *sophia* can be characterized both by the dignity *and* the universality of its objects. How can the wise man be said to know all things *and* to know the highest things? The path of Aristotle's inquiry in the *Metaphysics* suggests an answer. As we saw earlier, it begins as an inquiry into being as being and gradually becomes (in Books VII through IX) an inquiry into the being of *ousiai*, that is, the being of things, especially natural things. But Aristotle does not stop there. In Books X through XII, his inquiry into being becomes a search for the first cause or source of unity and change in things. Ontology becomes theology; first philosophy is transformed from an inquiry into what is first for us into an inquiry into what is first simply.

19. For an interesting account of the history of the meaning of *phronimos* and *phronēsis*, see Gauthier and Jolif, 3:463–69.

20. The word I've translated as "definitions" here is *horoi*. It can also mean "terms," as in "the terms of a discourse." (*Horos*, related to our word horizon, originally meant boundary marker or boundary—something used to mark off one field or region from another.) In Aristotle (and in Euclid) *horoi* in both senses establish the outer limits of a given intellectual discipline; they disclose the characteristic shape of a given mode of inquiry. Curiously enough, Euclid not only includes a definition of *horos*—"A *horos* is that which is an extremity (or limit) of anything"—among his *horoi*, but also implicitly uses it everywhere in his definitions of geometrical objects. All geometrical objects—lines, circles, squares, cubes, spheres and so on—are contained by or limited by *horoi*.

21. According to Gauthier and Jolif (3:469–70), Aristotle's emphasis on the wholeness of *phronēsis* in contrast to the arts "is inspired" by Socrates' definition of *sophia* in the *Republic* 428b–d.

22. See Klein's "The World of Physics and the Natural World" in *Lectures and Essays* for a detailed account of this fundamental difference between ancient and modern mathematics (1–34). According to Klein, ancient science is not "wholly bound up with universals" in the same sense as modern science. Ancient science lives within the tension between universal and particular. It employs general methods to make universal claims about particular objects. It has its eye on the universal but always keeps the particular in view. Modern mathematics and science, on the other hand, succeed by eliminating or making themselves oblivious to that tension. Their objects are self-generated generalities that are nevertheless taken to be concrete entities. To my mind, Klein gets it just right. He helps us to understand why the characteristic move in mathematics and physics is always in the direction of the general case; why algebraic structures and operations become a central topic of mathematical investigation; why we tend to speak with such casual confidence

of, say, energy or life as a something that takes on many forms; why we will always be tempted to think of electrons, protons, and the like as beings rather than mathematical fictions; and finally, why there is always something peculiar about modern attempts to recover basic insights. Seeing in such cases is very nearly the opposite of what Aristotle means by *noein*: What gets seen in such cases is always our own symbol-generating activity. The opening pages of two of Dedekind's essays, "Continuity and Irrational Numbers" and "The Nature and Meaning of Numbers," provide a wonderful illustration of this point.

23. This point has been a matter of some dispute among commentators on Aristotle. Sorabji (207–8) and Gauthier and Jolif (1:28–29; 3:563–72), in particular, are dissatisfied with the limited role which this interpretation assigns to practical reason. They want *phronēsis* to include a "rational apprehension" (Sorabji) or "connaisance" (Gauthier and Jolif) of the end of human life. As will become clear in the following section, I am in some sympathy with this view. But one must be careful to keep separate those passages in the *Ethics*, e.g., Book III, where Aristotle is describing the day to day workings of "ordinary" *phronēsis* and those passages where he points to the existence of an "extraordinary," somehow theoretical *phronēsis*. One must beware, in other words, of "thomisticizing" Aristotle, i.e., of supposing that, in Aristotle's view, ordinary reasoning about ethical matters and theoretical reasoning are formally or structurally identical. Cf. Jaffa's critique of Thomas's teaching on natural right and natural law (167–84).

24. Of course someone might say—Hegel would certainly say—that insofar as the prudent man employs *logos* in the course of his deliberating (and he does so by definition) he involves himself with the universal. (See the "Sense-Certainty" discussion in the *Phenomenology*.) But that is not the issue. The question is whether the prudent man must invoke universal principles in the course of sorting out what to do here and now.

25. This discussion should be compared with the discussion of the movement from experience to art to architectonic art in the first chapter of the *Metaphysics* (980b26–981b7).

26. Stewart provides a helpful diagram of this difficult passage (2:64). In his equally useful commentary on it, he notes that nearly the same division of political labor is to be found in the *Politics* 1297b37, and that there the verb *theōrein* is used to describe the "architectonic" activity of the legislator.

27. Even here, of course, it might be argued that there is some room for universal or quasi-universal reasoning, perhaps especially in judicial argument. As Burnet points out, one can imagine *nomoi* functioning as major premises in certain forms of political argument (270). I agree and suspect Aristotle would agree, too. But it looks as if Aristotle's point here is just the opposite—in the course of daily life within the city, political discussion which *could* be put into syllogistic form is not, but remains at the level of the particular. *Nomoi* that are "in themselves" universal are chiefly present *in* the particular habits and desires of its citizens, and when they are articulated, they generally take the form of particular maxims or examples. Cf. the *Rhetoric* 1418a1–5, where Aristotle claims that arguments from example, that is, from particular instance to particular instance, are best suited to deliberative speech.

28. Thus I take it that Aristotle would regard men like Madison and Jefferson, Marshall and Lincoln as our legislators in the strict sense of the term. Laws passed by Con-

gress would, by contrast, fall into the category of *psēphismata*, i.e., propositions voted upon or decrees. See Liddell and Scott on *psēphisma*, and Burnet's note, 270–71.

29. I use comparatives here to suggest that what I have been calling kinds of prudence are probably more like end-points of a spectrum. In the daily course of our own lives, we are guided for the most part by *who* we are, i.e., by our particular virtues and vices; insofar as we deliberate, we do so within the horizon established by our characters and characteristic desires and aversions. But in times of crisis, the larger questions that generally hover in the background, haunting our dreams but never making into the light of day, begin to make themselves felt and even heard. If we heed them, if we begin to reflect on them, then we are likely to begin moving along the spectrum in the direction of architectonic prudence. The same thing happens in public life. The great speeches we find in Thucydides provide a marvelous illustration of this point: The clash of fundamentally different ways of conceiving of political life—Thucydides calls his war "the greatest commotion"—forces out into the open, into *logos*, issues that ordinarily remain concealed. We can also see the same thing in our own history: Our greatest expressions of architectonic prudence come from the time of the founding and the Civil War. Think only of the Declaration of Independence (which even has the form of a syllogism), the Federalist Papers, and above all Lincoln's speeches.

30. Here, for instance, are four examples of *universal* propositions concerning human things that I can imagine any potential "architect of the good" would need to keep in mind. Each one has been ripped from its context and naturally requires a certain amount of qualification: "Every art and every inquiry, and likewise action and choice, seems to aim at some good" (1094a1–2). "... the human good turns out to be an activity of the soul in accordance with virtue, and if the virtues are several, in accordance with the best and most complete one" (1098a16–18). "... man is by nature a political animal ..." (*Politics* 1253a1–5). "All men by nature desire to know" (*Metaphysics* 980a22).

31. The position I am articulating here corresponds to Aristotle's other answer to the question of whether *phronēsis* can be said to give orders to *sophia*. Likening *sophia* to health and using language that puts one in mind of his description of *technē*, Aristotle says that *phronēsis* does "not employ it [that is, *sophia*], but sees how it might come into being; it gives orders, then, for the sake of that, but not to that" (1145a6–9). This answer is not necessarily incompatible with the gods-to-politics analogy. The analogy may simply be intended to suggest that *within* a given soul *sophia* occupies a far higher place than *phronēsis*. I shall have more to say about this question in what follows.

32. I say "ultimately" because, as I have tried to make clear, "equitable," "magnanimous," "just," and "prudent" also retain their pre-philosophic meanings in the *Ethics*. This, in fact, is what makes Aristotle's book so difficult to read: Aristotle's attempt to preserve and simultaneously point beyond (or point through) the everyday meanings of such terms obliges the reader to exercise a kind of double vision at every moment.

4 ‖ Friendship and Happiness

1. Put slightly differently: Nothing in Aristotle's definition of happiness or in the "official" program of study he sets out at the end of Book I prepares us for his lengthy

account of self-restraint and unrestraint in Book VII—much less his much more lengthy account of friendship in Books VIII and IX (1102a5–14; 1103a4–11). (At least Aristotle mentions self-restraint and unrestraint in the course of setting out his program [1102b13–22]—he has said next to nothing about friendship in the first six books of the *Ethics*.) Why, then, does Aristotle spend nearly a tenth of the *Ethics* on self-restraint and related issues and a full fifth of the *Ethics* on friendship? One answer is surely that these subjects are of intrinsic, that is to say, "theoretical" interest. Anybody interested in "the philosophy of human things," anyone interested in reflecting on the peculiar being of human beings, will want to think about human frailty and perseverance, human friendship and love (1181b12–16). But I also think—and this will be my focus in the current chapter—that Aristotle's treatment of these topics, as well as his double treatment of pleasure, is meant to prepare us, quietly and indirectly, for the discussion we might expect to come right after Book VI, the discussion of contemplation and action that comes only in Book X.

2. In this way, Aristotle conceals his own understanding of a virtue that lies "beyond" the city beneath Homer's: Hector dies because he chooses to remain—literally—outside the walls of his city, against the advice of his father and friends. But Hector's transcendence of Troy—his attempt to become the new Achilles—is illusory. He chooses to stay outside because of his fear of dishonor; his "heroic virtue," his extraordinary courage, remains grounded in the ordinary understanding of the good citizen (*Iliad* XXII 37–130). Cf. also Aristotle's discussion of "political" courage, where he alludes to the passage in question (1116a17–29). It goes without saying that Aristotle's new beginning also returns us to the starting point of his own discussion of the particular virtues; heroic virtue and self-restraint appear, at any rate, to correspond respectively to a higher form of courage and a lower form of moderation.

3. I have nicked these translations of *enkrateia* and *akrasia* from Joe Sachs. The traditional translations, "continence" and "incontinence," come with their own set of problems, and in any case the "strain" in self-restraint captures very nicely the tension in the soul of the self-restrained man.

4. That is, it might be argued that although wisdom is higher than the ethical virtues, the ethical virtues are accessible to the ordinary run of men and hence deserve a place in the understanding of *human* happiness. Aristotle seems to be moving in this direction in Book I (1099b18–21). But by Book VII his perspective has shifted.

5. Thus I think it is no accident that Aristotle does not describe in any detail the process of reasoning from universals to particular actions until Book VII (1147a1–1147b5). As I have argued in the preceding chapter, the moderate man, whose desires are by definition well ordered, need not reason from universals; his (already) right desires inform and guide his deliberations. The self-restrained man, by contrast, cannot depend upon his desires to guide him. The war within his soul forces him to appeal to (universal) reason for guidance; he must, as it were, continually refound himself. I do not, of course, mean to suggest that this state of soul is better than the state of the moderate man's soul, but only that it prefigures a better state.

6. Let us recall that Aristotle derives these criteria in Book I from the everyday understanding of happiness. Thus Aristotle is not arguing in Book X that wisdom meets certain standards that only the wise man would accept as standards for happiness. Rather he is showing us that, although wisdom has no place in the ordinary understanding of happiness, it nevertheless meets the criteria supplied by that under-

standing to a greater degree than any of the ordinary virtues; he argues *from* the everyday understanding to a position that transcends it.
7. Cf. *Politics* 1253a25–29. The distinction between gods and beasts is, of course, also implicit in Aristotle's distinction between divine or heroic virtue and bestiality in the opening chapter of Book VII.
8. This is roughly the position adopted by Gauthier and Jolif (1:28–29) as well as Stewart (1:5). On the other hand, with the exception of Rorty, the authors in *Essays* who treat the question of *theōria* and *praxis* tend to shy away from Aristotle's claim in Book X that contemplation is the ultimate standard or measure for all human activity. Thus Nagel presents what he calls the "intellectualist" view of happiness as Aristotle's own but concludes his essay with various proposals for refuting it ("Aristotle on *Eudaimonia*," especially 7–8 and 13). Ackrill argues that the "intellectualist" view is not in fact Aristotle's, that according to Aristotle *theoria* is one among many activities that define a life as happy ("Aristotle on *Eudaimonia*"). And Wilkes argues that both the "intellectualist" and "inclusive" positions are to be found in the *Ethics*; the latter position is, however, in her view the correct one ("The Good Man and the Good for Man"). The tendency on the part of these authors to favor the life of action does not seem to stem—as one might expect it would—from a keen appreciation of the dignity of the ethical life but from an impoverished understanding of *theōria*. Cf. Wilkes, in particular, who seems to identify *theōria*, not with the *activity* of understanding some *thing*, but with mere "static" reflection on a "theory" one has constructed or one's solution to a problem (353). Rorty, by contrast, seems both to understand and to appreciate the force of Aristotle's defense of *theōria* in Book X; she, too, argues for an "inclusive" view of happiness but does not do so at the expense of *theōria* ("The Place of Contemplation in Aristotle's *Nicomachean Ethics*").
9. We also get two references to contemplation in the treatment of pleasure in Book VII at 1152b35–1153a2 and 1153a20–23. I take it that Aristotle partly introduces this multitude of references to the pleasures of contemplation and thought—which he does, by the way, without much fanfare—as part of his quiet preparation for the up and coming defense of contemplation.
10. I am thinking here partly of Aristotle's surprisingly spirited defense of pleasure in Books VII and X, and partly of the striking contrast between his straightforward yet generous accounting for why so many men are helpless in the face of bodily pleasure in Book VII and his spirited denunciation of pleasure-lovers back in Book I (1154a21–1154b16; 1095b19–22). The latter has always struck me as something of a pose—Aristotle adopting the posture of the "cultivated and active" man who denounces the life of pursuing pleasure partly as a way of elevating (and thus winning honor for) his own. Perhaps the serious man's life looks less serious—and the pleasure-lover's less frivolous and more interesting—when viewed *sub specie aeternitatis*?
11. Some bodily pleasures are natural in that they accompany the restoration of our bodies to their natural state or condition: Imagine drinking a cool glass of water after a long summer hike (1152b33–1153a2). Such pleasures are only "incidentally pleasant," since they are generally accompanied by pain and dim once the body is back in kilter (1153a2–5). Other pleasures are natural in a higher sense in that they are or accompany the unimpeded activity of the body already in its natural state: imagine suddenly and unexpectedly coming across the smell of freshly baked bread

during your summer hike (1173b15–19). In this case we have gain with no pain. Contemplation is a non-bodily example of the latter (1152b35–1153a2).

12. Kraut (178–82) argues that the wise man *qua* wise also needs the other ethical virtues (although, as he argues, this should not be taken to imply that they are mere tools for theoretical activity). As should become clear later on, I am sympathetic to this view, but on other grounds than those articulated by Kraut. His argument for courage makes some sense to me, the argument for generosity less sense, and even he has trouble making the argument for justice.

13. Or at any rate Aristotle virtually limits the discussion to this narrow territory. In VII.6 he briefly discusses lack of restraint with respect to anger and thus indicates the possibility of a much fuller and broader treatment of the subject.

14. For the distinction between the good life and (mere) life, see *Politics* 1252b28–31, 1278b18–31, 1280a31–b5, and 1280b30–35.

15. Broadie (370) lays out the problem very clearly: "If the *Nicomachean Ethics* had come down to us minus Chapters 7 and 8 of Book X, our overwhelming impression from the work would be that Aristotle means to define the essence of happiness in terms of morally virtuous activity informed by practical wisdom." Broadie's whole discussion of the issue merits careful study. The discussion of the meaning of *theōria* (401) and the account of the place of *theōria* in the *Eudemian Ethics* (383–89) are especially helpful. Chapters one and three of Kraut's book also contain an extended interpretation of X.7–8 that is well worth careful study. Kraut's primary target is the "inclusivist" thesis (as expressed above all by Ackrill). But even readers who have different principles of interpretation than Kraut and who are not particularly interested in that debate can learn much from Kraut's extremely intelligent and focused reading of the *Ethics*.

16. Cf. Stewart: "The city exists for the sake of its thinkers. A materially prosperous city without thinkers would be *ateles*, like the body without life. Political institutions and moral rules are what they are, because the end of the city is to be the home of a few thinkers" (1:5).

17. The phrase "gracious ruse" is taken from Maimonides, *The Guide of the Perplexed* III.33. There Maimonides claims that the Law or portions of the Law are a "gracious ruse" employed by God to restrain the desires, and thus make possible "domestic governance" and "speculation."

18. Cf. Cicero *Laws*, where Cicero, the philosopher, employs his leisure in the fashioning and re-fashioning of Roman law.

19. Cf. "The Place of Contemplation in Aristotle's *Nicomachean Ethics*" in *Essays*, where Rorty, too, looks to Aristotle's account of friendship for help in understanding the connection between *theōria* and *praxis*. Rorty's essay is also interesting in that she attempts to make sense of Aristotle's placing of his discussion of friendship between his two accounts of pleasure. In contrast to the "historical" school, she argues that "[t]his interruption, this sequence, is no accident, no haphazard reshuffling of the notetaker's papyrus" (389).

20. Of the authors of the standard commentaries, Stewart comes closest to taking this position. That is, he argues that Aristotle's discussion of friendship is intended, among other things, to further articulate his brief account of equity at the conclusion of Book V (2:266–67). Two further signs that Aristotle's account of friendship is meant to supplement or even supersede his accounts of magnanimity and justice are: 1) In the discussion of magnanimity Aristotle called honor the greatest

of external goods; here friends enjoy that title (1123b20–21; 1169b9–11); and 2) In the discussion of justice, "need" or "demand," the conventional measure of which is money, is said to "hold together" communities of exchange because it "hold all things together," i.e., make them commensurable; here friendship does that work (1133b5–10; 1133a25–31).

21. Aristotle repeats this important point a little later and gives it an interesting twist. He notes that affection (*philēsis*) is or is like a feeling (*pathos*), while friendship (*philia*) is or is like a *hexis*, a steady disposition or condition of the soul (1157b28–29). He then adds that it involves choice (1157b29–32). Once we notice that earlier in the same chapter Aristotle had observed that friendship, like the virtues, can either be "at work" or not, we have in place all the elements needed to see that friendship is structurally identical to the ethical virtues—a further bit of evidence that friendship is meant to replace one or more of the ethical virtues in Books III–IV (1157b5–11).

22. Aristotle's examples are of gods and kings, but think of all those boy-meets-girl stories about the struggles that perfectly decent couples must face when one member or the other comes from "the wrong side of the tracks." *Pride and Prejudice* comes to mind.

23. See Jaffa, 125–26. But see also Kraut, 175–84. Kraut claims that in neither passage is Aristotle limiting himself to philosophical friendship. I agree up to a point. I certainly think that Aristotle would say that friendship is possible between ethically virtuous men and that some part of their friendship would consist of conversation "about matters that affect the well-being of their fellow citizens" (184). I am less sure than Kraut seems to be that good character or ethical virtue is the basis of complete friendship: As far as I can see, aside from some remarks about trustworthiness, Aristotle never specifies the content of the goodness or virtue that such friends mutually benefit from and delight in. In addition, I see no reason not to assume that Aristotle is referring primarily to philosophic conversation in the passage from IX.9.

24. For this, consider in particular the last two chapters of Book VIII and the first two chapters of Book IX.

25. For other discussions of the relation between mother or parent and child, see Plato *Symposium* 207a–208b; Hobbes *Leviathan*, chap. 20; Locke *Second Treatise*, chaps. six and fifteen. See also the opening of Book VIII, 1155a16–21, where Aristotle emphasizes the naturalness of motherly love, and *Politics* 1252a24–35, where he argues that the desire "to leave behind another such as oneself" is one of the two natural grounds for human community.

26. Notice that Achilles, our earlier prototype of the great-souled man, compares himself to a mother bird in Book IX of the *Iliad* and that Aristotle brings up mother birds as a prototype of natural affection in the introduction to his own Book VIII—right after citing a passage from Book X of the *Iliad*, the book in which Odysseus and Diomedes are forced to carry out a very dangerous and somewhat questionable special ops mission because Achilles has rejected the pleas of his "chicks" (*Iliad* IX 323–327; *Ethics* 1155a12–21). Is Achilles the exemplar of "vulgar" magnanimity—is he the magnanimous man who can't quite make the move to true beneficence because he cares too much for honor? Or do we see him achieve the heroic equivalent of true beneficence, true motherhood, in Book XXIV when, without any prodding from the gods, he feeds an old man and gives him the time to bury his son properly?

27. Cf. 1120b11–14 as well as Plato *Republic* 330b–c. Curiously enough, the natural ground of stinginess toward strangers—those who have earned their own wealth tend to hold on to it—also seems to be the ground of generosity toward one's own.

28. Compare the passage in question with Aristotle's initial description of the "cultivated and active" (1095b26–28). Is the root of the inability of most men—or at least the best among ordinary men—to achieve true beneficence a lack of confidence or trust in their own goodness—and therefore, by implication, a lack of self-knowledge? Is this why Aristotle says what must surprise our modern ears, that smallness of soul is more vice-like than vanity (1125a16–19; 32–34)?

29. Cf. Rorty 388–391. Notice how much the ground has shifted at this point, from the need to be recognized to the need to recognize. Love of honor is born of a kind of high-level neediness: Men want external recognition because they lack assurance that they are good (1159a22–24). They want, to use Hegel's term, *Anerkennen*—an acknowledgement that is also an affirmation. But the good man already knows that he is good (and is quite willing, if need be, to disappear into the woodwork). His need is of a different order. A friend is the greatest external good because he allows the good man to complete the admiration for goodness (*eu-noia*), the love of excellence, that lies at the root of all genuine friendship (1167a3–21). The friend allows him to take in and take delight in the being at work of goodness. Hence the tremendous concentration in this chapter of words cognate to *noein* and *theōrein*.

30. For the burgeoning philosopher as "puppy," see Plato *Republic* 375a–376c and 539b–c. As for the burgeoning philosopher as "child," Aristotle provides a mini-portrait of the philosopher as young man near the beginning of Book IX. There he contrasts the friendships of "those who have shared in philosophy" with the squabbling that goes on when other friendships collapse (1164b2–3). We might think at first that he is referring to the friendship of philosophic equals and their "sharing in conversations and thought" (1170b10–14). The context makes it clear, however, that he is talking about a young man's initiation into the philosophic life and that he means to draw a precise parallel between parents and philosophers: "For its worth (*axia*) cannot be measured by money, and an honor equal in weight to it could not arise, but perhaps, as in the case of gods and parents, what is possible suffices" (1164b3–6). I, for one, cannot read this passage without being reminded of Aristotle's own allusion to Plato and their philosophic friendship in Book I (1095b11–17). Is Aristotle doing his best here to pay the unpayable debt he owes his teacher precisely by calling what have become Plato's "teachings" into question? Is his re-opening of the questions that lie behind those teachings his way of "honoring before" the truth and the activity of thinking they once shared—while at the same time pointing to the principle or source (*archē*) of philosophic friendship?

31. Aristotle points to this difficulty in chapter three of Book IX. There he takes up a series of delicate questions about the breaking point of friendships: What are people to do when their friends go bad or turn out to be bad? Or when they find themselves outgrowing their friends in virtue or intellect? All of us have no doubt had to face such questions: they are the stuff of ordinary life. But it does not take much imagination to see that Aristotle's discussion also applies, *mutatis mutandis*, to the extraordinary man's relation to others; Aristotle's emphasis on extraordinary differences in intellect and virtue make this particularly clear (1165b23–29). His sober yet humane advice—keep in mind your past closeness (*syn-ētheia*), do what you can as long as you can, but do not let what is best in yourself be compromised—and his

stated principle—enduring friendship depends on *some* connection between friend and friend—likewise apply directly to issue before us (1165b13–20; 29–36).

32. Cf. 1152a19–24, where Aristotle likens the unrestrained man to a city that "decrees all the needful things and which has good laws, but employs not one of them." In the same passage he likens the bad man to a city with bad laws that obeys them. Here, however, he seems to say that the worse a man is, the more rent and wretched the "state" of his soul. Could Aristotle be suggesting that vice, as he describes it in Books III through V, is even rarer than virtue—that even the worst of men have some tincture of goodness in them, a tincture revealed by and in their very wretchedness? See his discussion of pleasure in Book VII, where he, as it were, pardons those who dedicate themselves to the pursuit of bodily pleasures by arguing that they know nothing better and that such pursuits provide them with relief from the travail their bodies force them to endure (1154a22–15).

33. In Book X, too, Aristotle insists that, although from one point of view *nous* is divine, i.e., trans-human, from another "each man would seem to be this, since it is the authoritative and better [part]: hence it would be absurd (*a-topos*) if someone would not choose the life of it but of something else" (1178a2–4). The implication seems to be that most men are—literally—displaced. Trapped somewhere between the "life of cattle" and the life of the divine, they need the city and its laws in order to achieve some measure of order and reason in their lives.

34. See also Aristotle's defense of self-love or self-friendship (rightly understood) in chapter eight of Book IX. Although Aristotle's emphasis in this chapter is (reasonably enough) on the decency and nobility of the man who loves himself wisely and well, he also makes it clear that intellect (*nous*) is the primary object of his love.

35. Cf. Socrates' discussion of education in the *Republic*, where he suggests that those who would be philosophers (and kings) must first acquire the habits of those who can only be guardians. The capacity to discern the order of the whole rests on the capacity to discern the order or beauty in human things (Plato *Republic*, especially the beautiful passage at 401a–402a). Of course, one might ask in the case of the *Republic* just the question I have been asking here: How new is the new beginning Socrates makes in Book V (450a7–b2)? In other words, how closely tied is the education of the philosopher to the education of the warrior guardian?

36. We are now in a position to understand the full meaning of Aristotle's claim in Book IV: "Now greatness of soul seems to be, as it were, a sort of *kosmos* of the [ethical] virtues; for it makes them greater and does not come to be without them" (1124a1–3). We are also in a position to understand another crucial difference between "vulgar" magnanimity and what we can now call philosophic magnanimity. The great-souled man as he first appears is not *thaumastikos*—not liable (or able) to wonder. "For nothing is great to him" (1125a2–3). Too focused on his own superiority and too concerned that others affirm it, he is unable to be astonished by anyone or anything else. The man with philosophic magnanimity is of a different sort (*Posterior Analytics* 27b17–26). He is big enough to feel small in the presence of things larger than himself, sure-footed enough to dwell within uncertainty, free enough to let himself wonder and therefore philosophize, for "on account of the activity of wonder (*thaumazein*) human beings both now and at first began to philosophize" (*Metaphysics* 982b12–13).

37. The distinction is wielded (for the first time) but not explicated in Aristotle's first discussion of pleasure, at the end of Book VII (1153a7–10; 15–17; above all 1154b26–28). Elsewhere in the *Ethics*, the focus is on the distinction between *en-*

ergeia (activity) and *hexis* (disposition, condition). The distinction between activity and motion also comes to the fore at a critical juncture in the *Metaphysics*, as Aristotle prepares us for the claim that *ousia* and form (*eidos*) *are* activity (*energeia*) (1048b18–35; 1050a23–1050b2).

38. The passage at 1048b18–28 in the *Metaphysics* is less clear on this score than one would like. (None of the examples Aristotle gives is an instance of action in the ordinary sense of the term.) The Book X discussion of pleasure is even less clear cut. Aristotle never tells us whether action, *praxis*, should be thought of as an activity, a motion, or some sort of hybrid. I assume this is because the basic character of *praxis* is one of several issues he wants us to think through in the second half of the *Ethics*.

39. In Book VII Aristotle identifies pleasure with unimpeded activity (1153a9–15). In Book X he considers and then rejects this formulation and in its stead proposes that "pleasure completes activity, not as an already present condition (*hexis*) does, but as an extra end that comes along afterwards, like the bloom that comes upon men at their peak" (175b30–35; 1174b31–33).

40. A defense of *praxis* can also be mounted from the side of *theōria*. No doubt genuine *theōria* is humanly possible. As the very word *theorem* suggests, real insight and understanding are available at least in mathematics. Moreover, the coherence of our everyday experience seems to rest on an elemental type of *theōria*: as Aristotle's identification of *eidos* with *logos* suggests, the very forms of things speak to us. Still, it's undeniable that much of what passes for theoretical activity—for instance, all learning and inquiry—is more like motion than pure activity. To be learning is to be on the way. (See, for instance, the *Physics* III.3, where Aristotle explicitly treats learning as a type of motion; since at the same time he identifies teaching with learning, it follows that teaching too is a motion. But as we learned in Book VI, teaching is a mode of *epistēmē*: apparently the sheer activity of knowing, when directed at the receptive intelligence of another, *is* the motion of teaching-learning.) Thus any attempt to write off *praxis* on the grounds that it is mere *kinesis* rather than sheer *energeia* would have to write off most of *theōria* as well. (In fact well-considered actions and even ordinary motions might seem to be more whole and therefore more *energeia*-like than open-ended inquiries, but this impression is misleading. What gives coherence and shape to every serious inquiry is the object of thought, which makes its presence felt in our questions and even in our moments of greatest perplexity. To see what's missing is to see.)

41. This, I think, is just what Cicero does in his *Laws*—with a mixture of playfulness and seriousness. The laws he proposes have the "look" of antique Roman laws, yet they also forbid prosecution for impiety and contain a provision for a temple dedicated to Mind (*Mens*). They quietly promote and preserve the conditions for philosophy (11.19).

42. Remember that Aristotle calls his inquiry *tis politikē*, "a sort of political [inquiry]," by which he means presumably that it is not only "about" politics and directed toward men engaged in politics but also a form of political activity (1094b10–11).

43. The phrase "philosophic deliberation" is meant to capture the peculiar character of Aristotle's inquiry in the *Ethics*, its persistent and deliberate straddling of the divide between theoretical and practical thought. From one point of view, the *Ethics* is a sustained act of deliberation that moves from an end—happiness—through a consideration of the possible means to that end—fortune, pleasure, the virtues, and so on. It is the activity of prudence in its most comprehensive, most architectonic form, for the question it seeks to answer is not what to do in this or that situation in

64033576

life, but what to do with life simply. From another point of view, the *Ethics* is a sustained philosophic exploration of a what-is question—What is the good, the end, the proper form of human life?—in the course of which the fundamental features of human being come to light. It is the activity of *theōria* in its most self-reflective form. What makes this conjunction of theoretical and practical thought possible is the common structure they share: Not only mathematical analysis and deliberation but philosophy, too, is a mode of *zētēsis*, inquiry, the most basic form of which is the humble activity of *anamnēsis*, recollection (1112b20–24; *On Memory and Recollection* 452a7–10; 453a7–14).

44. In the final book of the *Physics*, his study of beings that have their source of motion in themselves, Aristotle concludes that there must be a first unmoved mover, without parts and magnitude—an eternal source of eternal motion (266a6–12). Toward the end of the *Metaphysics*, his account of the causes and sources of beings as beings, Aristotle comes upon this same source again, now characterized as the sheer, potency-free thinking of thinking that moves the whole by being an object of desire or erōs (1071b12–22; 1072a24–27; 1072b3–4; 1074b33–35). Note also that in the very first line of the *Metaphysics*, Aristotle tells us that by nature all men desire to be in the state or condition of knowing (*to eidenai*)—that is, to engage in the activity of seeing for its own sake (980a21–27).